FOUNDING FATHERS

The Celebration of Champlain and Laval in the Streets of Quebec, 1878–1908

The late nineteenth and early twentieth centuries saw an unprecedented wave of public celebration of the past. Throughout the western world, heroes and great events from earlier times were celebrated by staging lavish parades, constructing intricately designed monuments, and mounting theatrical re-enactments of pivotal moments in history. In Quebec, two individuals occupied centre stage in these commemorations: Samuel de Champlain, the founder of Quebec City, and often referred to as the lay father of French-Canadian civilization, and Mgr François de Laval, the first bishop of Quebec, commonly seen as French Canada's religious father. Between 1878 and 1908 these men were fêted in four commemorative mega-events staged in the streets of Quebec City.

Based largely on the archival documents left behind by the lay and ecclesiastical leaders who organized the celebrations of Champlain and Laval, Ronald Rudin's study describes the complicated process of staging these spectacles. The vast array of leaders – lay and clerical, French- and English-speaking – rarely saw eye to eye about either the form or the goal of commemorative celebration. Accordingly, the tens of thousands who came out to view these affairs witnessed events with numerous messages. An examination of the four spectacles, which took place over a period of thirty years, provides an opportunity to view both changes in the nature of commemorative celebrations across the western world and tensions within Canadian society.

RONALD RUDIN is a professor of history at Concordia University and is the author of *Making History in Twentieth Century Quebec* (1997).

FOUNDING FATHERS

*The Celebration of
Champlain and Laval
in the Streets of Quebec,
1878–1908*

Ronald Rudin

UNIVERSITY OF TORONTO PRESS
Toronto Buffalo London

© University of Toronto Press Incorporated 2003
Toronto Buffalo London
Printed in Canada

ISBN 0-8020-3645-7 (cloth)
ISBN 0-8020-8479-6 (paper)

∞

Printed on acid-free paper

National Library of Canada Cataloguing in Publication

Rudin, Ronald
  Founding fathers : the celebration of Champlain and Laval in the
  streets of Quebec, 1878–1908 / Ronald Rudin.

  Includes bibliographical references and index.
  ISBN 0-8020-3645-7 (bound)   ISBN 0-8020-8479-6 (pbk.)

  1. Québec (Quebec) – Centennial celebrations, etc.   2. Champlain,
  Samuel de, 1567–1635 – Anniversaries, etc.   3. Laval, François
  de Montmorency, 1623–1708 – Anniversaries, etc.   4. Québec
  (Quebec) – History.   I. Title.

  FC2946.36.R83 2003   971.4'47103   C2003-900022-2
  F1054.5.Q3R83 2003

This book has been published with the help of a grant from the Humanities
and Social Sciences Federation of Canada, using funds provided by the
Social Sciences and Humanities Research Council of Canada.

University of Toronto Press acknowledges the financial assistance to its
publishing program of the Canada Council for the Arts and the Ontario
Arts Council.

University of Toronto Press acknowledges the financial support for its
publishing activities of the Government of Canada through the Book
Publishing Industry Development Program (BPIDP).

To the memory of two founding fathers:

ABE RUDIN
(1919–1998)

HAROLD WOLL
(1910–2001)

Contents

Acknowledgments

Books such as this one, much like the commemorative spectacles discussed in the pages that follow, are not quite what they seem. Those spectacles appeared to be straightforward affairs when they were in their final, polished form for presentation to the public. The tens if not hundreds of thousands of people who witnessed them must have believed that they were seeing the natural unfolding of celebrations that could not have been staged any other way. In fact, those spectators were being exposed to the final versions of scripts that had gone through many revisions after intense negotiations between groups of people who did not always see eye to eye about the point of the exercise. In a similar manner, academic monographs when published with the author's name on the cover seem to be the work of a single person, when nothing could be further from the truth.

This book would have never seen the light of day without the financial assistance of the Social Sciences and Humanities Research Council of Canada, which allowed me to visit the various sources that needed to be consulted. My visits to the relevant archives and libraries were also facilitated by Concordia University, which assigned me teaching loads that allowed me to research the book and granted me a sabbatical during which I wrote nearly all of it. The funds made available by SSHRC also allowed me to hire Crista McInnis and Eric Reiter to translate several documents from Latin into English and to employ Derek Parent to prepare the maps that are included. At the University of Toronto Press, I was helped along by two editors: Siobhan McMenemy showed interest in the project from its infancy, and Len Husband shepherded it along to publication, providing much needed sympathy at crucial moments. Both agreed with me that I needed to translate the considerable amount of material originally in French into English so as to make the book accessible to an English-language market.

The project also benefited from the various archivists and librarians who went out of their way to assist me. Special thanks go to the succession of archivists who looked after me over a number of years at the Archives du Séminaire de Québec: Jeanne d'Arc Boissonneault, Julie Bouchard, Madeleine Faucher, and Lan Tran. While in Quebec City, I was also treated with great generosity by both Armand Gagné and Pierre Lafontaine at the archives of the Archdiocese of Quebec and by Martine Ménard of the archives of the Ville de Québec. Also in Quebec City, Jacques Morin of the Archives nationales du Québec helped me find appropriate photographs from the archives' massive collection.

Closer to home, I was greatly aided by the staff of the Annexe Aegidus-Fauteux of the Bibliothèque nationale du Québec (where I am seated as I write these lines). I have been meaning to provide this small gesture of appreciation for a long time but have always somehow forgotten. Louise Tessier and her staff have answered hundreds of questions for me over the years and have provided me with a tranquil environment for writing much of five books. I can now go public about this gem of a library, without fear that it will be overrun by others looking for a quiet place to work, since it will soon disappear with the creation of the Grande bibliothèque du Québec. The staff and the collection may be moving to a brand-new building, yet I strongly doubt that its friendly atmosphere will be reproduced. It will sorely be missed.

I have also been aided along the way by my friends and colleagues at Concordia: Graham Carr, Shannon McSheffrey, and Mary Vipond. They kindly read parts of this manuscript when they were burdened with obligations of their own. I also appreciate the generous advice about the 1908 tercentenary provided by Viv Nelles of York University, whose book on the subject is a must read for anyone interested in turn-of-the-century commemorative celebrations. However, the two individuals who deserve my greatest thanks are the two who have had to hear about Champlain and Laval over the dinner table for years. My wife Phyllis has endured a number of books by now, so perhaps she has become used to my occasional disappearances to go off to the archives, and my occasional absent-mindedness as I think about writing a sentence when I should be listening to what is on her mind. In any event, I am forever appreciative of her patience with me and her talents as the proofreader of my manuscripts. As for my son David, this book is the first he has had to live through from beginning to end. I would like to think he was a bit unhappy about my leaving home from time to time, but he never complained or made me feel guilty. I also appreciated his constant questioning of me on the way home from school about the latest developments on the book front. I always suspected that this was a strategy to prevent me from asking him about school, but I appreciated his interest just the same.

I dedicate this book to David's two grandfathers, founding fathers in their own right, who died over the course of this project. My dad, Abe Rudin, was a tireless worker with a great sense of humour and an uncanny knack for getting along with others. As for my father-in-law, Harold Woll, he had a business card that read 'honest, conscientious and reliable' – a motto he always lived up to. In a world where there is much talk about the absence of positive male role models, here were two men who lived simple lives dedicated to their families. I can only hope to be such a good role model for David.

FOUNDING FATHERS

The Celebration of Champlain and Laval in the
Streets of Quebec, 1878–1908

Introduction

This is my second book touching on how French-speaking Quebecers – a people who claim 'Je me souviens' as their national motto – have remembered their past. In *Making History in Twentieth-Century Quebec* I was interested in the emergence of history as a profession, paying particular attention to how and why these professionals communicated various versions of the past to the larger population.[1] Clearly, however, most people derive at least as much of their understanding of the past from sources other than books written by historians. This point has been driven home in a fascinating study indicating that the views of the past held today by Quebec university students are based on ideas that were rejected by professional historians nearly thirty years ago.[2] While it may be true that previous generations were influenced to a greater degree by the printed word, the fact remains that even before the emergence of electronic media there were other, more accessible ways of learning about the past.

Having come to this conclusion, I was drawn back to the late nineteenth and early twentieth centuries – a period I had written about before. In particular, I was drawn to this era by the substantial and fascinating literature that has been produced over the past twenty years regarding the wave of public commemoration that swept across the western world at the turn of the twentieth century. It would have been difficult for ordinary citizens of that era to be unaware of the intricately choreographed spectacles taking place in the streets of their cities on both sides of the Atlantic – spectacles held so that their leaders might communicate messages grounded in the past. Heroes and great events from earlier times were celebrated through such devices as lavish parades, elaborate monuments, and theatrical re-enactments of pivotal moments in history.

Most of those who have written about turn-of-the-century commemorative activities have viewed them as a calculated response by lay and clerical leaders who perceived their authority as under attack due to industrialization, secularization, immigration, and other destabilizing forces. As Pierre Nora has put it, the construction of monuments evoking the past – what he called 'les lieux de mémoire' – was a calculated strategy to fill the void left 'at the end of the century, when the decisive blow to traditional balances was felt – in particular the disintegration of the rural world.'[3] In rural areas the social order had been maintained through a common memory of its longstanding legitimacy; this was not possible in the new urban societies. Cities were impersonal places inhabited by large numbers of workers and immigrants, who felt no particular compulsion to follow the dictates of their betters and who had been placed in a position to select their political masters through universal manhood suffrage. As Eric Hobsbawm has argued, 'formal rulers and dominant groups [were faced with] unprecedented problems of how to maintain or even establish the obedience, loyalty and co-operation of [their] subjects or members.'[4] Providing evocative symbols from the past was a rather self-conscious 'compensatory strategy' to persuade the population to support such constructs as the state and the nation, lest they be seen – like other aspects of traditional society – as the detritus of an earlier age.[5]

Quebec was hardly immune to this process. For example, between 1880 and the early 1920s the number of statues erected in the province's public places increased from 3 to 177. However, though some excellent studies have been produced on particular aspects of the public celebration of the past in Quebec, few works have explored the evolution of these activities in their heyday.[6] This book, which focuses on the celebration of two founding fathers, one lay and the other clerical, in the streets of Quebec City, does not claim to be a comprehensive study of such public spectacles. Nevertheless, I hope that when I show how Samuel de Champlain, the founder of Quebec City and first governor of the colony, and Mgr François de Laval, the first bishop of Quebec, came to be lavishly feted in four commemorative mega-events over a period of thirty years, the reader will see reflections of changes in Quebec society, as well as shifts in the commemorative repertoire available at any given moment.

In line with numerous other studies of the construction of public celebrations, we will see that the process of feting Champlain and Laval was not nearly as neat as is suggested by Hobsbawm's characterization of the packaging of the past for public consumption as 'the invention of tradition.' This expression suggests that there were 'inventors' – that is, leaders who need their considerable resources to foist on an unsuspecting public whatever vision of the past suited their purposes. We will see that in fact there was considerable conflict among these leaders regarding which messages to convey to the public and how best to communicate them. In turn-of-the-century Quebec City, most of the leaders involved in commemorative activities were French-Canadian clerics and laypeople, whose efforts often attracted the involvement of English-speakers as well.[7]

These French-speakers argued over questions of message and technique, yet generally they understood that their audience consisted largely of French Canadians, whose sense of national identity touched on their relationships with Canada, the British Empire, France, and Catholicism. Over much of the past thirty years, questions about Quebecers' sense of identity have taken a back seat in historical writing. Beginning with the Quiet Revolution of the 1960s and continuing till the 1990s, Quebec historians were preoccupied with tracing the province's integration into the urban-industrial world that was emerging in the late nineteenth and early twentieth centuries. Earlier historians had concerned themselves mainly with the factors that led French Canadians to view themselves as different from their North American neighbours; the 'revisionist' historians (as I have referred to them elsewhere) focused on social and economic concerns and pushed questions of national or religious identity to the margins. Yet questions regarding identity were important enough to turn-of-the-century French-Canadian leaders that they invested considerable time and energy in mounting commemorative spectacles. Indeed, Quebec historians have recently paid greater attention to such matters, and in the process began to develop a postrevisionist view of Quebec's past in which the various elements of French-Canadian cultural history form an important part of the narrative.[8]

In spite of their frequent differences, French-Canadian leaders were of one mind in lavishing particular attention on Champlain, often referred to as 'le fondateur de l'état civil' for having given French Canada a firm foothold along the St. Lawrence, and Laval, who was viewed as 'le fondateur de l'état religieux' for having provided the institutional basis for Catholicism across not only what would become Quebec, but also much of North America, which fell within his diocese.[9] Of all the heroes who could have been chosen from French-Canadian history, these two were paid the most sustained attention in the heyday of public commemoration because together they embodied the secular and religious roots of French-Canadian identity. When considered as a pair, it might be expected that Champlain was celebrated for his secular and Laval for his religious accomplishments; yet when the two men were considered individually, Champlain was often praised as a devout Catholic while Laval was honoured as a participant in the governing of New France. Many of us perceive secular and religious forces as hostile to each other; from the perspective of most leaders in turn-of-the-century French Canada, they were not.

There were, of course, other figures who could have been celebrated, most notably Jacques Cartier, the first French explorer to navigate the St. Lawrence. Cartier spent the winter of 1535–6 at the site that would later become Quebec City – a feat that perhaps should have been as celebrated in the late nineteenth century as that of John Cabot, over whom considerable fuss was made in English Canada.[10] Cabot was Italian, yet he sailed for England, so his exploration of the Atlantic coast could be seen as the beginning of Canada's British connection. Cartier, in contrast, represented the French claim to the St. Lawrence Valley – a claim that evaporated on the Plains of Abraham in 1759. Since Cartier did not really 'build' anything that endured in the way that Champlain and Laval had, he could be celebrated only as representing a French connection that no longer existed and that was not always viewed in a positive light in turn-of-the-century Quebec.

In an era of public commemorative spectacles, Cartier did not have the right stuff for adulation. His limitations were underscored by the only significant celebration of his legacy in Quebec City – a rather minor event compared with those that honoured the founding fathers, and one that he had to share with others. This celebration was built around the unveiling in 1889 of what came to be known as 'le monument Cartier-Brébeuf.' On one of the monument's faces was a tribute to Cartier; the others were reserved for three Jesuit martyrs, most notably Jean de Brébeuf. Laval and Champlain could stand on their own as representatives of a people defined in both secular and religious terms; this could not be said of Cartier. Nearly all the leaders, both lay and clerical, who spoke at the unveiling pointed to the need to bring Cartier and the martyrs together so as to pay tribute to both 'l'église et l'état.'[11]

Founders held sway in turn-of-the-century Quebec because they symbolized the roots of a civilization that had managed to survive in spite of all obstacles. Accordingly, in contrast with Cartier's reserved celebration, there was a much more enthusiastic one in honour of the 'founder' of Montreal. In 1895 an estimated 20,000 people assembled for the unveiling of a statue in honour of Paul de Chomedy de Maisonneuve, who had combined both secular and religious motives, thus making him worthy of celebration as a hero in his own right, without the sort of assistance required by Cartier. In the end, however, some aspects of this celebration underscored the fact that though Maisonneuve had been a founder, his feat was a rather local one. In contrast, the legacies left by Champlain and Laval were viewed as central to French Canadians' existence as a people. Thus, while the founding fathers were repeatedly celebrated in Quebec City, Maisonneuve had just this one day in the sun. Moreover, while all the spectacles to be discussed in this book were carefully choreographed affairs with many components, the unveiling of the Monument Maisonneuve was a relatively brief affair, held on the morning of 1 July, but with no connection to other celebrations taking place the same day. Ultimately, the difference between Maisonneuve, on the one hand, and Champlain and Laval, on the other, was best expressed by an article in *La Presse*. On the day following the unveiling of the statue to the founder of Montreal, it noted in a headline: 'Thousands of People Stayed Away from the City.' As we shall see, the celebrations of the founding fathers did not scare people away; rather, they attracted large numbers of visitors to Quebec City from across North America and, in the case of dignitaries, from as far away as Europe.[12]

This book is the story of four lavish celebrations of Champlain and Laval in the streets of Quebec City. Each is the subject of a chapter. To the extent that this story has a starting date, it is 1877, the year of the unearthing of Laval's long-missing remains. This discovery quickly led to the mounting of a sumptuous and highly orchestrated series of events, culminating in Laval's reburial in the spring of the following year. This event, unprecedented in its scale, sparked a campaign to secure Laval's canonization. Throughout the late nineteenth and early twentieth centuries, this campaign led to various public manifestations of support for Laval's cause, even if such displays clearly violated the church's own rules for elevating an individual to sainthood. Alongside the campaign for Laval's canonization, there emerged a competing and much more public drive to erect a statue to Champlain – in a sense to provide the founder of Quebec with his own form of immortality. This drive culminated in the unveiling of the Monument Champlain in 1898 – an event every bit as lavishly choreographed as the Laval reburial. The two men then vied for attention in the early years of the new century in the prelude to 1908 – the bicentenary of Laval's death and the tercentenary of Champlain's founding of Quebec. For the leaders of Quebec City, lay and clerical alike, the manoeuvring over who would be celebrated in 1908 and in what form was the logical culmination of the commemorative politics that had begun with the discovery of Laval's remains. In the end, two celebrations were held within weeks of each other in the summer of 1908. The first was a lavish ceremony to mark the unveiling of a statue in honour of Laval; this was followed by an even more imposing celebration of Champlain.

These four extravaganzas presented different versions of Champlain and Laval to the public and were staged in different social, economic, and political contexts. British imperialism had not been much of a factor in 1878, but it played a key role in the commemorative events of 1908. Ultramontanism (the brand of Catholicism that suggested that the church should take precedence over the state) had been a powerful force at the time of Laval's reburial, but it had weakened by the early twentieth century. As for France, its relationship with French Canada went through a number of peaks and troughs, coloured to a considerable extent by the treatment of Catholics under the Third Republic. There were also occasional strains in the relationship between French- and English-speaking Canadians as a result of various political crises and the increased concentration of economic power in English-run businesses.

At yet another level, these celebrations reflected changes in the business world, as methods of scientific management made their presence felt. Over time, relatively informal committees were replaced by hierarchical organizations staffed by professionals employed for their particular expertise in staging commemorative spectacles. The increasing complexity of the organizations running these events made it possible to stage fetes that went on longer, incorporated more individual elements, and brought more participants into the process. This bureaucratization also increased the costs of such affairs, with the result that during celebrations of their own heroes, French-speakers often had to take a backseat to English-speakers, who had the means to foot the bill.

Much changed between 1878 and 1908, yet these four celebrations also had much in common. In each case, Champlain and Laval provided the raw material for the civil and ecclesiastical leaders, who functioned as producers of public performances staged on the set of Quebec City. Here were the sites of the beginning of a French-Catholic civilization in North America, vestiges of a time when 'outsiders' had not yet arrived. When the celebrants of the legacies of the founders took control of the streets, they were reclaiming the same routes their heroes had traversed. However, Quebec City was more than the starting point for French

Catholic civilization in North America; it was also the place where one could see the most reason to hope for the survival of the French-Canadian people under the difficult circumstances of the late nineteenth and early twentieth centuries. Immigration and industrialization were transforming Montreal into a linguistically diverse city; an English-speaking elite was overseeing its emergence as an important major business centre. In contrast, Quebec City was becoming even more solidly French-speaking and Catholic. Without so much as a rail link to connect it directly with the south shore of the St. Lawrence, the town was largely untouched by the immigrants and the economic changes that had, according to some, corrupted Montreal. As a solidly French-speaking centre, which after 1867 was home to the only government in North America where francophones were in control, Quebec City was the logical site for commemorative events drawing on images from a time when French Catholics were entirely in control.

All four celebrations were coloured by certain traditions of public celebration in Quebec. The community leaders were aware of the latest tools in the commemorative repertoire that was evolving in this, the heyday of such spectacles, but they were careful to incorporate elements that had a particular meaning to French Canadians. The issue of public space was central to these events: monuments were constructed and spectacles staged on land that was normally open to all. However, the most dramatic use of these spaces came with the movement of people through the streets, and in this regard the leaders were careful to draw on the distinctive processional forms linked to the Corpus Christi (Fête-Dieu in French) and St-Jean-Baptiste holidays. Both of these had roots in Quebec stretching back to the seventeenth century. French Canadians took to the streets in a distinctive manner on these occasions, and the organizers seized on this language of performance to help tell the stories these spectacles were designed to communicate.

This communication process was far from straightforward. Nevertheless, we might get a different impression from much of the literature on the subject, which views the spectators of these celebrations as little more than pawns to be manipulated by leaders working together to bolster their positions in society. In fact, we will see that these four spectacles were the product of intense and often messy negotiations among groups that did not necessarily see eye to eye about either the form of the celebrations or the messages to be conveyed thereby. Much of what follows is based on the documentation left behind by these leaders, who took their organizational work very seriously. Nothing was left to chance;

every decision was carefully considered, from the timing of the various events, to the routes to be followed and the order of marchers, to the design of public monuments and mounting of theatrical events. These leaders, most of them from Quebec City, invested huge amounts of time and energy in these details in order to send contemporary messages to the tens if not hundreds of thousands of participants and spectators. In addition, messages were sent to an even larger number of people who learned of these spectacles through lavish descriptions and illustrations in newspapers.[13]

By and large, the intended audience for these performances, whether they attended or only heard about them later, was French-speaking. The leaders who shaped the spectacles were much more diverse in terms of national origins. Francophones always dominated in numbers, but their control over certain events was tenuous. Yet, for all of the leaders drawn into the commemorative process, the main point of the exercise was to influence French-speakers' views of themselves, their place in Canada, and their role in the empire. Accordingly, this is largely a study of the efforts of leaders to impose certain perspectives on the past – and by extension views of the present – on French Canadians.

The documents that provide the basis for this story – mainly the records of the organizations responsible for the various celebrations, and the local newspapers of the time – tell us much about what the lay and clerical organizers were hoping to achieve. Yet they tell us very little about what the public actually drew from these events. The one exception to this is the fascinating journal of Abbé Alfred Paré, a professor at the seminary in Quebec City who conscientiously recorded his reactions to three of the four spectacles. But even Abbé Paré was hardly an 'ordinary' resident of Quebec City, although he stood outside the inner circle of leaders that organized these events. It is hard to imagine that spectators could have been left unmoved by the spectacles that passed before them, but we can only speculate about whether French-speaking Catholics came away as the organizers hoped, with an altered sense of their national or religious identity. This speculation is further compromised by the fact that often, ambiguous messages were being communicated by events, which tended to be designed by committees within which different points of view had to be accommodated. In the end, this is not so much a study of the impact of commemorative events on the larger population, as one that focuses on the intense involvement of various types of leaders when it came to mounting celebrations of Champlain and Laval that they hoped would shape public opinion.

chapter one

The Discovery and Display of Mgr de Laval, 1877–1878

Roberge and Simard Strike Gold

The era of the commemorative mega-event in Quebec City began late on the afternoon of 19 September 1877. Towards 4 o'clock, Charles Roberge and Benjamin Simard, two young workmen from the St-Roch district, were busy cleaning out the basement of Quebec City's Basilica to make room for repairing some rotting beams, when they came across a lead coffin containing the remains of Mgr François de Laval, the first bishop of Quebec. Laval had died in 1708, leaving behind instructions that he should be buried in the seminary he had founded. Unfortunately, the chapel of the seminary where his remains were supposed to have been deposited had burned to the ground in 1701 and had not yet been reconstructed by the time of his death. So he was buried underneath the Cathedral (as the Basilica was known until 1874) for what was supposed to have been a temporary stay.[1] However, due to a number of renovations made to the building, Laval's coffin was moved, and as a result clerical officials lost track of its whereabouts. Roberge and Simard's discovery came as a complete surprise.

The two workmen would probably have been surprised by the discovery of any coffin, but they must have been shocked when they read the words 'Franciscus de Laval' that formed part of the Latin inscription chiselled into the cover. They immediately reported their discovery, and by early the next morning word had spread throughout the local ecclesiastical establishment, ultimately reaching Archbishop Elzéar-Alexandre Taschereau. He immediately called together other leading members of the local clergy, and together they headed off to the basement, where they interrogated Roberge and Simard to make sure they had not in any way tampered with the contents of the coffin. The workmen were then dismissed, and the official party opened the coffin to remove the bones. These they deposited in a box, which was sealed and transported to the basement of the seminary for safekeeping. Taking no chances, they forbade all access to the discovery – probably a good idea, since one of the priests in attendance, Cyrille Légaré, admitted in his journal, 'I took one of these bones and placed it against my lips with the same respect that I would have accorded to the relics of a saint.'[2] As the archbishop noted only two days after Laval's remains were unearthed, 'We have taken all necessary precautions in order to guarantee the authenticity of the relics of Mgr de Laval, just in case he is canonized one fine day.'[3]

Between the discovery of the bishop's remains and the lavish ceremonies surrounding his reburial beneath the seminary chapel in May 1878, the issue of Laval's canonization would regularly surface. The decision to deposit Laval's bones at the seminary was easily arrived at, given the institution's desire to repossess what rightfully belonged to it according to Laval's own wishes; and the date was just as easily selected, since it coincided with a meeting of the council of Quebec bishops that had already been set for the following May and that would be presented with a request to begin the formal process for Laval's elevation to sainthood. The ceremonies for Laval's reburial extended over several days, comprised a number of intricately planned events, and brought tens of thousands of people into the streets of Quebec City. This spectacle was unlike anything the city had ever seen. To make sense of its significance, we must understand who Laval was and how his legacy had been communicated to Quebecers in the 170 years since his death.

Who Was Mgr de Laval?

François de Montmorency-Laval de Montigny was born in France in 1623 to a noble though not especially wealthy family.[4] From an early age, François de Laval (as he was commonly known) was destined for a clerical life; he took holy orders before his ninth birthday. For most of the next fifteen years, until his ordination in 1647, he was educated by the Jesuits, who gave him the taste for missionary life. Though not a Jesuit himself, his connections with that order cost him a position as the pope's representative (vicar apostolic) in Indochina. The perception in Rome was that his backers had grown too independent of the Vatican. In the end, however, Laval's failure to secure that post made him available for one in New France.

By the middle of the seventeenth century, both the French state and the Catholic church were looking for ways to strengthen their presence in the St. Lawrence Valley. The state's interest in this regard led to the imposition of direct rule from Paris in 1663. For the church, the process was complicated by the relationship between France and Rome, as well as by feuding within the church. As support grew for the idea of naming a bishop, who would hold authority over the church's activities in New France, the interests of various parties had to be accommodated.

Up till this time, missionaries – most of them Jesuits – had enjoyed a wide range of autonomy, so they looked upon the creation of any authority over their affairs with some suspicion. Eventually the Jesuits recognized that some bishop was going to be named and began looking for ways to cut their losses. In 1657 they successfully blocked the naming of the candidate of the Sulpicians, a religious order that oversaw the affairs of the church in Montreal and with which they had been wrangling for some time. The Jesuits and Sulpicians were divided by their quest for power, but they were also divided by ideology, with the former taking the ultramontane position that church should dominate over state, and the latter taking the gallican view that allowed for state involvement in church affairs. Having blocked the Sulpicians' candidate, the Jesuits recognized that there would be considerable resistance if they nominated one of their own for the bishop's post in New France. So they set their sights on François de Laval, who was sympathetic to their interests but was not a member of their order.

After 1657, although there was really no other candidate for the bishopric of Quebec, obstacles remained in Laval's path – in particular, questions regarding his relationship with church authorities in both France and Rome. In France, the Archbishop of Rouen was claiming that he had previously been responsible for affairs in New France, and wanted Laval to be subject to his authority, which he claimed to derive from traditions of French clerical independence from Rome. At the same time, some Vatican officials were concerned that Laval's links to the Jesuits would make him too independent of their authority. In the end, as a result of this in-fighting, in 1658 Laval was named vicar apostolic, rather than bishop, of Quebec. This preserved Rome's authority over affairs in New France, which angered the Archbishop of Rouen, who prevented Laval from sailing to the New World until the following year. Laval wisely kept quiet during these intense negotiations between Rouen, Paris, and Rome. Nevertheless, for those who wanted to remember his legacy in the nineteenth century, he emerged as a symbol of a victory for Rome over the parochial interests in France. This made him attractive to ultramontanes in Quebec, who were eager to defend their church's interests against those of the state.

Laval's legacy was even more strongly marked by the half-century he spent in New France, where he served as leader of the church until retiring in 1688. In the thirty years that he exercised authority, he never put a complete stop to the efforts to curb his power that had begun before his appointment. He continued to battle with the Archbishop of Rouen, this time over his securing the title of bishop with uncontested control over his diocese – a struggle he finally won in 1674. More significantly, however, Laval constantly struggled with the state over efforts to limit his influence. Louis XIV seemed at first sympathetic to Laval, and in 1663 when a Sovereign Council was established to administer New France, he was willing to accord him equal status with the governor, the highest state official in the colony. Over time, however, the king and his advisors recognized the dangers of allowing the bishop to wield power that might conflict with imperial designs, and efforts were made to reduce Laval's influence. The battle between church and state was most visible in the bishop's efforts to restrict the trade in alcohol with native people. The merchants and state officials insisted that this trade was necessary to protect France's commercial and imperial designs; Laval saw it as putting morality over material gain. This position would earn him praise from those who wanted to defend nineteenth-century Catholicism from the onslaught of the industrial world.

Laval's desire for power in New France was also symbolized by the special role he envisioned for the seminary he established in Quebec City in 1663. The seminary had all the characteristics of a theological school, but Laval had a second, more radical goal for it – to make it the base for all the priests of the diocese. In his conception, parishioners would pay their tithes to the seminary rather than to the local priest; in return, the seminary would guarantee the provision of services. As André Vachon put it: 'Clergy and seminary were all one in Bishop Laval's mind: the seminary of Quebec would be the clergy of New France.'[5] At first, this organization made sense, since it ensured that services would be provided to communities too small to be established as self-supporting parishes. Over time, however, as the colony's population grew and Laval showed himself reluctant to create new parishes, it began to appear that the seminary was really a device for him to monopolize control. In the end, Laval was forced to give in to royal edicts ordering the creation of parishes detached from seminary control. This again reinforced the bishop's image as an embattled victim of state intrusion into church affairs. Shortly after his retirement, his successor, Bishop St-Vallier, ended the special role that the seminary had played for more than a quarter-century. Thus, to the leaders of the seminary who took charge of Laval's reburial, Quebec's first bishop was not only their 'fondateur,' but also a visionary who had forseen a special role for their institution.

As this brief description suggests, Laval was a complex character who would offer many interpretative possibilities during the turn-of-the-century wave of public commemorative events. In his thirty years as bishop, he was a powerful proponent of Catholicism in Quebec, and he built the church into a strong institutional presence. Some saw his single-mindedness as an asset, others as a liability. In the 1840s, the less charitable view of Laval's episcopal career was communicated most force-fully by François-Xavier Garneau, author of *Histoire du Canada depuis sa découverte jusqu'à nos jours,* a multivolume work that earned him the mantle of Quebec's *historien national.* Garneau's *Histoire* went through three editions in his own lifetime, mainly because of clerical opposition to his rather liberal interpretation of Quebec's past. He did not always depict the church in the best light. Though he made many changes to his history to tone down his anticlericalism, he left intact most of his condemnations of Mgr de Laval. In particular, Garneau focused on the bishop's 'uncompromising and dominating spirit,' which led him 'into disputes with public officials, religious communities, and even private citizens. He believed that his judgments were infallible if he was acting in the best interests of the church.'[6]

Garneau was not alone in harbouring reservations about the bishop. Nearly forty years after the publication of *Histoire du Canada,* Abbé Henri-Raymond Casgrain published his own concerns as part of a review of the most recent edition of Garneau's work. Obviously thinking about Laval's candidature for sainthood, which had begun following his re-burial, Casgrain largely supported Garneau's negative view, noting that 'it is possible to venerate him like a saint, but at the same time to judge him like a man.'[7] Although Casgrain was rebuked by the superior of the seminary for criticizing Laval publicly, he was still casting doubt on Laval's legacy ten years later in a letter to a colleague.[8] Casgrain observed that although he regarded 'Mgr de Laval as if he were a saint,' he was troubled by Laval's heavy-handed tactics, some of which had humiliated his adversaries. Laval should have been working for co-operation be-tween church and state, and it troubled Casgrain that the bishop had acted at times 'to humiliate and belittle representatives of civil authority, and had done so over trifling matters.' He pointed to one occasion when Laval became enraged 'during a ceremony at the Collège des Jésuites, when the students saluted the governor before saluting the bishop.' Casgrain closed by distancing himself from Garneau, noting that he had no intention of viewing the bishop as 'an uncompromising and dominating spirit.' Nevertheless, here was further evidence that Laval was far from an entirely sympathetic character.[9]

Given the mixed messages it was possible to derive from his long reign as bishop, those who later invested considerable energy in promoting Laval's legacy were fortunate that he lived another twenty years after resigning his post. The man who emerged after 1688 was the very model of Christian virtue. The seminary remained Laval's proudest achievement, and he spent his last years there, rarely leaving the grounds except to attend to the poor. As André Vachon put it in the most recent biography of Laval: 'The prelate no longer gave thought to anything but prayer and mortification, limiting his outside activities to acts of charity ... He gave away everything he owned, asking for nothing that was not for his poor, for whom he even kept the greater part of his meals.'[10] In the same spirit, Laval's contemporaries wrote of his willingness to expose himself to illness in order to minister to the sick, and to wear clothes that could hardly protect him from the cold so as to provide newer garments to the truly needy.[11]

Perhaps because of his last years as much as his time as bishop, Laval's death was followed by an outpouring of popular sympathy. This may have been genuine, but it was not exactly spontaneous. His body lay in state for three days in the Cathedral, an event that prompted considerable public adoration. The intendant, Jacques Raudot, observed: 'As soon as he died, the people viewed him as having been canonized, exhibiting the same veneration for his body that one would have for a saint. They came from all around while his body lay in state, touching him with their rosary beads and their prayer books.'[12]

At the end of the third day, the body, dressed in full episcopal garb for the first time in two decades, was carried through the streets in a procession that included more than 150 priests and members of the male religious orders. Regarding how many laypeople either marched in the procession or watched from the sidelines, the evidence is silent. The record is similarly silent regarding the order in which the marchers passed through the city and the place of Laval's body in the procession. These questions would be of considerable significance for the organizers of the 1878 reburial. However, according to the *annaliste* for the Ursuline nuns, Laval's remains were carried through the streets by 'a group of six priests whose composition changed at each station.' The reference to stations linked the 1708 procession in honour of Laval to the ritual of marching past the Stations of the Cross, during which stops are made at various holy sites symbolizing stages in Christ's passage to his death. The stations in this case were the chapels of each of the town's religious orders, which were visited so that the cloistered nuns would be able to pay their last respects to Laval; much of this route would be replicated 170 years later. The procession eventually returned to the Cathedral, thus ending what the Ursulines' *annaliste* described as an unforgettable occasion: 'This land had never seen a comparable funeral procession.'[13]

Most of Laval's remains were then buried beneath the Cathedral. However, some parts of his body were not in the coffin that Roberge and Simard discovered in 1877. Before Laval was presented to the public in 1708, his heart had been removed for keeping at the seminary, which was not in a position to provide him with a proper resting place. After the corpse was opened up, Frère Houssart – who had been responsible for looking after the bishop during his retirement – had the idea of making parts of Laval's body available to the public, to encourage devotion to his memory. As Abbé August Gosselin, Laval's nineteenth-century biographer, observed: 'After the body had been opened up for the autopsy, [Houssart] soaked cloths with the blood of the bishop, cut away some of his hair, removed bone and cartilage from above his breast, and kept some of his clothing ... Over three thousand people wanted to possess one of these relics, in order to show their respect and devotion.'[14] There must have been some genuine adoration of Laval, considering that roughly 15 per cent of the Canadian population wanted to possess some part of him. Nevertheless, Houssart understood that action had to be taken to encourage reverence for Laval's memory. In a sense, he anticipated the fuss that would be made over what remained of Laval's remains in the late nineteenth century.

Laval Remembered Unobtrusively

By the late eighteenth century, Quebec City's clerical leaders had lost track of Laval's coffin and the general public had largely forgotten his legacy. During the first half of the nineteenth century, if the bishop became better known to literate Quebecers, it was largely through Garneau's less than kind treatment of the 'founder' of Quebec Catholicism. Even Abbé Gosselin, whose late-nineteenth-century biography of

Laval was meant to counter Garneau's criticisms, had to admit that Laval's impact had largely been forgotten. As Gosselin put it, the bishop's legacy might have survived 'in an ordinary society,' but not in the circumstances of eighteenth-century Quebec. Memories of Laval quickly receded: Quebecers had to get on with the business of surviving in a hostile environment; then later, in the second half of the century, they had to adapt to living 'under foreign domination, obliged to adapt to a new regime, and to abandon the majority of their long-held traditions.'[15]

If any institution worked to keep Laval's memory alive, especially after it had been sullied by Garneau, it was the seminary, which in 1859 organized a celebration of Laval on the bicentenary of his arrival in Canada. This public ceremony in honour of the bishop – the first since his funeral in 1708 – was an exceedingly modest affair, not only in comparison with the celebration of Laval in the 1870s, but even by the standards of Quebec City in the 1850s. In particular, the 1859 event paled in comparison with two events from the same decade organized around the celebration of the Battle of Ste-Foy, won by the French in the spring of 1760, seven months after their defeat on the Plains of Abraham. This battle was the last hurrah for the French Empire in the St. Lawrence Valley. Accordingly, there was considerable public interest when in 1852 three of the leaders of Quebec City's Société St-Jean-Baptiste – one of whom was none other than F.-X. Garneau – came across some human bones in a ravine not far from the site of the battle. There was no evidence to prove that these were soldiers from 1760, let alone French Catholic ones; even so, the Société St-Jean-Baptiste de Québec (SSJBQ), the leading lay organization for advancing French-Canadian interests, secured qualified episcopal approval two years later for the reburial of these bones in a proper grave. In early June of 1854 an imposing procession consisting largely of soldiers and SSJBQ members accompanied the remains of the 'unknown' soldiers through the streets of upper town to the Cathedral for a religious ceremony. It then proceeded to Ste-Foy, just west of the city limits, for their burial. One newspaper estimated that 10,000 spectators watched the event.[16]

This celebration focused on the heroic past of French-speakers, yet it was constructed to highlight cooperation between two ancient enemies. In the context of the Crimean War, in which France and England were allies, British officials were happy to lend their support to the SSJBQ to celebrate the memory of soldiers from both armies. British military officials provided guns to the marchers in the procession who represented the French soldiers of 1760. One British general observed: 'It really doesn't matter to which of the two armies these men had belonged.'[17] This was not what the leaders of the SSJBQ had had in mind when they began organizing the event, but by the time the big day arrived there was little evidence of any narrow national agenda.[18] Speaking at the burial, E.-P. Taché, a minister in the Canadian government, encouraged those who had accompanied the soldiers' remains to dedicate themselves to the construction of a monument on the site. However, he did not want it to be constructed 'in a mean-spirited or self-centred manner, but with generosity towards the memory of the soldiers of both armies ... Let us imitate the fine example which has been set by our citizens of British origin in the construction of the obelisk to the memories of both Wolfe and Montcalm ... Why would we want to be less generous than our neighbours of English ancestry?'[19]

It seems that Taché's advice was taken seriously in 1855, when the cornerstone for the Monument des Braves was laid. The ceremony, originally set to coincide with the Fête de St-Jean in late June, was delayed until the arrival in July of the French warship *La Capricieuse*, the first such vessel to sail up the St. Lawrence since the Conquest. The commander of *La Capricieuse* was accorded a special place in the festivities alongside the governor general; and the spirit of accommodation between French and English speakers was reinforced by the keynote speech of the day, delivered by P.-J.-O. Chauveau, the Superintendent of Public Instruction. The remains had at first been viewed as those of French soldiers; now Chauveau presented them as 'the mixed together bones of English Grenadiers, Scottish Highlanders and of all the combatants from this memorable day.'[20] This spirit of cooperation between people of various backgrounds was similarly reflected in the procession that passed through the town toward the site of the future Monument des Braves. An estimated 25,000 people watched French sailors (from *La Capricieuse*), English soldiers, Hurons dressed for war, and representatives of Quebec City's French-Canadian, English, and Irish communities march together.[21]

Conspicuous by their absence in the ceremonies of 1854 and 1855 were the leaders of the Catholic church, who had been lukewarm at best in supporting these celebrations. The leaders of the SSJBQ had wanted the bones buried alongside those of other French veterans in one of the city's Catholic cemeteries. Since there was no evidence that these were in fact the remains of Catholic soldiers, permission was denied, and the burial took place at the site of the battle. The archbishop permitted a religious ceremony at the Cathedral in 1854, but mass was not celebrated. As for the involvement of the church in 1855, it could not have been encouraged by the rather obvious efforts of British officials to court the French government and to make the celebration one of French–English cooperation. In particular, the church leaders must have been struck by the perfunctory visit they had been paid by the commander of *La Capricieuse*, compared to the effusive public tribute that he had paid to Garneau, who embodied the anticlerical strain in French-Canadian thought, most notably in his attacks on the good name of Mgr de Laval.

The celebrations of 1854 and 1855 had tried to play down the existence of distinctive religious and linguistic communities in Canada. In contrast, the 1859 bicentenary of Laval's arrival in Canada enabled clerical leaders to highlight the contours of an identifiable French-Catholic identity. The organizers of the ceremony for laying the cornerstone for the Monument des Braves had sought the participation of France so as to foster cooperation between French and English speakers. The Laval fête took a very different view of the French connection, coming as it did on the centenary of the French defeat on the Plains of Abraham. To the extent that France figured in the celebrations of 1859, it was in a negative manner: French Canadians were reminded that the defeat of France had been 'a Providential act.' Here was a people 'attached to its faith, its language, its customs and its clergy' – a people that had managed to survive in part by separating itself from the godless France that had grown out of the Revolution of 1789. Thanks to the Conquest, 'our ancient religion, our clergy, our churches, our seminaries, and our convents were preserved.'[22]

Everything about the two-day celebration of Laval's memory in June 1859 was designed to point to a people that had been able to survive on its own terms, without anyone else's help. The leaders of the seminary, who were responsible for the event, did not have bones at their disposal to generate a concrete and highly dramatic connection for the greater public between the past and the present; nor were they able to benefit from the broader trend across the western world toward staging sumptuous commemorative spectacles – a development that would be more pronounced by 1878. In 1859 the clerical leaders constructed a modest celebration, one designed to communicate a clear message but marked by a certain reluctance to involve the public at large.

The celebration of Laval's arrival in Quebec City was held on 15 and 16 June, to mark the exact date the bishop arrived in his new home. In the heyday of commemorative events, the timing would have been given much more careful thought; perhaps Laval's fête would have been given more visibility and nationalist significance by linking it with the St-Jean-Baptiste celebration that followed only a week later. Moreover, the spectacles staged later in the century would take to the streets to draw the public in, whereas this one was staged largely behind closed doors and lacked dramatic appeal. An obvious illustration of the organizers' lack of a flare for the dramatic is that they made a doctoral defence the main event of the first day. François-Alexandre-Hubert LaRue was a medical student at Université Laval, the first French-language university in North America, which had been established in 1852 as an outgrowth of the seminary.[23] Since the seminary had been Laval's proudest creation and had long championed his legacy, there was some logic in the seminary's decision to link a major event in the history of the university that bore the bishop's name with the anniversary of his arrival in Canada.

Beyond drawing attention to Laval's memory, LaRue's very public defence was designed to send the message that there existed a strong French-Catholic nation. As *Le Canadien* observed, the university's very creation was a tool 'which places our current generations on an equal footing with those in Europe in terms of the classical studies and the acquisition of higher education.'[24] The university might help integrate Quebecers into the modern world; however, judging from the subject of LaRue's dissertation, this integration would not necessarily diminish the role of Catholicism in Quebec society. LaRue had studied suicide, using the most modern scientific techniques, and aided by his 'moral and religious education which helped him steer his way through the sometimes unclear route towards scientific understanding.' In the end, he concluded that Quebec had the lowest suicide rate in the 'civilized' world, a situation attributable to the power of 'moral and religious ideas.'[25] Needless to say, LaRue, having been held up for public emulation, successfully defended his thesis. On the afternoon of the second day of the fête, he received his degree in another public event. (What would they have done on the second day if LaRue had failed his defence?) LaRue was the last to speak at the ceremony, and his words captured the spirit of the event. He recognized that he had been singled out for attention because the completion of his thesis had coincided with the 'bicentenary of the arrival in Canada of one of its greatest benefactors, Mgr de Montmorency-Laval.'[26]

This celebration of Laval's memory was dominated by talk. A debate between seminary students was scheduled as the main event for the first night of the fête. As with LaRue's defence, here was an opportunity to connect the past with the present by showing off the skills that had been acquired at an institution with a link to Laval.[27] However logical these events might have seemed to the leaders of the seminary, they could not attract crowds as large as those which had witnessed the processions honouring the veterans of the Battle of Ste-Foy.

Even when the organizers of the Laval fête constructed larger, more public events, they seemed reluctant to make them overly accessible. For instance, the second day began with a procession of clergy, professors, and students from the seminary to the Cathedral, where a lavishly organized mass was to be celebrated. Much care was taken to decorate the Cathedral and to provide a musical program worthy of Laval. As one newspaper put it, here was 'a solemn mass in which art and music combined with religion to enhance a serene atmosphere and to display the glories of our faith.'[28] In the end, however, seating inside the Cathedral was limited; the wider public was locked out, and could only see the procession that preceded the mass. Inexplicably, the route of this procession did not pass through city streets; instead it stuck to the more private paths connecting the seminary with the Cathedral. As a result, few Quebecers would have viewed, among others, 'the students and professors of the university dressed in their bright and highly textured ceremonial garb.'[29]

The public might also have come out in large numbers for the final event of the celebration, one that focused firmly on Laval through words and music. This event was staged in the Grande Salle of the university, but admission was restricted to men holding tickets of admission and women 'introduced by a gentleman, provided with a Card for that purpose.'[30] These tickets and cards were available only from the secretary of the university during very restricted office hours, yet they must have been grabbed up quickly, since the hall was full fifteen minutes after the doors opened. There were 2,000 people eager to partake of a 'an evening of music to celebrate the two-hundredth anniversary of the arrival in Canada of Mgr de Montmorency-Laval.' One newspaper described it as a 'concert-monstre' that involved two hundred performers, who constituted 'an army drawn from all parts of the population, from the young to the old.'[31]

By all accounts, the highlight of this four-hour concert was the debut of the 'Cantate en l'honneur de Mgr de Laval,' with words by Octave Crémazie set to music from Rossini's opera *La Donna del Lago*.[32] By now Crémazie had earned the mantle of French Canada's 'poète national,' with a status comparable to that of the historian Garneau. Crémazie's nationalism, unlike Garneau's, had a strong religious element; thus the poet could write to Abbé Casgrain that 'our language [is] the second defining characteristic of our nationality, since our religion is the first.'[33] He imagined a French-Canadian identity in which secular and religious influences were in some balance; in this spirit his cantata, although in honour of Mgr de Laval, gave equal billing to Champlain, the secular founder of the nation. With only two exceptions, Crémazie presented the name of Laval in conjunction with that of Champlain, just as he saw the origins of New France in both 'la croix' (the cross) and 'l'épée' (the sword), and the future of his people as both 'Français et catholique.' In this effort to remember two very different but not incompatible sides of French Canada's past, Crémazie closed with this patriotic appeal: 'Vive, Champlain! vive, Laval!'[34]

Crémazie's 'Cantate' became the unofficial anthem of the various celebrations of Laval and Champlain that are the focus of this book, and was so popular that by the early twentieth century it had been memorized by 'six generations of schoolchildren.'[35] This popularity was no doubt linked to the poet's conception of French-Canadian nationalism, which was broad enough to accommodate both the secular concerns of a Champlain and the more religious ones of a Laval. However, in two speeches that constituted an intermission for the 'soirée musicale,' Laval was presented in his own right as a two-dimensional figure. The first of the speakers, Abbé (later Archbishop and Cardinal) Taschereau, described Laval not only as a religious leader, but also as someone who had helped 'to organize the government of this colony on a solid and rational basis.'[36]

In the second of these speeches, by U.J. Tessier, a professor at the seminary, Laval emerged even more strikingly as a figure around whom all Quebecers, regardless of their differences, might rally. Tessier focused on Laval's legacy in education, in particular on his founding of the seminary, and he listed a significant number of lay and clerical leaders who had passed through that institution's doors. But the most dramatic part of his speech came when, while touting the legacy of the first bishop of Quebec, he paid tribute to 'the eldest of the surviving graduates of the seminary of Quebec; the most eloquent orator and the most sincere patriot of our land, the Honourable Louis-Joseph Papineau.' With these words, the crowd broke out in wild applause, as Tessier had succeeded in bridging the gap between the sacred, represented by Laval, and the secular, in the person of the anticlerical leader of 1837.[37] Thus, the final event of this celebration of Laval was a rallying cry for all French Canadi-ans to focus on what united them and distinguished them from the other inhabitants of British North America.

In the end, surprisingly few people would have known the 1859 fête had taken place. Though it was widely discussed in the French-language newspapers of Quebec City, and even resulted in a pamphlet under the aegis of the university, it probably made little impression on ordinary French-speakers, who were far removed from the circles of the seminary and the university and who would have been unable to witness it, since it took place largely behind closed doors.[38] And the local English-language press, which lacked close ties to institutions such as the seminary, simply ignored the celebration, which had made no effort to invade public space.

There is little evidence that Laval's memory was any more alive in the years after 1859 than it had been before the fête. This situation was underscored in 1874 when a celebration was staged for the bicentenary of the founding of the diocese of Quebec. Although Laval had been personally responsible for this development, his connection to the event was rather muted, as organizers chose instead to emphasize the tri-umphs of Catholicism across North America. When it came time to dress up the Cathedral, whose status was being elevated to that of a Basilica, none of the decorations made any reference to Laval's legacy.[39] And when the organizers inserted a musical extravaganza into the program, they opted for the symphonic ode 'Christophe Colomb,' ignoring the 'Cantate en l'honneur de Mgr de Laval,' which might have been more logical and which was more explicitly Catholic.[40] Be that as it may, the ode to Columbus was performed on two occasions so that as many people as possible could attend. This sense that the public should be drawn into the affair – a spirit totally lacking in 1859 – was similarly evident when a procession made its way through the streets surrounding the Basilica. Indeed, the organizers' decision to reach out to the public was reflected in the introduction to the volume published to describe the celebration, which placed this three-day event in the context of the 'centennial anniversaries' that were becoming more and more popular across the western world. Nevertheless, Laval did not benefit from the exposure. He was not even mentioned in the sermon at the end of the mass that followed the procession.[41]

A clear indication of the limited reverence for Laval is the failure of attempts to use the 1874 celebration to launch a fundraising campaign for a monument to him in the Basilica. Four years later, on the eve of

Laval's reburial, Mgr Edmond Langevin, the bishop of Rimouski, who had long been labouring to promote Laval's legacy, had to admit that he had succeeded in raising only $137. Now that Laval's coffin had been discovered, he was prepared to turn that money over to Archbishop Taschereau. As Langevin observed: 'I am going to explain to the contributors that the sum received will be handed over to the Archbishop to use as he sees fit. At the time, no one could have imagined that the body of the first bishop of Quebec would be exhumed and reinterred in the Chapel of the seminary. But since that is about to be the case, it is only fitting that the subscription be used to erect a monument in the same place where the remains of the venerable founder of the church in Canada will be deposited.'[42] The possibilities for promoting the memory of Laval had been transformed by the discovery of his remains.

Laval's Return in Troubled Times

Although Roberge and Simard unearthed Laval's coffin in the fall of 1877, the bishop's remains were not reinterred until the following spring. Nevertheless, by early in 1878 preparations were in place for the staging of a spectacular event.[43] This conscientious planning contrasted starkly with the slapdash organization of the 1874 bicentenary of the diocese of Quebec, which only took shape weeks before thousands of visitors were to descend on the city. In the case of Laval's remains, however, nothing was left to chance, since the clerical organizers recognized that this opportunity to promote Laval's memory would never arise again. Moreover, they had the incentive to put on as imposing a show as possible in light of two significant and potentially unsettling developments in the late 1870s, one religious and the other economic.

The discovery of Laval's coffin came at a time of intense in-fighting between ultramontane and liberal factions of the clergy. This conflict revolved in part around the role of the Catholic clergy in Quebec politics. Since the early 1870s, some elements within the church had been looking for ways to oppose the influence of the Liberal Party in Ottawa and Quebec City. These ultramontanes believed that the party was dominated by European-style 'liberals' who were sympathetic to the idea of eradicating the church's influence in society. In fact, the most extreme liberal thinkers in Quebec constituted only one element within the Quebec Liberal Party, and even they were far less radical than their European counterparts. But this did not matter to the ultramontanes, who persuaded the bishops to issue a pastoral letter in 1875 condemning

Catholic liberalism. This cast a cloud over the future of the Liberal Party. Archbishop Taschereau distanced himself in 1876 from this direct involvement in partisan politics; even so, some clergy obviously heeded the call, and as a result, several elections, at both the provincial and federal levels, were reversed by the courts in late 1876 and early 1877 because of the 'undue influence' of clergy.

Rome was troubled by the fact that bishops were arguing with one another, and that clergy were opposing candidates for office simply because they were members of the Liberal Party. It was also bothered by the bickering between ultramontane and liberal elements of the Quebec clergy over the nature of Catholic university education in the province. The founding of Université Laval in 1852 as the first French Catholic university in British North America led to a demand by the ultramontane bishop of Montreal, Ignace Bourget, for a separate institution in his city. Bourget viewed Université Laval as a bastion of liberal forces within the clergy – forces that had long held sway at the seminary and that had now extended their influence to the university. Ultimately, in 1876 the Vatican declared that there would be no separate university in Montreal, and that Université Laval was free to open a branch campus in Montreal. This raised for the ultramontanes the spectre of the further spread of liberalism. Rome perhaps hoped that this decree would settle the university question. It didn't, so in the spring of 1877, the Vatican sent an envoy to Quebec, Mgr George Conroy, to put an end to public quarrelling among church officials.

Conroy's presence in Quebec City in June 1877 provided the backdrop for one of the most famous political speeches in Canadian history. At the time of his speech on political liberalism, Wilfrid Laurier was a rising star in the federal Liberal caucus. His party was in power but lacked a strong presence in Quebec, in part due to the cloud that hung over it (as well as its provincial counterpart) as a result of clerical animosity. Laurier had been given the task of explaining that Canadian 'liberalism' had nothing to do with the revolutionary liberalism of the European sort. He successfully explained not only to the hall – which was packed with Liberals – but more importantly to Mgr Conroy that there was nothing contradictory about voting Liberal and being a conscientious Catholic.

Conroy came to Quebec already sympathetic to the point of view expressed by Laurier, which was held as well by the more 'liberal' elements within the Catholic hierarchy such as Archbishop Taschereau and the leaders of the seminary. In the end, though Laurier no doubt made it easier for ordinary Quebecers to vote Liberal – thus changing the dynamics of Quebec politics – neither his speech nor Conroy's presence entirely silenced the ultramontanes. Nor for that matter was Conroy able to placate the ultramontanes who were incensed by the envoy's determination to settle the university issue. He ultimately presided over the creation of the Montreal branch of Université Laval in January 1878, only months after the discovery of Laval's remains. Conroy's low esteem in certain quarters was noted by the superior of the seminary, who wrote in his journal on the envoy's death in the summer of 1878: 'this death was a joyous development for our fervent, ultramontane Catholics ... It appeared to these people that providence had delivered a severe punishment against *liberalism*.'[44]

The discovery of Laval's remains during Conroy's mission provided an opportunity for the various factions to work together to celebrate Quebec Catholicism. The liberal elements, especially those at the seminary, viewed Laval more as a builder of the infrastructure of the Quebec church than as an ideologue, whereas the ultramontanes drew from the lessons of Laval's life that spoke to the close ties between church and state. From the perspective of Archbishop Taschereau, whose authority had been challenged by the ultramontanes, this was an opportunity to take charge of a cause that everyone could support.

The same discovery also provided the opportunity to stage a celebration that would bring together the various classes in Quebec society. Social tensions were in the air as a depression that had begun in 1873 continued to drag on, with no end in sight. It had started with a banking crisis in the United States and Europe, and by 1878 a number of Quebec-based banks had collapsed, many large companies had gone bankrupt, and many industrial workers had been laid off or seen their pay reduced. As Joseph Auclair, the curé of Notre-Dame de Québec, observed only weeks before Laval's remains were reinterred, the people were living through some 'difficult circumstances ... hard times, a slowdown in commercial activity, the impoverishment of the working class, and the suffering of the poor.'[45]

So it is hardly surprising that workers fought back, waging strikes that often were perceived – not without cause – as a challenge to the social order. In the United States, only months before the discovery of Laval's coffin, there was the 'the great uprising of 1877,' a series of strikes that left 'over one hundred people dead and millions of dollars' worth of property destroyed.'[46] Later in the year there was a strike by hundreds of men working on the Lachine Canal in Montreal. This disruption was the

culmination of a number of smaller ones along the canal that year.
Quebec City saw a number of strikes the same year, by workers constructing the new legislative buildings. As it turned out, all these skirmishes
were the warm-up for a larger confrontation that took place only two
weeks after the ceremonies to reinter Laval's body. On this occasion,
thousands of construction workers went on strike, with the disruptions
spreading out from the Hôtel du Parlement building site. For roughly a
week, workers marched through the streets, trying to shut down other
work sites to bolster their ranks. Finally, on 12 June, the marching
erupted into a full-scale riot during which shops were looted. It ended
only after the Riot Act was read and troops called in from Montreal
intervened.[47]

No one could have anticipated the upheavals of early June of 1878;
even so, they were manifestations of the considerable social tension in
Quebec City in the months leading up to the reinterment of Mgr de
Laval. On the very eve of his reburial, some workmen on the parliament
buildings wrote to one Quebec City newspaper, making it perfectly clear
that they were unhappy with 'the way in which workers [had] been
treated since the beginning of the project.'[48] Perhaps all of this explains
why the organizers of the celebration often mentioned the support their
project was receiving from all social classes. The official report on the
reburial festivities drew attention to the involvement of 'citizens of all
social classes ... who have seen it as both a duty and an honour to take
part in this fitting and grandiose celebration.' Ultimately, the participation of the various classes made it possible for the procession carrying
Laval's remains to attract 'a crowd ... a human avalanche' of 30,000
spectators.[49] This procession took control of the streets, much as the
workers had done and would do again more forcefully in the weeks to
follow. The transfer of Laval's remains to the seminary provided an
occasion for clerical leaders to encourage cooperation both within
Quebec Catholicism and among the various classes in Quebec society.
With the stakes so high, the big event was planned with meticulous
detail.

Preparing Laval for Display

Throughout the spring of 1878, while the ordinary people of Quebec
City focused on their day-to-day existence, local church leaders occupied
themselves with planning the town's first commemorative spectacle. In
the process, the superior of the seminary, Abbé Thomas-Étienne Hamel,

and his associates reflected a nineteenth-century interest in the public display of the dead. As Serge Gagnon has put it: 'Such ostentation would be found offensive in our secular society ... However, in the nineteenth century, all segments of society would have responded positively to the creation of a fete around the remains, showing particular care to keep the skeleton intact in anticipation of the resurrection of the body.'[50]

Hamel's program for the celebration was as grandiose as he could make it without hurting Laval's chances of being canonized. Church rules established in the seventeenth century forbade the public veneration of any candidate for sainthood. Veneration was restricted to those who had already made their way through the canonization process, so it was important not to venerate those who had not yet been proven worthy.[51] Hamel wrote to a friend: 'We will not do anything that will resemble a cult. We believe that he died with the air of saintliness around him, and we would not want to hurt his chances for canonization. There will be a funeral ceremony, but it will be as solemn as possible.'[52] The seminary's superior was troubled enough by this matter that he wrote to a colleague, then in Rome, to confirm that he had not gone too far in his plans for the reburial. In turn, Hamel's Roman connection consulted lawyers in the Congregation of Rites (which was responsible for cases leading to sainthood), seeking reassurance that no line had been crossed.[53]

In the end, the organizers exercised some restraint, although it might not have seemed so to the general public, which watched several imposing processions pass through the streets. Abbé Gosselin came away from the event convinced that 'Quebec had never seen such a grandiose fête.' Nevertheless, he also observed that much had been done 'to avoid giving the slightest appearance that Mgr de Laval was being publicly venerated as if he were a saint. The rules of the church are so wise and so severe!' In particular, Gosselin pointed to the scaling down of the mass to be celebrated on the day of Laval's reburial and to the decision that only white and violet would be used for decorations over the course of the fête.[54]

Which colours to use was only one question among many as the organizers crafted the story they would tell. Abbé Hamel, in his original design for the fête, had proposed that Laval's remains be displayed 'on a cushion of red silk.' All of Hamel's suggestions except this one were eventually incorporated into the program. Red was not an acceptable colour since it suggested a direct connection with Christ, his apostles, and the martyrs of the faith. Because it would have promoted a cult around Laval, it was rejected. Laval would instead be displayed 'on a cushion of violet silk.' According to the official publication for the celebrations, violet was the predominant colour because it indicated 'a certain regret not to be able to celebrate without restraint. It masked the real triumph [of Laval's life] by giving the appearance of grief.' Along the procession routes, buildings were decorated with violet and white tapestries. Laval's coffin was adorned with ribbons of the same colours.[55]

Colour questions aside, Abbé Hamel was left to his own devices in preparing a highly choreographed celebration that took up much of May 1878. The fête actually began on 2 May when an official party entered the sealed room in the university where the box containing Laval's remains had been deposited earlier in the year. There were seals on the box, and after these were broken the bones were laid out on a table and arranged 'in their natural order.' Doctors confirmed that these were the bones of someone roughly the size of Laval and that certain bones were missing – further proof that this was the bishop's skeleton. It was well documented that his body had been carved up at the time of his death. The doctors then left the bones in the care of the Sœurs de la Charité, who cleaned them and immersed them in wax. The official account of these events pointed out that the wax was required 'in order to protect them against deterioration from contact with the air.' However, Abbé Hamel observed in his journal that the wax served 'to take away their disturbing appearance which might have been found repugnant by certain individuals. Once laid out, the wax-covered bones could not be found repulsive.'[56]

The bones were then fastened together with violet bands laid out on a silk cushion, and surrounded by garlands of wax flowers. The most intriguing decorations were the *couronnes* that had been prepared by groups or individuals. The use of crowns to adorn the heads of saintly figures has a long tradition in Christianity; the origins of this practice date back to Christ's crown of thorns. The precise nature of such crowns varies from culture to culture, but invariably they reflect the triumph of an individual who has achieved a heroic level of dedication to the faith. In this particular case, the crowns, after Laval's remains had touched them, were to be returned 'to the donors as a precious souvenir and, one hopes, as a relic.'[57] The organizers believed that if these crowns could be linked to miracles, they might some day provide evidence to support Laval's candidacy for canonization.

In all there were eighty crowns. Some of these were placed directly on Laval's remains; others were reserved to decorate his casket or the platform on which his coffin was to be displayed. Although Abbé Gosselin described 'a spontaneous movement that focused upon the bishop's

Laval's remains, 1878 (Archives nationales du Québec à Québec; Livernois Photo, P560, S2, P300370-664)

tomb,' with regard to the production of the crowns and to the whole celebration, little was improvised.[58] The seminary encouraged the crowns so as to secure as broad a participation as possible in the celebration of Laval. Some offers of crowns were more spontaneous than others. Clearly, the many crowns produced by the seminary students were prepared on demand. Others, however, were not the result of any direct request. In this category were the crowns contributed by individuals, families, and local businesses. Even the Quebec government contributed a crown *au nom du peuple Canadien*, which was inscribed with the nationalist mantra of the time: 'Nos institutions, notre langue et nos lois.' On its face, the celebration of Laval was a religious event, but the Quebec government did not hesitate to join in, viewing the event as a celebration of one of the founders of French Canada, who had played both civil and religious roles in seventeenth-century New France. Nevertheless, as we will see, the participation of the province would be a bone of contention, given that the government of the day was a Liberal one headed by a Protestant, Henri-Gustave Joly.

The most interesting crown by far came from Prosper Vincent, also known as Sawatennen, the first Huron to be ordained a priest.[59] Though natives would be encouraged, and on one occasion hired, to join the celebrations of the founding fathers, Vincent's involvement was apparently unsolicited. In 1878 he was the vicar of the parish of Ancienne-Lorette just outside Quebec City, which bordered on the Huron village where he was born. Thus, Vincent was ideally positioned to bring natives into the Laval celebration by contributing something quite out of the ordinary. Most of the crowns were made out of flowers; he described his as 'a small savage crown made from precious stones of antique porcelain, the product of my ancestors from before the arrival of Mgr de Laval in Canada ... These small stones were of great value for the Hurons; they were presented to the first chiefs of the tribe as a symbol of their importance ... Although violet and white are the only colours permitted on this occasion, I think that as a Huron I should be allowed to add another one, because we never use fewer than three colours ... I have chosen green, the sign of hope; we all hope that soon the process will begin for the canonization of our saintly bishop.'[60]

The preparation and decoration of Laval's remains was a lengthy process that took up the first two weeks of May. Clearly, the organizers took great pride in the result, since they arranged to have the bones photographed by Jules-Ernest Livernois, the 'official's photographer of late-nineteenth-century Quebec City. Livernois's 'customers included all the nation's most prominent figures: religious leaders, renowned lawyers, politicians, businessmen, scientists, scholars, and noted visitors.' The firm made a special point of maintaining close connections with the Catholic church, and Jules-Ernest was himself extremely devout.[61] Accordingly, his family's studio was the logical choice when it came time to record for posterity what Laval looked like as he passed before the public. The photograph would be employed in the campaign to promote Laval's legacy. *L'Événement* observed during the celebrations: 'Everyone wants to have a copy of this precious souvenir. On the back of the photograph, there is a prayer for the glorification of Mgr de Laval, signed by the archbishop.'[62]

The photograph done, it was time to finish preparing Laval's remains for public display. The violet cushion on which the bones, the garlands, and the crowns had been arranged was placed inside a coffin, which had glass sides, in accordance with Hamel's instructions. However, the flowers and crowns were piled so high over the bones that a glass cover had to be built for the coffin; this rose, in the shape of a pyramid.[63] Some of the ornaments were hung from the inside of this cover so as not to block the public's view of the bones.

The Language of the 'Procession de la Fête-Dieu'

All of this careful preparation led up to two separate and heavily choreographed public processions. On 15 May the elaborately decorated coffin was transported from the tightly guarded office at the university to the seminary chapel, where the public would be allowed to view it over the following week. Then on 23 May, Laval was taken to the streets once again; this procession made its way from the seminary to the Basilica, where a mass was celebrated; after this he was returned to the seminary for reburial. The seminary, the university, and the Basilica were adjacent to one another, so there was no need for circuitous routes through the city. But these processions of course had nothing to do with transportation and everything to do with controlling public space in order to put on a show permeated with messages.

Every element of both processions was carefully considered with the goal of maximizing the impact on the population. Decisions had to be made about who would march, the order in which they would march, and the routes the marchers would follow. In the end, Hamel and his colleagues adhered to certain local traditions for public processions – traditions with roots in Quebec that went back to the time of Laval. To

Laval's coffin, 1878 (Archives nationales du Québec à Québec; Livernois Photo, P560, S2, P300370-663)

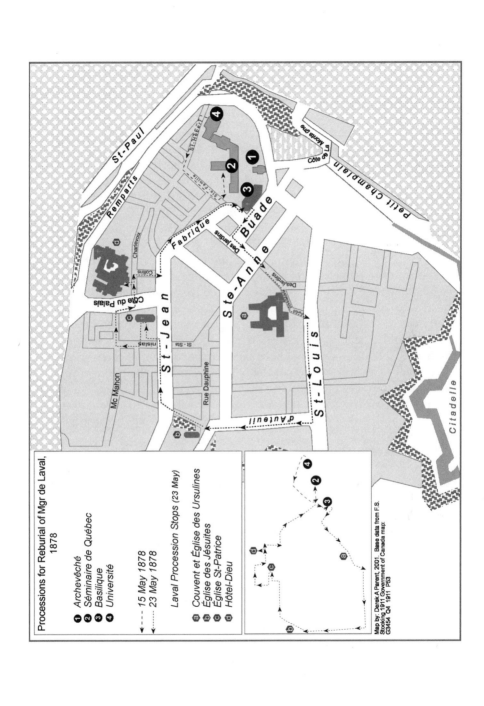

Processions for Reburial of Mgr de Laval,
1878

1 Archevêché
2 Séminaire de Québec
3 Basilique
4 Université

---- 15 May 1878
······ 23 May 1878

Laval Procession Stops (23 May)

a Couvent et Église des Ursulines
b Église des Jésuites
c Église St-Patrice
d Hôtel-Dieu

Map by: Derek A Parent, 2001. Base data from F.S.
Stocking 1911 Government of Canada map:
G3454 Q4 1911 P53

the untrained eye of the early twenty-first century, the processions of May 1878 would have had little meaning; but to French Canadians of the late nineteenth century, the processions had their own 'language' and were telling a story connected with the Catholic holiday known in French as the 'Fête-Dieu' and in English as Corpus Christi.[64]

In the earliest days of New France, even before the arrival of Mgr de Laval, the Fête-Dieu was celebrated every year in each parish.[65] Participation was obligatory, according to church ritual that stretched back to the thirteenth century, when the Feast of Corpus Christi was added to the Catholic calendar on a date that could fall any time from the end of May to the end of June, depending on the timing of Easter.[66] The holiday was part of a larger campaign within the medieval church to celebrate the Eucharist as constituting the body of Christ. Unlike any other feast day, 'Corpus Christi [was] the feast of a symbol, a concept, a world-view rather than [that] of a saint, or a commemoration of a particular historic event.'[67] In the years leading up to the creation of the holiday, rules and regulations were put in place regarding the preparation and use of the host, especially in the context of holy communion. Among the practices that became commonplace was the taking of the host to the ill; this soon resulted in the staging of 'a veritable procession with followers and an audience ... People were taught to fall to their knees and recite prayers when they heard the ringing of the bells announcing the passage of the viaticum (the vessel that held the host in transit).'[68] Based on this experience, when a feast day was finally proclaimed to celebrate the presence of Christ's body on earth, it was only logical that the procession take centre stage.

By the time the Fête-Dieu procession made its way to New France, it had been precisely shaped by four centuries of European experience. The holiday traditionally began with a mass at which the host was blessed; following this it was taken to the streets, carried by a priest, who marched beneath a canopy at the centre of the procession. No one from the community was denied the right to march, but all were arranged in a manner that privileged those closest to the host; this reflected how ecclesiastical and secular power was distributed in the community. It was no coincidence that the body of Christ was associated with the community assembled as a body. As Mervyn James has observed: "'Body" was the pre-eminent symbol in terms of which society was conceived. Other images were available – the social order might be seen as a tree, or as a ship ... All had the advantage of suggesting structure ... But it was the idea of the social order as body which had the widest connotation

Fête-Dieu procession (Archives de la Ville de Québec, negative 8201)

[because] it suggested the intimacy and naturalness of the social bond ... The language of body provided an instrument by means of which social wholeness and social differentiation could be conceived and experienced at many different levels.' In sum, the Corpus Christi procession was designed to show that it was possible for a divided body to function as a whole.[69]

For all the efforts of lay and clerical leaders, there were always some in the community who refused to accept their assigned places with good grace.[70] Nevertheless, every year a procession did take place that at least gave the appearance that something was natural about the roles to which people had been assigned. The sense that the Fête-Dieu procession was somehow natural was reinforced by other elements of its organization. For instance, the host was positioned in the middle of the procession; this was intended to reflect the order of the universe, in which the various planets were arranged around the centre. Also to reflect nature, trees were placed along the route, flowers were cast in front of the host as it passed through the streets, and incense was burned so that 'the city had the fragrance of the forest and flowers.' The idea was to transform the route of the procession into a space 'decorated and transformed into a Garden of Eden.'[71]

Everything about the Fête-Dieu procession was designed to convey a message. This included the route it took, which usually formed a loop so as to consecrate the space thereby enclosed – usually the parish. As Claude Macherel put it, such processional routes 'impose a loop upon urban space; ideally, a circle is employed in order to demarcate a completely enclosed area.'[72] To reinforce its claim to a certain route, the church often erected *reposoirs* (street altars) along the way where marchers could stop and pray. The location of these *reposoirs* was significant; often they were placed before the houses of prominent citizens, further reinforcing the hierarchy in civil society. Also, the route was often decorated with ornate *arcs de triomphe*, usually bearing religious messages, under which the marchers passed. On a more symbolic level, these *arcs* were modelled after similar structures that had long been constructed along streets in Europe 'in order to celebrate the entry of a ruler into a conquered city. The *arc de triomphe* of the Fête-Dieu occupies the same function. In this case, the ruler is God who in the form of the host is led triumphantly through the streets.'[73]

The traditions of the Fête-Dieu procession were implanted in New France, which was first settled during the Counter-Reformation, during which emphasis was increasingly placed on the Eucharist as a symbol differentiating Catholics from Protestants.[74] In New France, beginning in the mid-seventeenth century, the Fête-Dieu was a time for the population of each parish to come together in the streets, claim the territory of the parish as holy, and draw attention to the social order. In the mid-nineteenth century, when the hierarchy of the Quebec church was trying to reinforce the role of Catholicism in the wake of the rebellions of 1837–8, the Fête-Dieu procession took on special significance. As Mgr Bourget, the bishop of Montreal, proclaimed: 'We will celebrate everywhere, and with as much pomp as possible.'[75] By the time Laval returned to the streets of Quebec City, this procession had long been a fixture of the French-Canadian calendar. Its language was well known to the French Canadians who watched the two processions that constituted the centrepiece of the bishop's reburial.

Taking Laval to the Streets

The first procession was referred to as *une translation intime* (an intimate movement of the remains), because only those directly associated with the seminary or the university, who claimed to constitute Laval's 'family,' were allowed to march alongside the casket as it made its way from the university to the seminary. As the marchers passed before the crowds lining rue Hébert and rue Ste-Famille, there could be little doubt that the procession had been choreographed with attention to the conventions of the Fête-Dieu. What could have been more natural than to transfer Laval's body in a procession inspired by the body of Christ? The event was uncharacteristic of a normal Corpus Christi procession, in that it limited participation to those with ties to the seminary or the university; but everything else about the event would have triggered memories of the annual spring ritual. The route of the procession was more or less circular, consecrating space shared by the university and the seminary. More significantly, the participants marched in an order that mirrored that used by the Fête-Dieu. The organizers claimed they didn't want to present Laval as if he were a saint, yet his remains were at the centre of the procession and rested on a cushion just like the host in the Corpus Christi celebration. Students were at the start and the end of the line, while the leaders of the seminary and the university were clustered around Laval's coffin; thus, the most important marchers were at the centre near Laval's remains. Even the use of incense ordered by Abbé Hamel reflected centuries of Fête-Dieu tradition.

In spite of all the preparation, the *translation intime* was relatively brief, lasting less than thirty minutes. Even so, it provided a dramatic start to a celebration that would continue for nine days and that would end with a much more elaborate procession. In between the two events Laval's remains were displayed to the public in the seminary chapel, which had been lavishly decorated in violet and white. The chapel also contained a new supply of crowns, which the students had carried as they marched in the *translation intime*. These crowns were then deposited around the coffin, which had been placed on a platform. This arrangement made it look as if Laval was floating on air, supported only by four hundred floral crowns.

While Laval's remains were lying in state, 'a crowd of a countless number of people' approached the first bishop of Quebec. 'The eagerness of the people to venerate the blessed casket, and the zeal that they showed to touch it with different holy objects were truly moving.'[76] People who were troubled by personal problems, and those with physical afflictions, came to seek help from Laval. Religious orders, school groups, and delegations from nearby parishes were given appointments to ensure that they would have time alone with Laval's remains. On the afternoon of 22 May, these visits came to a close; the time had come to prepare the coffin for its passage, the next day, through the streets of the city. This second procession was to be the highlight of the fête.

The procession of 23 May defied Fête-Dieu tradition by restricting participation to well-defined groups of marchers. Although the cast of characters had been considerably expanded since the *translation intime*, there was still no role in this event for *le peuple*, who were consigned to the sidelines as spectators. In almost every other regard, however, this procession – really two processions in one – conformed to the conventions of the Fête-Dieu both in the route it followed and in the way the marchers were organized.

The first part was referred to by organizers as '*[une procession] particulière*' (a private procession), because participation was largely limited to members or students of various religious orders and to individuals associated with specific Catholic groups. This was an intricately planned event; participants joined or left the procession at various points along the way. These comings and goings suggested a certain openness to the community that was typical of Fête-Dieu processions. Yet in spite of all the changes in the cast of characters, Laval's remains never lost their place of honour at the centre of the line, which followed a route 'almost identical to the one followed through the city on the day of his funeral.'[77] In this fashion, the events of 1708 were being recreated in the streets of Quebec City.

Crowds started taking up places along the route as early as 5:30 a.m., though the great event was not scheduled to begin for another two hours. At 7 a.m., students from the Ursuline convent made their way, 'marching as if they were already in a procession, carrying decorative banners,' to the courtyard of the seminary, where they joined members or students of other female religious orders. Thus, as the procession set off, many of the participants were female, adding to the inclusive spirit of the event. After the firing of the first of one hundred cannon shots that would be heard during the procession, the marchers headed off for their first stop – the Ursuline convent, which Laval's remains had last visited 170 years before, and which for this occasion was decorated in the obligatory white and violet. The procession then split in two; while the roughly nine hundred male students at the front of the procession remained outside, the clergy, followed by Laval's remains and the women and girls, entered the Ursuline church. Inside, the casket was placed before a grille, behind which the Ursulines fell to their knees and prayed, as their forebears had done early in the eighteenth century.

The women and girls now dropped out of the procession as the students and clergy left the church with Laval's coffin, followed by a new group of marchers – men and boys belonging to various local chapters of the 'Congrégation de Notre-Dame.' These congrégations originated in the sixteenth century when a Jesuit, Père Léon, came up with the idea of organizing laymen under clerical supervision 'to honour the Mother of God by a common cult and to seek through her maternal protection and the emulation of her virtues their personal sanctification and the well-being of those near to them.' The original Quebec City chapter was established in 1657, two years before Laval's arrival, but only received a chapel of its own in the early nineteenth century. In 1849 the Jesuits, following their return to Canada after their banishment by London and dissolution by Rome in the late eighteenth century, were placed in charge of this chapel, which came to be known as the Chapelle des Jésuites.[78] It was here that the congréganistes assembled from various parts of the city before making their way to the Ursuline church, where they took the place of the women at the end of the line. The procession then retraced the steps of the congréganistes, taking Laval's remains to the Chapelle des Jésuites. Here, once again, the students stood guard outside while the rest of the party went inside for prayers in honour of the first bishop. The organizers were retracing Laval's 1708 itinerary whenever possible; here, the Jesuit chapel stood in for the Jesuit church of the

French regime, which had been demolished in 1800 after the order's misfortunes.

The exchange of marchers was repeated twice more that morning. The *congréganistes* dropped out to be replaced by priests and laymen from the Irish Catholic community as the procession made its way to St. Patrick's Church. Later, after celebrations inside their church, the Irish contingent dropped out and was replaced by representatives of the various local chapters of the Société St-Jean-Baptiste, who joined the end of the line as Laval's remains made their way to the end of the first part of the procession, the Eglise de l'Hôtel-Dieu. It was here that Laval's 1708 procession had made its final stop before continuing on to the Cathedral.

While the representatives of the SSJBQ waited outside to take their place in the second part of the procession, in which lay leaders would play a significant role, the clergy entered to place Laval's coffin on a specially prepared platform in the chapel, which had been decorated, of course, in white and violet. As the chronicler for the Sœurs Augustines observed: 'We worked for three days to complete the decorations, but we paid little attention to our fatigue while thinking about the honour of receiving in this church the venerated remains of the first bishop of Quebec.' The sisters were grateful for the opportunity 'to come close to the coffin holding the body of the holy man, which was positioned very close to our grill ... Seeing these dried up bones brought tears to the eyes of many of us.'[79]

The arrival of the cortege at the Hôtel-Dieu brought the first part of the procession to an end. It had been intricately choreographed, and had presented Laval as *fondateur* in two very different contexts. As the procession visited various sites along its route, much as a Fête-Dieu procession would stop at *reposoirs*, he was displayed mainly in terms of his Catholicism, and his remains were honoured by men and women, clerics and laypeople, French and English speakers. Laval's status as a 'universal Catholic' was symbolized by his coffin's visit to St. Patrick's Church, even though the Irish had obviously not been on the scene in the bishop's lifetime.[80] At the same time, other aspects of the *procession particulière* reflected Laval's place in the narrower French Catholic community. The sites that were visited, other than St. Patrick's, had been on the route of Laval's 1708 funeral procession; this conveyed the message that a French Catholic nation with roots in the French regime had been able to survive in spite of all hardships. This more narrowly nationalistic message would dominate the second part of the procession.

Laval's remains at the Hôtel-Dieu, 1878 (Archives du Monastère des Augustines de l'Hôtel-dieu de Québec; Livernois Photo; Décoration de l'église des Augustines pour la translation des restes de Mgr de Laval, 23 mai 1878)

While the *procession particulière* was making its way to the Hôtel-Dieu, a smaller procession was setting off for the same place from the archbishop's palace, led by Archbishop Taschereau, the other bishops from Quebec, and Archbishop Taché of St-Boniface. The leaders of French-Canadian Catholicism (defined in its broadest geographical sense) were 'bedecked with black capes and white mitres. Each bishop was accompanied by two chaplains. This august procession, something entirely new, something that Quebec had never seen before, passed between two lines of respectful onlookers who were packed closely together and who were deeply moved by the spectacle.'[81]

On their arrival at the Hôtel-Dieu, the bishops were joined in the chapel by various civic leaders of French Canada, including most of the Quebec Cabinet. Also on hand was the lieutenant-governor, Luc Letellier de St-Just, who was billed in official accounts of the festivities as 'the successor to Vaudreuil,' the last French governor of New France, who happened to be Canadian born. This depiction of Letellier stands in contrast with that of Champlain, who in celebrations in his honour was identified as the first in a series of colonial governors whose line extended to the Governor General of Canada. In the 1878 celebration of Laval, the lieutenant-governor was seen as a successor of a French colonial governor; this elevated Quebec to a higher status than would be acceptable to English Canadians, who would strongly influence the Champlain celebrations. In their view, Canada rather than Quebec was the successor state to New France. National identity was being promoted in the second part of the 1878 procession. So Letellier was viewed as the representative of 'the French Canadian nation at the tomb of its most illustrious founder.'[82]

Laval's image as a resolutely French Catholic hero was reinforced by the choice of Archbishop Taché to preside over the ceremonies in the chapel of the Hôtel-Dieu, just before the procession returned to the streets. Taché highlighted Laval's role, two centuries earlier, in sending 'humble missionaries to the banks of the St. Lawrence and into the depths of our forests.' Now, from his position in the Canadian West, Taché had the power (as had Laval) to send out missionaries who might extend the influence of French-Canadian Catholicism. He symbolized the extended French-Canadian family, which now took to the streets.[83]

The marchers passed without stopping from the Hôtel-Dieu to the Basilica in what was called the *procession officielle* because both civic and clerical leaders of the French-Canadian community were in attendance. Although *le peuple* were still conspicuous by their absence, this was in

Arrival of procession with Laval's remains at the Basilica, 1878 (Archives de la Ville de Québec, negative 19762; reproduced from *Opinion publique*, 6 June 1878, AVQ negative, 19672)

some ways a more 'typical' Fête-Dieu affair than the first part of the procession; civic and clerical representatives of the French-Canadian community were now marching together in an order that reflected the power of the various participants. At the head were some two thousand students 'dressed up with crowns, banners and flags,' followed – in order of increasing importance – by two hundred priests, the episcopal party that had been at the Hôtel-Dieu, and then Laval's coffin in its familiar position at the centre.

The rest of the procession consisted of laymen (there were no women), who were organized in decreasing order of importance. Leading the way was the lieutenant-governor, followed by members of the judiciary and representatives of the federal and provincial governments. Next came representatives of various foreign governments, and a Huron delegation from Ancienne-Lorette, that had been drawn into the affair by contributing a crown. A delegation from the municipal governments of the Quebec City region brought the parade of state officials to a close. Next came French-Canadian professional groups and the members of such lay organizations as the SSJBQ and the Institut Canadien. A small contingent of Irish residents had been sandwiched into this last section; their presence was the only interruption in a line that displayed the hierarchy of French-Canadian society.

When described in such a manner, the assembling of thousands of people must have seemed 'natural' to the 30,000 spectators. Of course, this was one of the main reasons for staging a Fête-Dieu sort of procession – to display the pecking order as if it had been accepted without complaint by all the participants. In fact, almost from the moment that plans for the procession were announced, Abbé Hamel had been receiving complaints from participants who were unhappy with their assigned places. For instance, the lawyers wrote to say that they would participate, although they could not 'acknowledge the place assigned to [them] in the order of procession indicated in the official program.' Another complaint was filed by Jean-Thomas Taschereau, a Supreme Court justice and the archbishop's brother, who felt that the justices had not been assigned the position to which they were entitled. This same complaint was made by Albert-Alexis Lefaivre, the French consul to Canada, who felt that France was being denied a status worthy of Laval's country of birth. In the end, Justice Taschereau agreed to participate in the procession, but Lefaivre boycotted. This foreshadowed the difficulties that France would pose in the decades to come for those who organized celebrations of the founding fathers.[84]

Grievances of another sort were expressed, mainly in the local press, over the participation of the premier of Quebec, Henri-Gustave Joly. As both a Protestant and a Liberal, Joly was *persona non grata* to the ultramontanes, who wanted to see not so much a celebration of the French-Canadian nation, as one of Catholicism. Joly had become premier only a few months earlier, after the lieutenant-governor – himself a Liberal appointee – removed the Conservative government in a highly controversial move. In the elections that followed this action in early May, only weeks before Laval's fête, conservative Catholics expected voters to undo Letellier's work. Instead, Joly won a very narrow victory, and on 3 May, Liberals celebrated their success in the streets of Quebec City. *La vieille capitale* would soon become white and violet, but for at least that moment it was quite another colour. As one newspaper observed: 'Yesterday, the Liberal Party procession was marching in a victory parade through the streets of our city. Red was everywhere. There were red flags, the men were dressed in red outfits, and wagons, along with their horses and their drivers were coloured red ... These must be the types of processions that the Liberals will give to the people to make them forget their more traditional, national ones.'[85]

Throughout the month of May the harangues in the local Conservative press against Joly continued unabated. The premier was characterized as hostile to French-Canadian interests.[86] *Le Canadien*, one of Joly's fiercest detractors, sourly complained about his participation in the grand procession in honour of Laval: 'Monsieur Joly was marching in the procession on Thursday. This will come back to haunt [Joly] who claims that he wants to abolish such remnants from the past.'[87] In response, the Liberal papers declared that Joly had the right to be present. *L'Événement* defended his participation, viewing both the premier and Laval as members of a large family, as linked 'by the ties of blood.'[88] *Le Journal de Québec* remarked: 'The presence of the premier in the ranks of the procession on 23 May seems to have shocked one of the other newspapers. For our part, we take the contrary view. We think that it is only natural that he should have participated in the veneration of the remains of a great man ... Representatives of both political and civil power have followed popular opinion by taking part in this day of commemoration.' With both the lay and religious leaders marching together, here was 'a celebration that was simultaneously national and religious in nature.'[89] This was essentially the perspective of the procession's organizers, who were pleased to have Joly in their midst. The celebration was meant to take in the entire French-Canadian family, even Protestants such as the premier.

The End of the Journey

The arrival of the procession at the Basilica was not the end of the journey, but rather another stopover or *reposoir* before Laval's remains returned (in typical Fête-Dieu fashion) to the seminary, from which they had set off earlier in the morning. That being said, the arrival of the marchers at the Basilica marked the end of the day's most public events. Constables were hired to make sure that only individuals possessing *cartes spéciales* (special passes) were admitted. In this way, access was restricted largely to the participants in the procession and to those who owned pews within the Basilica. Men without special passes would be admitted if space remained after the procession arrived. There was also this unambiguous rule: 'Women would no longer be admitted.'[90]

As the fête retreated from public view, there was a further change in the depiction of Laval. To the crowds that watched the last stage of the procession, the bishop had been presented as a French-Canadian hero; now he was presented as the Catholic figure he had been at the start of the day. Inside the Basilica, many of the decorations were in the obligatory violet and white; more striking than these, however, were the various banners bearing slogans exalting the grandeur of Catholicism. None of these made any particular reference to Laval or to the French-Canadian context of the day's events.[91]

This emphasis on Catholicism in its broadest sense was reinforced by the seating of Mgr Conroy, the papal envoy, in the 'the habitual throne' of the archbishop. Similarly, in his funeral address, which concluded the festivities inside the Basilica, the bishop of Sherbrooke, Mgr Antoine Racine, made only passing reference to Laval's role in establishing the institutions of French-Canadian Catholicism. Rather, he emphasized Laval's role in preparing the ground for Catholicism across North America: 'The name of Laval is too great, too venerable, too dear to all the Catholics of North America to be the exclusive property of the seminary that he founded, of the city that he sanctified by his virtue, of the diocese that he governed with such wisdom; this glorious name is the property of all the dioceses that have successively detached themselves from that of Quebec; he is blessed by the *Canadiens* who constitute his first family; he is honoured and blessed by our Catholic brethren, the children of Catholic Ireland, who make up his second family, with its unbreakable attachment to the church of Jesus Christ.'[92] Racine closed by expressing the hope that Laval would be canonized in the not too distant future. Here he was making explicit one of the goals of the entire enterprise.

With the end of Racine's remarks, the procession formed yet again – this time with Mgr Conroy taking the senior position closest to Laval's remains – for its final journey to the seminary.[93] There, a small party remained behind to refit the coffin for its interment. The glass cover and the decorations surrounding the bones were removed; a solid wooden plank was put in place as a lasting seal. The coffin, still with its glass sides, was then placed in a second coffin, which in turn was placed in a third one of lead. Two inscriptions were engraved on the lead coffin. One was identical to that which Roberge and Simard had seen when they discovered Laval's original coffin. The second commemorated the events of the day. By 3 p.m., all was ready for Laval's passage to his new home in a specially prepared vault beneath the seminary. This was sealed behind a wall and two doors, the outer of which bore the inscription: 'Mgr de Laval de Montmorency, died 6 May 1708, interred here 23 May 1878.'[94]

In the same way that the host was returned to the church from which it had set off in a typical Fête-Dieu procession, Laval's remains had been returned to their starting point from early that morning.

Sainthood

The very long day of celebrations in honour of Mgr de Laval ended, much as had the 1859 fête, with a concert at the university attended by civic and clerical leaders. Its highlight was the 'ever popular Cantate en l'honneur de Mgr de Laval.'[95] At the 1859 concert, the intermission had consisted of two speeches, one by the future Archbishop Taschereau (then an Abbé) and the other by U.J. Tessier, a professor at the seminary. Tessier's speech had been more noteworthy; he had closed the day with a reference to the diverse French Catholic family, of which Laval had been one of the founders and Louis-Joseph Papineau a distinguished son. In 1878 the family in all its diversity was evoked by P.J.O. Chauveau, whose intermission speech complemented the one that Mgr Racine had given earlier in the day. Racine had delivered 'a splendid tribute to a Christian hero'; Chauveau, who had been the first premier of Quebec, presented Laval's legacy 'from a civil and political, as well as religious perspective.'[96] Laval had been involved in the governing of New France; even more significantly, he had encouraged 'the development through both word and example of the patriotic spirit which is responsible for the existence of the French Canadian people. After so many setbacks and so many calamities, that spirit is more lively today than ever.' Chauveau called on French-speaking Quebecers, who now had a province of their own, to emulate 'the spirit of sacrifice and the courage of Mgr de Laval' in facing up to the challenges before them.[97]

At around 10 p.m., the concert ended, and the fête was over. That day, Laval had been presented as both a Catholic and a French-Canadian hero. The multiple messages of his legacy were again evident the following day, when the Quebec bishops met to discuss Laval's accession to sainthood. One of the subjects throughout this spectacle had been the hope that Laval might some day be canonized, and in that context the meeting of the bishops was the final act in this highly choreographed affair. On the day of the reburial, Quebec's civic and clerical leaders had sent them a letter asking that proper recognition be paid to 'the very father of the entire Canadian race.' The bishops, in their response dated the following day, approved the request, but did so for an individual whose significance transcended French Canada and extended across 'the American regions.'[98]

Laval's candidacy for sainthood was an opportunity for ordinary Quebecers to come forward to testify as to what the celebration of 1878 had meant to them. This evidence, which was concealed from the larger public in the late nineteenth century, provides us with a small window – not available in the aftermath of most commemorative events – through which we can glimpse the impact of the bishop's reburial. Between 1880 and 1883, evidence was collected in order to determine whether it was generally believed in the late nineteenth century that the bishop had a reputation for sanctity and miracles. Having passed through this phase of the process, Laval achieved the first rung on the ladder to sainthood, and was henceforth referred to as 'venerable.' Between 1898 and 1902, still more witnesses were called, this time to offer evidence that Laval had displayed 'heroic' virtues or had been responsible for miracles. Many of those who came forward referred to the events of 1878.[99]

Some witnesses claimed that they had experienced miracles simply from having attended Laval's reburial. The Rev. Georges-Pierre Côté claimed to be the first person to see Laval's casket after the workmen had stumbled across it in the fall of 1877. By the following spring, while decorating the Basilica, he was suffering from 'an intestinal ailment ... Irritated that I continued to suffer while I was working for such a good cause, I complained bitterly to Mgr de Laval that he was letting me suffer while I was trying to honour him; and this was the last time that I experienced this discomfort ... I have always attributed this cure to Mgr de Laval.' Laval was also credited with having cured Cléophas Auser, who had been suffering from intestinal problems for a number of years: 'In 1878, the year of the movement of the remains, the pain that I was experiencing was worse than ever. I found myself in Quebec City on the day of the movement ... When I was not far from the Cathedral, I was struck by a pain that was so strong that I almost loss consciousness, and I searched for a carriage that might take me back home. At that moment, I saw the procession pass by. It then occurred to me to ask for the intercession of Mgr de Laval ... At that very moment, the pain left me instantly and completely. Since that time, I have never had any intestinal discomfort.'[100]

Laval's miraculous powers extended beyond his reburial ceremony, thanks to the distribution among the population of pieces of the casket in which he had been buried in 1708. The casket was not reused in 1878. Mgr Gravel, the bishop of Nicolet, could thus report: 'I distributed thousands of fragments from the tomb, and I have never been able to keep up with demand. An incredible number of people have come to tell me that they had experienced miraculous cures thanks to the intercession of the Venerable Mgr de Laval.'[101] Gravel provided the specific example of Rosa Hébert, whose story had already been published in the late 1880s. According to Mgr Henri Têtu's telling of the tale, Rosa was thirteen years old and had become deaf after contracting scarlet fever. Gravel asked her to 'carry on her body a fragment from the tomb of Mgr de Laval ... Almost immediately, it resulted in a remarkable transformation.' Years later, providing evidence during the second phase of Laval's 'trial,' Rosa's doctor confirmed Mgr Gravel's explanation of what had happened: 'It is my opinion as well as that of my colleagues that it was impossible for this child to recover her hearing ... I am not able to explain her cure as anything other than the result of some supernatural intervention. From my perspective, this was a true miracle.'[102]

Speaking more generally about the transformation of the popular image of the bishop after his reinterment, Abbé Gosselin testified that there had been little appreciation of Laval before 1878: 'But the great celebrations that took place at that time, the large-scale participation of both laymen and clerics from all parts of the country, and even from the United States, the joy and the piety that was fixed on the faces of those in attendance proved that his reputation for saintliness had not evaporated; it was rather latent. It was sufficient for an event such as this one to make it appear once again. I have no hesitation in saying that since 1878 the reputation of saintliness surrounding Mgr de Laval has only grown.'[103]

In the end, none of this testimony was able to move Laval toward sainthood, at least in the short term.[104] Nevertheless, the reburial ceremony rekindled interest in his legacy for those who had either experienced or were prepared to believe in his power to perform miracles. More generally, Laval's reburial provided an occasion for thousands of people to march through the streets of Quebec City, in the process telling stories about national identity to the even larger numbers who watched from the sidelines.

chapter two

A Monument for Champlain, 1879–1898

In Search of Champlain's Remains

In November 1866, more than a decade before Mgr de Laval's remains were discovered, *Le Journal de Québec* trumpeted that the grave of the other founding father, Samuel de Champlain, had been located: 'We are happy to be able to announce today some news which will interest people not only in Canada and North America, but as far away as Europe. Messieurs les abbés Laverdière et Casgrain, after long and serious research, are close to discovering the tomb of Champlain, something that our most eminent archaeologists have long wanted to find.'[1] Just as Laval's remains had long been missing, so too had there been much mystery surrounding the location of 'le tombeau de Champlain.' When the founder of Quebec City died in 1635, he was placed in a temporary grave, in which he rested briefly until a chapel in his honour was built. In 1640 that chapel was destroyed by a fire. Though it had been rebuilt, there was no record of it beyond the 1660s. Until it was established where the chapel had stood, Champlain could not be found.[2]

Newspaper reports to the contrary, Laverdière and Casgrain had not really discovered Champlain's grave; rather, they had a theory as to where his remains might be found. This theory was based on a chance conversation that Laverdière had had with a local printer, Stanislas Drapeau. Before that chat, the abbés had assumed that Champlain had been buried beneath the Cathedral; they went so far as to conduct 'a careful search under the pavement of the Church, but all in vain.'[3] During their search for Champlain, they probably came close to finding Laval. Be that as it may, their research was going nowhere until Drapeau told Laverdière that in the 1850s a city engineer had found some bones in the lower town. Though they had little reason to believe these were Champlain's, the two priests made their announcement just the same. Not surprisingly, Drapeau felt pre-empted, and went public to contest their findings. Thus began what became known as the 'querelle des antiquaires.' This debate, carried out largely through a series of pamphlets, ended only in 1875, when Casgrain admitted that he and his colleague had been wrong.[4]

The search for Champlain continued, encouraged by the Spanish consul in Quebec City, a participant in the procession that had carried Laval's remains to their new resting place. In 1879 he offered a prize to the author of the best essay on Canadian history; this was won by Narcisse-Eutrope Dionne, who would later write a biography of Champlain. In his winning essay, Dionne suggested possible sites in the upper town where Champlain might be found. Apparently unwilling to allow anyone to share the limelight on this question, Drapeau offered groundless speculations of his own to counter Dionne's suggestions. Several other equally weak theories were advanced in the late nineteenth century before the issue died down. Then in the 1950s interest was rekindled by the archaeologist René Lévesque, who made this search his life's work. In 1951 and again in 1988, he arranged permission to open various coffins, but Champlain still refused to be found. On the second occasion, *Le Soleil* echoed *Le Journal de Québec* at the time of Laverdière and Casgrain's 'discovery,' with this page one headline: 'L'énigme du tombeau de Champlain enfin résolu?' (The mystery of Champlain's tomb finally solved?)'[5] Various researchers, including the indefatigable Lévesque, are still looking for Champlain's grave, but the founder of Quebec City still hasn't been found.

The search for Champlain reached its peak of intensity in the late nineteenth century, when public celebrations of past heroes were being staged with greater regularity and grandeur and more and more monuments were being raised to them. Statues of great men had become so ubiquitious by this time that Maurice Agulhon declared this era as one of 'statuemania.'[6] In the spirit of the times, Stanislas Drapeau observed in 1880 that the site that he believed was Champlain's resting place would be the ideal location for the long overdue monument to Quebec's 'founder and first governor.' As J.M. Harper put it a few years later: 'What city would not be proud to have such a monument raised on the sacred spot of its founder's grave? Is there anything in us or around us to prevent us from making a public effort in behalf of the scheme? In a word, is there anything to keep the citizens of Quebec, from joining with those who would largely assist us in raising a Maison de Champlain on the ground where the stalwart frame of our first governor had its resting place?'[7] The discovery of Laval had provided the pretext for the celebrations of 1878; in the same way, Champlain's discovery would have provided the pretext for the raising of a monument in his honour. But he hadn't been found.

Though his remains were never discovered, Champlain was immortalized by a monument a decade before one was raised in honour of Laval. Around the same time Laval's remains were discovered, various local leaders – a very different group from the one that had organized the celebrations for the bishop's reburial – began a campaign for a Monument Champlain. In 1898 their efforts bore fruit, and a huge celebration every bit as elaborate as Laval's was organized around the unveiling ceremonies. This celebration, and the monument itself, had stories to tell that were quite unlike those communicated during Laval's fête. To make sense of those messages we must first establish who Champlain was, or more importantly, who late-nineteenth-century Canadians *thought* he was.

Who Was Champlain?

Interest in Laval's legacy hardly extended beyond French Catholic Quebec; in contrast, Champlain was a pan-Canadian figure, and a hero to the English and the French, because he had founded the first permanent European settlement on 'Canadian' soil and was the first person to hold the title of 'governor' in what would become Canada.[8] Champlain was written about in both official languages, and though it would be an oversimplification to say that each linguistic group had its own distinctive view of Champlain's life, the contrasts were striking. Until the last third of the nineteenth century, however, neither linguistic community showed much concern for Champlain's legacy. He had been largely 'relegated to obscurity.'[9] This began to change in 1870, when his account of his voyages to the Americas was published. This account is still the source of most of what we know about his life in North America. As Marcel Trudel has put it: 'From 1607 to 1625 [a period that included the founding of Quebec City], the only facts that we know about Champlain are those that he told us himself.'[10]

Champlain's *Œuvres* were published by the Université Laval, which in 1864 assigned responsibility for the task to Abbé Charles-Honoré Laverdière, only two years before his co-'discovery' of Champlain's remains. The university's clerical leaders gave this project a high priority, and provided Laverdière with a house and staff. The eventual result of their investment was the publication of Champlain's text, complete with explanatory notes and an introduction. Thus it can be said that Champlain did not exactly speak for himself; his text was shaped by Laverdière, whose criticisms of those who wrote history 'with preconceptions and biases' did not stop him from emphasizing Champlain's legacy as a French Catholic hero. This characterization would dominate accounts in French of Champlain's life for the next forty years, until the time of the tercentenary of 1908. Recognizing the impact of Laverdière's text, Abbé Gosselin (Laval's biographer) noted after the Monument Champlain was raised that the *Œuvres* were 'the real monument in honour of Champlain.'[11]

Laverdière's Champlain was an unambiguously Catholic figure, even though there is considerable doubt as to whether he had even been born into that faith. In fact, there is as much mystery about Champlain's early years as there is about the location of his remains. A lack of information did not prevent people from speculating about where he was buried; in the same way, it did not prevent biographers from speculating about his life. Marcel Trudel lamented that 'under these conditions, it is difficult to construct an image of Champlain that conforms to reality.' If anything, the absence of documentation about Champlain fostered the development of two diametrically opposed views, one in French and the other in English. Laverdière outlined the French version, which was expressed in its clearest form only later, in Narcisse-Eutrope Dionne's two-volume biography.[12]

It is not clear exactly when or into what social class Champlain was born. Nevertheless, Dionne was certain that his subject had been of 'noble origins.'[13] We know he was born in the west of France not far from La Rochelle, but this 'fact' has only led to speculation that he may have been born a Protestant – an important consideration later on, during the celebrations in his honour. La Rochelle was in a part of France heavily populated by Huguenots, and in Brouage, Champlain's place of birth, Samuel was a name usually given to Protestants. Yet for Dionne – as for Laverdière before him – there was no doubt that Champlain's parents had been 'Catholics, as was evident from their baptismal names.' Dionne conceded that Champlain's parents may have been Protestant for a time, possibly at the moment of Samuel's birth, but even if so, it was of no significance, since it would only have indicated that they had been forced to abandon their 'true' faith.[14]

Whether born a Catholic or not, Champlain was certainly one by 1603, when he first arrived in Canada. By then he was already in his forties. It seems that he had been trained as a draftsman; this provided him with skills he needed to map uncharted lands. Moreover, it seems that he had already been across the Atlantic, most likely with Spanish ships sailing to the West Indies. When he returned to France he was invited by Commander Aymar de Chaste, who held the trade monopoly at the time, to sail to New France. Champlain had no official status on this journey, during which he travelled as far inland as Hochelaga (the future site of Montreal). Though he did not really 'discover' anything new, his discussions with the natives enabled him to produce an 'amazing reconstruction of the Great Lakes.'[15]

Over the next three decades Champlain crossed the Atlantic another twenty times, all the while moving up in the French colonial bureaucracy. Though he held no official title as part of the expedition led by de Chaste's successor, Pierre Du Gua de Monts, he was involved in the establishment of short-lived settlements at Île Sainte-Croix (on what would become the Maine–New Brunswick border) in 1604 and Port-Royal (in present-day Nova Scotia) in 1605. By 1608, when he set off on the journey that would result in the founding of Quebec, he held the title of lieutenant to de Monts. By 1613 he was effectively the governor of New France, having been made the lieutenant to the viceroy responsible for the colony. Although he would have various titles, he would continue in that function for the next two decades.

During his years as governor, Champlain had to balance the often conflicting demands of fur traders interested in a quick profit, missionaries concerned with the souls of natives, and advisers to the king intent on settling colonists in the St Lawrence Valley. To assist the various fur-trading companies, he allied the French with the Hurons, Algonquins, and Montagnais, all of whom were enemies of the Iroquois, whom the French were now willing to fight on their behalf. There was often tension between traders and clerics; notwithstanding these, Champlain's ties with the natives aided the missionary efforts of the Recollets and Jesuits. Regarding settlement, he proposed to establish, at the site of Quebec City, the town of Ludovica. Had this been done, it would have been home to hundreds of French settlers, along with a resident clergy.

Because Champlain's career was so varied, late-nineteenth-century biographers were able to read his legacy in different ways. In the 1840s, Garneau presented a Champlain who was 'naturally religious.'[16] Yet at the same time Garneau – like some of the English-language biographers who followed – never used the word 'Catholicism' in connection with Champlain's career. As so often happened, French Canada's *historien national* was out of step with clerically influenced writers such as Laverdière and Dionne, who credited Champlain as the founder of French Catholic civilization in the St. Lawrence Valley. They paid little attention to his dealings with the fur traders, who were sullied by 'their mercenary tendencies.' Rather, they viewed Champlain as the father of a rural way of life in which Catholicism played a central role.[17]

In this French Catholic depiction of Champlain's life, his relationship with his wife loomed large. Champlain married Hélène Boullé in 1612, when she was fourteen. They lived together for only a few years in the 1620s, when she joined him in New France. In fact, because Champlain lived most of his life without the company of a woman, Dionne depicted him as a quasi-religious figure: 'Living as if he were a priest with a vow of chastity, our hero never did anything that might have sullied his reputation of saintly modesty.' Though she spent little time with Champlain, Hélène was still important in the construction of Champlain as a Catholic hero. Dionne insisted that Champlain had been born a Catholic; he was just as eager to depict Hélène as a born Protestant who had become 'an excellent Catholic under the tutelage of her husband. He taught her about the faith, and led her to embrace the religion to which she remained strongly devoted until her death.' More generally, Champlain's entire life had been dedicated to 'the great and noble cause of his religion, without ever neglecting the honour of his country.'[18]

In keeping with this portrait, Dionne painted the fur traders as villains who stood in the way of Champlain's loftier goals – a theme also present in English treatments of the subject. Dionne used the fur traders to remind his French-Canadian reader of the dangers presented by the English-speaking businessmen who exercised so much power in late-nineteenth-century Quebec; English-language authors saw fur traders as precursors of the turn-of-the-century 'robber barons.'[19] In this spirit, J.M. Harper, in the introduction for a play written for the 1908 tercentenary, described the behaviour of the fur traders as 'a definite, tangible illustration of the old story of bad faith – a pertinent proof of the callousness of corporations in their greed for the largest dividends.' Only a few years later a McGill history professor, Charles Colby, wrote that Champlain had been forced to 'withstand the cabals of self-seeking traders who shirked their obligations.'[20]

Similarities between English and French language treatments of Champlain broke down when it came to the role of Catholicism. Harper was silent about the religious zeal that had consumed Hélène Boullé.[21] As for Colby, his text began with an imaginary entry for Champlain in a *Who's Who in History* that made no reference to Catholicism. Colby commented later on Champlain's religious zeal, but only in the context of his last years, when 'his piety was confirmed by the reflections of advancing age and his daily contact with missionaries.' Colby obviously saw this phase as an aberration in Champlain's life, and was quick to reassure readers that 'it is not to be inferred from the prominence of Champlain's religious interests that he neglected his public duties.'[22]

Laverdière and Dionne made Catholicism a central element in their celebrations of a life that had assisted in the birth of a French-Catholic civilization. English-language authors saw Champlain as the founder of a Canadian nation that included both the French and the English. In this spirit, Colby closed his text with this observation: 'It is a rich part of our heritage that [Champlain] founded New France in the spirit of unselfishness, of loyalty and of faith.'[23] As was typical of him in his biography, Colby was resorting to the term *faith* – or alternatively *Christianity* – to make Champlain a universal character that all Canadians (or at least all Christians in Canada) could celebrate.

Unlike Laval, Champlain fascinated both French and English Canadians, who drew different lessons from his life. But these differences were not restricted to the pages of biographies, which most Canadians would not have read. Rather, they spilled into the streets of Quebec City on two separate occasions during the heyday of public celebration of past heroes. The larger of the two celebrations of Champlain was in 1908, the tercentenary of his founding of Quebec. Long before that event, however, Canadians from both linguistic communities had been campaigning for a statue in Champlain's honour. The Monument Champlain was unveiled in 1898, but only after protracted negotiations over the messages it would convey to the public.

The Campaign for a Monument

The first significant effort to raise a monument in Champlain's honour began in the spring of 1879, roughly a year after the reinterment of Mgr de Laval. The largely English-speaking Literary and Historical Society of Quebec passed a resolution reflecting the point of view that would soon prevail in English-language biographies. Champlain was deemed worthy of a statue because he had been 'a discoverer, a geographer, an undaunted leader, a man of letters, a Christian gentleman, the founder and first Governor of Quebec.'[24] He was not seen as a Catholic, which probably guaranteed that this campaign would generate little support from French speakers. In any event, as one newspaper later pointed out, the Literary and Historical Society, though it 'endorsed the project, appointed no collectors of funds to erect the shaft. Of course, what was everybody's business became nobody's business and the matter dropt [*sic*] out of sight.'[25]

Nothing more came of the idea of a monument until 1890, when it was taken up by the Société St-Jean-Baptiste de Québec (SSJBQ), which approached the project – in the spirit of Champlain's French-language biographers – as an affirmation by French Canadians of 'their faith and their patriotism.'[26] The leaders of the SSJBQ were looking ahead to 1892; they were hoping to mark the fiftieth anniversary of their society by unveiling the Monument Champlain. The president of the society, J.B. Caouette, wanted 'something new and interesting to catch the eyes of visitors, because otherwise they will not trouble themselves, and the anniversary of our society will pass without much notice.'[27] In putting the matter in these terms, Caouette was recognizing that the statue would do more than celebrate a great man; it would also create an event through which messages could be communicated.

Although Caouette did not mention it, the SSJBQ was also motivated by a series of events that had been triggered by a devastating fire in the St-Sauveur district of the city in the spring of 1889. Two English-speaking soldiers, Major Short and Sergeant Wallick, died fighting the fire, and a campaign soon developed to raise a statue in their honour near the Château Frontenac on Dufferin Terrace overlooking the St. Lawrence. Since this had been the site of Champlain's Fort St-Louis, there was an immediate uproar over this proposal. The promoters of the Short-Wallick statue could hardly be blamed for staking a claim to the site, since no one else had really taken up the challenge of building a monument for Champlain – that is, until the SSJBQ moved into action, claiming the location for just that purpose.[28]

The SSJBQ soon recognized that it was incapable of carrying out the project on its own, and began searching for partners. First it looked to the provincial government, following the lead of the premier, Honoré Mercier, who had proposed that three monuments be erected, one of them to Champlain. They would be raised in front of the city hall, which was about to be built across from the Basilica. Mercier had suggested that one of the other monuments be to Laval; as to the third, that was left in the air.[29] The city hall site was not the one coveted by the SSJBQ; even so, the society's leaders began using the premier's initiative as a means to leverage public support for a Monument Champlain on Dufferin Terrace. The society hoped the province might help finance this statue, leaving the other two to a later date. In the end, Mercier offered little help, suggesting that the municipal government and the seminary should build the monuments to Champlain and Laval respectively. The province would take care of the statue in honour of the still unidentified hero. His final words to the president of the SSJBQ were clear: 'It would be wise, I believe, for you to continue to try to encourage contributions.'[30]

Heeding the premier's advice, the society began a fundraising drive – a common method for financing monuments in the late nineteenth century that would be used again for the Monument Laval in the early 1900s. Though campaigns like this never raised funds from all segments of the population, the effort in itself was crucial to conveying the sense that the monument represented the broader community's understanding of the past. As Kirk Savage, a historian of 'statuemania' in the United States, has observed: 'Sponsors usually worked hard to sustain the fiction that they were merely agents of a more universal collectiv[ity] whose shared memory the project embodied ... The more widely the monument campaign appealed, the more enthusiasm it seemed to generate, the more convincing its public would come to resemble the democratic vision of one people united by one memory.'[31]

The SSJBQ hoped to collect $10,000 – an amount that would turn out to be grossly inadequate for the job at hand. To raise that sum, it called a meeting late in 1890 that brought together 'all the presidents of mutual aid societies, and other organizations such as sporting organizations' in order to create 'a permanent committee for the erection of a monument to Samuel de Champlain, by means of contributions.' This meeting, attended by representatives of the various *sociétés françaises de Québec*, made little concrete headway. Sobered by the absence of money on the table, the committee met again a week later, this time for the sole purpose of asking the mayor to widen the fundraising drive by calling a meeting of all citizens of Quebec City.[32]

In October the mayor had been told by the SSJBQ that Champlain deserved to be honoured as one of the heroes of French Canada 'who have stood apart from the crowd because of their intelligence, their virtue, their bravery and their patriotism.'[33] But two months later, in the absence of financial support from the French-speaking community, Champlain became the 'property' of both linguistic groups. A Comité du Monument Champlain, which would oversee the project through to the unveiling ceremony, was created, headed by Judge Alexandre Chauveau, a former president of the SSJBQ and son of the first premier of Quebec. Chauveau would have two vice-presidents, both English speakers. Two secretaries and two treasurers were also appointed, one from each linguistic community. In addition, two subcommittees were created, a *comité de direction* that would choose the site and the design for the monument, and a *comité exécutif* to raise funds. Once more, each committee was carefully crafted to balance the participation of French and English speakers. The complexity of all this was in sharp contrast to the situation twenty years earlier, when Abbé Hamel organized the ceremonies for the reburial of Mgr de Laval largely on his own.

In the years that followed, the monument committee was barely visible.[34] We know, however, that fundraising progressed very slowly. In 1892 Chauveau announced that roughly $16,000 of the required $30,000 had been pledged; if so, few of the subscribers had honoured their promises, since there was less than $5,000 in the committee's bank account. Two years later, Chauveau complained that little headway had been made in attracting new subscribers due to 'a variety of unfavourable circumstances ... The enthusiasm among the public has cooled off a bit.'[35] *L'Électeur* even published a rebuke of those who had failed to respect their pledge to the project:

> We cannot reproach someone who fails to repay a debt if he does not have the means to do so. However, this excuse cannot apply to everyone. More than one wealthy man has been known to add his name to a list of donors, and then fails to pay anything towards the construction of the monument. Is this simply a question of getting his name on a list of generous donors, without having to pay up? We would like to think that such is not the case, but rather laziness and apathy. We hope that these words are heeded by those who fit into this category, and that all of those who have promised to help defray the costs of the Monument Champlain will fulfill their obligations just as they would repay a promissory note, which ought to be honoured when due, with legal consequences should they neglect their duty.[36]

Besides criticizing those who had not paid up their subscriptions, *L'Électeur* took the SSJBQ to task, noting that it had been too passive in promoting the Champlain project. Though it had been willing 'to hire musical corps and to organize the banal procession of 24 June,' with regard to this project the society 'remains inactive and indifferent! It is really hard to believe!'[37] If the committee had little reason to expect further support from the city's leading civic organization among French speakers, it had similarly limited prospects when it came to the Catholic clergy. Only a few weeks after the rebuke of the SSJBQ's behaviour, Cardinal Taschereau wrote to his clergy in a manner that could hardly have encouraged Chauveau and his colleagues. The archbishop observed that 'the Quebec City clergy has already done more than its duty ... After the enormous sacrifices that this clergy has made over the past few years, it is impossible to expect them to make a considerable contribution [to the Monument Champlain]; and this is exactly what I explained to the Honourable Monsieur Chauveau.'[38]

With some of the most obvious sources of funding drying up, the Comité du Monument Champlain decided in early 1895 to look to potential donors who had so far been neglected. A special committee was created to solicit funds 'from our English-speaking citizens and from various institutions.' At the same time, 'two other sub-committees were also formed, with the responsibility of raising contributions from the Senate and the House of Commons, respectively.'[39] These actions must have made some difference, because the coffers of the committee began to fill throughout 1895 and 1896, till they reached $20,000 – roughly the total that would be contributed by individuals.

The shortfall was made up by various levels of government, which contributed a total of $9,000 after individuals had done their duty.[40] It is no surprise that the Quebec provincial and Quebec City municipal governments made contributions, since both had long supported the project. More unexpected was the involvement of the Ontario government, which would also offer generous support for the Champlain tercentenary in 1908. In both situations, the province was guided by the sense that Champlain belonged to all Canadians, French and English alike. In fact, Chauveau made precisely this point when he encouraged the federal government to contribute to the raising of a monument to 'the founder not only of Quebec City, but of all of Canada.'[41]

Ottawa's contribution was arranged by François Langelier, a Liberal MP with long ties to Prime Minister Laurier. In 1880 Langelier, Laurier, and other prominent Quebec City Liberals such as Henri-Gustave Joly (the former premier of Quebec) founded L'Électeur in order to advance the party's interests in the *vieille capitale*. Throughout the 1890s, until it was transformed to become *Le Soleil* in 1896, *L'Électeur* was the newspaper of record for the Comité du Monument Champlain. This means that almost everything we know about it was what *L'Électeur* chose to publish. This underscores the links between those involved in the monument and the Liberal Party – or to put it another way, the gap between the committee and the local ecclesiastical establishment, a gap that only widened as the project moved closer to completion.[42]

Designing Champlain

By early 1895 the committee's finances were reasonably firm, and plans could begin in earnest for the actual building of the monument. First a site had to be selected, although there was little doubt that it would be somewhere along Dufferin Terrace. The sole dissenting voice on the special committee that had been struck to deal with this matter was Mgr Joseph-Clovis Kemner Laflamme, who preferred 'the site of the old parliament building' across the road from both the university, where he was rector, and the seminary, where he was superior.[43] Had Laflamme been heeded, the Monument Champlain would have been integrated into the centre of the Catholic presence in the upper town. In the end, the rector's choice could not compete with Dufferin Terrace, which had strong historical links with the site of Champlain's fort. The committee was even more impressed, however, by the possibilities the monument offered for attracting tourists.

The connection between commemoration and tourism had not drawn the attention of the clerical authorities who had organized Laval's reburial; they had been more concerned about the bishop's canonization than about attracting tourists to the city. In any event, there was nothing really left behind to see once Laval's remains had been sealed into their resting place. In contrast, the Monument Champlain might add to the cachet of the city for tourists staying at the Château Frontenac, which had opened in 1893. In this vein, the committee that recommended the site near the hotel touted the fact that 'every visitor who comes to Quebec City is attracted by the incredible view from this terrace; and since the construction of the Château Frontenac, this part of town has become and will be in the future a major attraction.'[44]

One of the jewels in the Canadian Pacific Railway's hotel chain, the Frontenac was an immediate success; it drew nearly three thousand guests in August 1894, during its first summer in operation. Most of its guests were from the northeastern United States and were drawn from the expanding middle class, who were wealthy enough to visit Quebec but not to visit Europe.[45] Quebec City offered an inexpensive taste of the Old World, and a monument to Champlain would contribute to the European flavour. The American tourists might not understand the significance of Champlain to Canadian history, but they would recognize him as a French explorer, and in that role he would contribute to the aura of the town. This attention to tourism was crucial to Quebec City, whose population had barely grown since the 1870s, having suffered from both the demise of the square-timber trade and the phasing out of the construction of wooden ships. In the absence of a rail link with the south shore of the St Lawrence, Quebec City could still appeal to tourists looking for something exotic. Without them, the city's economic prospects were bleak.

The site having been chosen, the next task was to select a design – no small question, with the stakes so high. There is always conflict over the precise form of any monument, and the Monument Champlain proved no exception. Yet after it was raised it would take on a life of its own. As Kirk Savage put it:

> A funny thing happened once a monument was built and took its place in the landscape of people's lives: it became a natural fact, as if it had always been meant to be ... Public monuments exercised a curious power to erase their own political origins and become sacrosanct ... The individuals and interest groups that vied for representation in monumental space understood that there was a great deal at stake in the form and content of public monuments. They were competing not merely for the right to speak for the people but for the chance to etch the people's voice in stone, where it would remain forever.[46]

In the case of the Monument Champlain, even before the selection process began, at least one Quebecer was lobbying local leaders to return to the earlier notion of making Champlain's statue one of a trio. A week after the Dufferin Terrace site had been formally selected, Charles Baillairgé, the city engineer who had played a key role in the design of the Terrace in the 1870s, wrote to the mayor of Quebec City, the rector of the university, and the assistant to the archbishop. Though his letters were not identical, they all said basically the same thing – Champlain's statue ought to form part of a wider celebration of a French Catholic civilization. In his letter to the mayor, he proposed statues to Champlain, Laval, and Brébeuf (even though the last of the three already had been immortalized with the raising of the Monument Cartier-Brébeuf in 1889). In the end, Baillairgé was open to other suggestions, and he encouraged the mayor to work with Cardinal Taschereau to arrive at 'the most appropriate choice of two individuals who would form the trio along with Champlain.' The religious motif was also stressed in Baillairgé's letter to Taschereau's assistant, Mgr Louis-Nazaire Bégin, who would replace the cardinal by the time of the unveiling. Baillairgé wrote to Bégin that it would make good sense to link Champlain with Mgr de Laval because 'there is currently a movement for the canonisation of [the bishop], so that one should also erect a statue in his honour.'[47]

Nothing in Baillairgé's career suggested that he was especially close to the local Catholic establishment. In fact, his biographer found that he broke with the archbishop of Quebec in the 1850s in a dispute over the design of a church. According to Christina Cameron, Baillairgé had 'cut himself off from his most faithful client,' yet he was still designing church buildings in the 1860s and in 1886 proposed 'a 10-storey illuminated tower to commemorate Archbishop Taschereau's investiture as cardinal.'[48] Clearly, his 1895 proposal for a trio of statues that would point to Quebecers' Catholic legacy was not entirely out of character. Ultimately, Baillairgé, much like Laflamme, would be ignored when it came to promoting Champlain's Catholic legacy. The Monument Champlain project was being negotiated mainly by civic leaders, both French and English speaking. In this context, there was little room for an explicit celebration of Catholicism; that would have to wait for the construction of the Monument Laval in the new century.

The contest for the design began in earnest in the summer of 1895 with the publication of a call for submissions. Potential competitors were told they were free to design any style of monument, with the understanding that 'a statue of Champlain of heroic dimensions should constitute the main element.'[49] For all the freedom the artists were given, the various submissions stayed close to what Maurice Agulhon has described as the standard formula of the time for public representations of great men. Each maquette depicted Champlain realistically, in period costume and carrying out some activity linked with his career. Moreover, each submission included one or more allegorical figures designed to emphasize some particular aspect of his life.[50]

Notwithstanding this adherence to convention, the maquettes presented various versions of Champlain. Thanks to the efforts of an unnamed reporter from *La Presse*, who sneaked into the hall where the maquettes were being displayed early in 1896, we know that several presented him as a Catholic figure. The reporter referred to one submission as 'a failed Champlain; it wasn't really him, but rather a missionary, with a cross in hand upon his chest. The whole conception was very Christian.' In spite of his reservations, the reporter had to admit a

A Christian Champlain: maquette entered in competition for the Monument Champlain (Musée de la Civilisation, fonds d'archives du Séminaire de Québec, Maquette – Projet du Monument de Champlain [Anonyme], 1896, N° Ph 1986-0853)

certain fondness for this particular maquette, which did not advance to the short list of four. Another design that failed to advance past the first round presented a rather bland Champlain flanked on one side by 'an interesting group of characters ... a savage directing a missionary towards the horizon.' The only other submission that touched even vaguely on a Catholic theme presented an imperial-looking Champlain surrounded by three allegorical figures 'symbolizing the cross, the plough and the sword.' This submission was one of two offered by the noted Canadian sculptor Louis-Philippe Hébert, who was already well known for public monuments such as the one in honour of Montreal's founding father, Paul de Chomedy, sieur de Maisonneuve, which had been unveiled in 1895. Both of Hébert's designs made the short list for the Champlain competition, but neither won.[51]

All of the other designs, including the remaining maquettes selected for the final round, focused on Champlain as a secular figure. One of these, Hébert's other submission, presented a Champlain who was 'given a vigorous pose, without affectation: his left hand was on the shield of his sword, while the right was resting on a volume of his "memoirs."' On the front of the pedestal three figures were grouped together, one representing Quebec City, others the French army and navy; on the back was another group depicting settlers bringing in the harvest. Although Hébert did not win the commission for this design, he was able to recycle it a decade later as the starting point for his statue in honour of Mgr de Laval.[52]

The winning design presented Champlain as a secular figure but also as a representative of France. Accordingly, the statue presented him 'standing on the rock of Quebec, saluting his new country on his arrival from France. In his left hand, he [holds] the commission of Henri IV, to which is attached the great seal of France.'[53] The reporter from La Presse liked this maquette, but it was not his first choice, mainly because he did not care for the statue, which he found rather lifeless. Nevertheless, he considered the work 'a first-class project' because of the three allegorical figures grouped around its base: 'The group on the front was remarkable, so dynamic and full of life.' The smallest of the three represented 'le Génie de la navigation,' to recall Champlain's exploits as a navigator, which had preceded his founding of Quebec. Only a few years before the unveiling of the Monument Champlain, 'le Génie' was also displayed prominently alongside an arch constructed for visitors to the Columbian Exposition of 1893 who approached that site by water.

The conventions of the time were also reflected in two imposing

Winning maquette, the Monument Champlain (Musée de la Civilisation, fonds d'archives du Séminaire de Québec, Maquette-Projet du Monument de Champlain [Projet Gagnant], 1896, N° Ph 1986-0860)

figures of women. One, representing Quebec City, had her back turned to the public as she gazed admiringly at Champlain. She wore a crown in the shape of the town's walls and was writing into a book words that she had taken from Champlain: 'May God allow the success of this enterprise dedicated to His name and His glory.' There was also the female allegorical figure 'la Renommée' (Fame), whose roots stretched back to classical antiquity. This sort of figure was usually presented as winged, to symbolize that she was hard at work day and night delivering news, often with a trumpet. Here she was trumpeting the achievements of Champlain so that they might become widely known. Champlain's feats were further celebrated by the wreath of victory that Fame held in her other hand.[54] *La Presse*'s correspondent concluded that thanks to these figures, 'this monument in its straightforward manner has considerable value.'

The French Connection

Each artist who submitted a design for the Monument Champlain signed his work, not with his name, however, but rather with some distinctive mark or signature.[55] In this way the identity of the artist was concealed from the jury until after the final decision, presumably to avoid any favouritism. Even so, there was some grumbling when the entry by two Frenchmen, the artist Paul Chevré and the architect P.-A. Le Cardonnel, was selected in February 1896 from the twenty submissions considered. On the day the jury began its deliberations, Mgr Laflamme wrote in the seminary's journal: 'Rumour has it that the cabal is in place, thus giving the whole affair the appearance of being political.' The final decision was announced the following day. To this, Laflamme responded: 'It was the French design which won the prize. There is a certain amount of disappointment which is going to lead to even more unhappiness in the days to come.'[56] The morning after the jury's decision, when it became clear that there was little dissatisfaction with the choice, Laflamme was still wishing the commission had gone to Hébert. Nevertheless, the superior of the seminary was satisfied that there had been 'a good, strong competition. There were a number of beautiful designs, so that the judges did not have an easy task to carry out. Now, everyone is happy with the verdict of the jury, or so it seems.' His only real regret remained with the choice of the site. He observed rather quixotically: 'Now we have to think again about changing the site, to see if it is possible to switch to the location of the old parliament buildings.'[57]

Laflamme's disenchantment with the winning design is perhaps understandable, considering the thoroughly secular character of Chevré's proposal; but there is no reason to believe the decision was somehow predetermined. If anything, Laflamme would have been mollified by the presence on the nine-member jury of a priest, Abbé Bouillon, as well as the artists Napoléon Bourassa and Charles Huot, both of whom were well known for their paintings, which decorated many churches. Furthermore, all the jurors were French Canadian – rather striking, when one considers that the Comité du Monument Champlain usually attempted to ensure some balance between French and English speakers. In fact, the only aspect of the jury's composition that might have troubled Laflamme would have been that it was chaired by Henri-Gustave Joly, the former premier of Quebec whose Protestantism and Liberalism had disturbed some clerical leaders when he participated in Laval's reburial ceremony.

In the end, Chevré's design was widely praised. That being said, it is inconceivable that the English-speaking Protestants who provided so much of the funding and who were so active on the committee would have accepted an overtly Catholic version of Champlain. The French speakers on the jury could not trumpet Champlain's Catholic heritage; they could, however, emphasize his 'Frenchness' – something that was possible in the late nineteenth century before France and Rome severed their ties in the early 1900s. Although the Third Republic had been trying for some time to limit the influence of Catholicism, there was a truce of sorts between Paris and the Vatican in the 1890s. Pope Leo XIII was looking for allies in his battles with the Italian government. In that context, the Vatican published a papal encyclical in 1892 that 'advised French Catholics to proclaim their allegiance to the Republican regime.'[58] If Rome was prepared to get along with France, it was difficult for most French Canadians to object too strongly.

At the time, English speakers perhaps had more difficulty than their French-speaking counterparts with presenting Champlain as a representative of the French state. During Gabriel Hanotaux's tenure as foreign minister, which spanned all but a few months of the period between 1894 and 1898, France was trying to expand its empire, especially in Africa. This brought it into conflict with England on various fronts. The single greatest threat of war emerged in the Sudan, where in 1898 the two countries became embroiled in what came to be known as the Fashoda crisis. This showdown would colour the unveiling of the Monument Champlain. However, in 1896, while the French submission for the statue was being accepted, relations between England and France were not yet at the boiling point. English speakers had no reason to object to the fact that a representative of France's seventeenth-century imperial grandeur was being celebrated. They were satisfied that Champlain's Catholic legacy had been pushed out of the picture, and prepared to accept this depiction of his French connection.[59]

The Monument Champlain's ties with France did not end with the acceptance of Chevré's design. In the years leading up to the unveiling, care was taken to use the monument as a tool for reinforcing the links between Quebec and France. These ties had been growing stronger since the 1880s, when Hector Fabre was sent to Paris as the representative of the Quebec and Canadian governments. Fabre's efforts were reciprocated, especially in the 1890s, when France was flexing its imperial muscles. While it was trying to expand the 'empire' of the Third Republic, it looked back with considerable fondness on the imperial glories of an earlier time. This led to its own celebration of Champlain's legacy. In 1893 a fete in honour of the founder of Quebec was held at Saintes, a town near Champlain's birthplace. This event attracted only minor officials and seems to have been prompted largely by the announcement of regular steamship service between La Rochelle and Quebec City. However, there was a much more elaborate celebration in 1898, and this one was directly linked to the Monument Champlain.[60]

This second celebration was held at Honfleur, the Norman town from which Champlain had left for Canada many times, just a month before the September unveiling of the monument in Quebec City. Earlier that year the organizers in Honfleur had asked the Comité du Monument Champlain if it would provide a scaled-down model of the monument and an appropriately prestigious figure to represent Quebec at a celebration, which was intended 'to coincide with the unveiling of the Monument Champlain in Quebec City.' The committee asked Chevré to produce the replica, which he did. He then brought it to Honfleur, where he was feted: The Quebec minister of colonization, Adélard Turgeon, was sent to represent the committee. This choice reflected the project's secular nature, since Turgeon was a minister of the Liberal government that earlier in the year had introduced legislation to establish a Ministry of Education. Had it been passed, this legislation would have significantly reduced the power of Catholicism in the province.[61]

Turgeon described the coming celebration in Quebec as 'a fete in honour of the French family, all branches of the French family.' Quite aside from the obvious historical links by which Champlain connected France and Quebec, Turgeon pointed out that the Monument Champlain 'comes from the chisel of a Frenchman; and to reinforce its French character, the granite used for the base as well as all other materials came from French sources.' To be more specific, this stone came from the same quarry that had provided the material for both the Arc de Triomphe and the Église du Sacré-Cœur de Montmartre. Turgeon recognized, however, that there were dangers in playing the 'French' card, since the English-speaking benefactors of the monument back home would be reading his comments. For their benefit, he recounted a conversation he had had with one of his cabinet colleagues, an English Protestant, who had told him: 'Assure your compatriots of our complete support. We are not able to forget that England is the product of two bloodlines: it comes from the fusion of the Saxon and the Norman, who together have formed the powerful English nation.' English-speaking Quebecers, with Norman blood in their veins, could thus feel a part of a Norman celebration.[62]

The monument's role as a symbol of the ties between Quebec and France was also emphasized by one of Turgeon's hosts. As A. Boudin, a professor at a local school, observed:

Let me tell you just how dear France is to the people of Quebec City. Not only have they provided the most beautiful site in their city for a statue in honour of Champlain, the founder of their town, but they have insisted that it be French in terms of both the artistic spirit which inspired it and the artist who brought it to life. The people of Quebec City have also insisted that the Monument be transported upon a French ship, sailing under the flag of France, and that French workmen (on the site at this very moment) place it on the spot where it will be unveiled.[63]

Boudin then suggested that Champlain represented the glories of France's imperial past, which might be revisited in the late nineteenth century: 'We are trying to find the spirit of our past, in order to construct a new version of Jacob's Ladder, so that our people might rise up to the greatest heights possible.'[64] These comments were especially pertinent in the summer of 1898, with the English and French vying for supremacy in Africa. In July 1898 French forces commanded by Jean-Baptiste Marchand reached the Sudanese town of Fashoda. This was only a month before the ceremonies at Honfleur, and just two months before the British under Lord Kitchener reached Fashoda themselves. By September, just as the Monument Champlain was being unveiled, British and French forces were staring each other down in the Sudan. However, in August 1898 the French perhaps believed that they had the upper hand in the Sudan and that the glories of their imperial past, symbolized by Champlain's founding of Quebec, were about to be repeated in Africa.

This sentiment was reflected in a lengthy article, first published in Paris and later reprinted in Quebec City newspapers only days before the unveiling, by Gabriel Hanotaux, who until June 1898 had been the French foreign minister. Hanotaux was no longer a minister by the time of the unveiling, but as a trained historian he maintained an interest in the Monument Champlain. He had written extensively about Cardinal Richelieu, so he had a longstanding interest in New France. As foreign minister he 'turned to the colonial history of his nation for inspiration, and often based his African policies on the past.'[65] He praised Champlain for having thought in terms of the French controlling not just the St. Lawrence Valley but all of North America, a territory '1600 lieues [roughly 9000 kilometres] long and 500 [2800 kilometres] wide! These are the dimensions upon which empires are operating nowhere other than in Africa.'

Hanotaux regretted that someone with Champlain's vision had not been present when France was abandoning its North American empire in the eighteenth century. Nevertheless, there was a message for the present day in Champlain's legacy. Hanotaux noted that the French of the late nineteenth century harboured doubts as to whether they were up to the task of running an empire: '"Does the Frenchman have the ability to be a colonizer?," this is a pertinent question which is being discussed at the very moment that we have a vast empire which, once more, is being built upon the conscientious efforts of our missionaries and our soldiers. "Does the Frenchman have the ability to be a colonizer?" – The answer to this question can be found in the life of Samuel de Champlain.'[66] Hanotaux's reasons for championing Champlain's French legacy were different from those of the French and English speakers on the Comité du Monument Champlain. But clearly, there was no escaping the French character of the Champlain who would soon be presented to the public.

The Inscription Debate

Chevré and Le Cardonnel had designed the Monument Champlain but were not responsible for the texts that would be engraved on its base. On the front would simply be the hero's name. The text for the other three empty sides was to be decided on by a special *comité des inscriptions*, which was struck a few weeks after the contract was awarded to the Frenchmen.

Like the committee that selected the winning design, this one was also made up entirely of French Canadians. Two of its most active members were priests. The committee was chaired by Abbé Lionel Lindsay, at the time a school inspector in the Quebec archdiocese. He recruited Abbé Henri-Raymond Casgrain – one of the 'discoverers' of Champlain's coffin – to help him push through an inscription in Latin. At first, things seemed to be going Lindsay's way. Though there was some debate among committee members as to what the inscription should say, they all seemed to agree that it should be presented in Latin. At one point the committee found itself deadlocked, but after a few weeks off to 'let everyone cool down,' in 1897 it unanimously approved a Latin text pointing to Champlain's continuing influence: 'Through his writings, inspired by God and country, he still inspires the [French] Canadian people, now having reached maturity, towards the highest and most noble goals.'[67]

There was much less enthusiasm for the use of Latin when the text was forwarded to a joint meeting of the *comité des inscriptions* and the *comité de construction*, which had responsibility for the whole project. Had the Latin faction been able to avoid internal bickering, it would have prevailed over those on the construction committee, who had little enthusiasm for the use of a dead language, let alone one so closely connected with Catholicism. No one had objected when, less than a decade earlier, Latin was used on the Monument Cartier-Brébeuf, but that project had not been financed by governments that represented large numbers of English-speaking Protestants and by members of Quebec City's English-speaking community. In October 1897, Herbert Price, a prominent figure in that community, introduced a motion to bar Latin, reminding the others that the Monument Champlain should be 'a practical monument ... accessible to the intelligence of American tourists.'[68]

Price's motion carried by a single vote. Much of the 'blame' for this result was assigned to Abbé Casgrain, who to the surprise of many voted with the anti-Latin faction. Casgrain's vote angered Lindsay, who perhaps should have remembered the abbé's reluctance to support Laval's candidacy for sainthood before asking him to join the *comité des inscriptions*. Casgrain stated that he had simply changed his mind about the quality of the Latin text that was on the table; Lindsay retorted that he had voted against the use of *any* Latin text, not one text in particular. Lindsay well realized that because of Casgrain's vote, an opportunity had been lost to recognize Champlain's Catholic legacy: 'Canada is a great Christian country, and Champlain was a great Christian. So, how can we now erect a religiously *neutral* monument to the illustrious founder of

Quebec City? In order to avoid offending anyone, the decision has been taken to reduce to the *minimum* the indispensable Christian aspect.'[69]

Much the same point was made by the historian Thomas Chapais, who had also argued hard for a Latin text. He observed bitterly that 'the majority had decreed in a learned fashion that we at Quebec are too advanced intellectually to revert to the worship of Latin epigraphy.' Yet another observer, Raoul Renault, remarked rather naively: 'Latin is the language, par excellence, for inscriptions, because Latin is a classical language, so that it has the ability of transcending the passions of the various races that constitute a heterogeneous country such as ours.'[70] In the end, the only Latin visible on the day of the unveiling was in a souvenir volume provided to the various dignitaries who took part in the ceremonies.[71]

At the same meeting that rejected the use of Latin, the committee approved a French text authored by Narcisse-Eutrope Dionne, Champlain's biographer. The Latin text had pointed to the qualities that Champlain had transmitted to successive generations, and had not included a single reference to any specific date; in contrast, Dionne's inscription as described by Chapais was 'a simple listing of historical dates' that reflected the committee's desire 'to concentrate upon the banal.'[72] Though he may have provided little more than a list of Champlain's exploits, Dionne did sneak in a reference to Champlain's Catholicism, as could have been expected, since he had emphasized exactly that in his biography of the hero. Thus, after indicating Champlain's place and date of birth, Dionne's inscription noted that Champlain 'served, during the time of the League, in the armies of the king.' This was a reference to the Holy League of the late sixteenth century that had united Catholics against Huguenots.[73]

Having presented Champlain as a Catholic hero, Dionne was aghast to find that the actual inscription engraved on the left and right sides of the base, in both French and English, made no reference to the League, but only to Champlain having 'served in the French army ... under Henri IV.' In other places besides this, Dionne's text had been altered so as to make the text – which is still visible for all to see – historically inaccurate. For instance, Dionne referred to Champlain as having been the 'lieutenant of the viceroys of New France,' but the version chiselled into stone mentioned that Champlain had been the 'lieutenant-governor' – a position that simply did not exist during the time in question.[74]

When Dionne saw the changes, he was 'more than a little shocked. Why was there such a revision when the sub-committee had not, to my knowledge, requested it? Who is responsible for such an intrusion? This is quite a Mystery.'[75] He did not have to look far for the culprit: Casgrain was openly admitting that he had revised the inscription in order to eliminate its 'editorial weaknesses.'[76] He offered no explanation as to why he had purged the reference to Catholicism, but others were quick to point to the implications of his editing. Dionne observed: 'My learned editor has seen fit to suppress the fact that Champlain served "during the time of the League." But why? Is it because this episode in Champlain's life is not worthy of attention? Or was it because it seemed offensive to place him before the public as a good Catholic, ready to shed his blood for a cause that he considered as both just and holy?'[77] Ernest Gagnon was less restrained, noting that Casgrain had 'transformed [the inscription] in a clumsy manner ... sapping it of its value. We know already the underhanded dealings regarding the Latin inscription; we can now add to that episode the intrigue surrounding the French inscription ... It was important to show that Champlain founded not merely a city, but also a people, a French-Catholic civilization.'[78]

Three of the four sides had now been filled. Only the back was left. The text for this seemed straightforward enough: it noted that the monument had been paid for by citizens' subscriptions and by contributions from various levels of government. Even so, a complaint about this was published in *Semaine religieuse*, the journal of the archdiocese, which by the summer of 1898 was openly expressing its frustration with the repeated marginalizing of Champlain's Catholic legacy. The journal complained that the text failed to 'mention the contributions from a number of priests and layman from the diocese of Quebec, even though the amounts donated were rather small.'[79]

By early 1899 the Monument Champlain had been unveiled, but public debate continued over both the inscriptions and how they had been agreed upon. All this grumbling prompted Judge Chauveau to write to Casgrain: 'This is typical behaviour for Quebec City! If it were possible to tear the monument down brick by brick, someone would probably be happy to do it, in spite of all the energy invested and difficulties overcome in the monument's construction.'[80] Yet one suspects that if Chauveau was frustrated, it was just as much over the bickering surrounding the unveiling ceremony.

Constructing the Unveiling

By the turn of the century there was nothing especially novel about the unveiling of a statue. For nearly twenty years similar monuments had been raised across Quebec as part of the general wave of 'statuemania' sweeping the western world. Leaders invested considerable time and energy mounting elaborate unveiling ceremonies that would attract the public's attention and reinforce the messages the statues had to tell. The general public perhaps missed some of the subtleties in the stories communicated via realistic statues, allegorical figures and carefully worded inscriptions, but they were well versed in the language of processions. Accordingly, tens of thousands of people were organized to march through the streets of Quebec City in processions which formed central elements of the ceremonies that marked both the unveiling of the Monument Champlain in 1898 and that of the Monument Laval ten years later.

Planning for the unveiling ceremonies for the Monument Champlain did not begin until late May 1898, when a meeting of interested citizens was held at the city hall. There is little evidence that this *ad hoc* committee played any role in the months that followed; it vanished as quickly as it was created, its powers assumed by Chauveau's committee, which had hovered over all other aspects of the project. That being said, the *ad hoc* committee included in its ranks various French-Canadian leaders whose feathers had been ruffled during the years of fundraising and monument building, and whose support would be useful in the coming months. Mgr Laflamme, who had been dissatisfied with both the location and the design of the monument, was appointed to the committee; so was the president of the Société Saint-Jean-Baptiste de Québec, Judge Adolphe-Basile Routhier.

Routhier was made president of this committee as part of an effort to draw the SSJBQ into the project. Chauveau announced in late May that while work on the monument was well underway in France, it would not be completed until August. Accordingly, he wanted to schedule the unveiling for September. He hoped the SSJBQ would help draw French speakers into the fete by delaying by three months the annual celebration of their favoured saint – normally held on 24 June – so that it would coincide with the big event.[81] The SSJBQ had played no particular role in the plans for the monument since relinquishing control to Chauveau's committee in the early 1890s. As an organization committed to preserving the French and Catholic aspects of the French-Canadian identity, the society could not have been pleased as decision after decision downplayed Champlain's Catholicism.

By the end of May, when they were approached about delaying their fête, the society's leaders were angry. They had just learned that Routhier had been made president of the committee to organize the unveiling ceremonies; at the same time, they were beginning to realize that their society was considered unworthy of more than a 'secondary role' in the project. In particular, there was considerable grumbling over the fact that in the tentative program that was being circulated, Routhier – a noted orator – had not been included on the speakers' list. The directors were gearing up for a fight as they sent a delegation to meet Chauveau.[82]

Within a few days, these differences had been papered over. Routhier was placed on the program, and the SSJBQ was given a central role in the celebration, which would feature the St-Jean-Baptiste parade as the first event on the schedule.[83] By bringing the SSJBQ directly into the event, the Comité du Monument Champlain had done a great deal to legitimize it among French speakers. Nevertheless, sufficient reticence remained that the society had to hold assemblies in different parts of the city on the two Sundays immediately preceding the unveiling 'in order to reignite enthusiasm.'[84] Another sign of coolness was alluded to by the *commissaire-ordonnateur*, the grand marshal, whose responsibilities for the parade included selling decorative cards to finance it. Less than a week before the unveiling, he observed that French speakers had not rushed out to buy these cards. While 'there has been a satisfactory sale of cards, the Société still has a certain number of them on hand.'[85] Nearly two thousand cards had been sold in 1892, when *la fête de St-Jean-Baptiste* (or *la St-Jean*) also marked the fiftieth anniversary of Cardinal Taschereau's ordination. In 1897, when the fete was linked to the celebration of Queen Victoria's Diamond Jubilee, roughly eight hundred had been sold. In 1898, fewer than seven hundred cards were sold.[86]

Yet any coolness had obviously dissipated by 21 September, the day of the unveiling. The grand marshal commented a few weeks before the big day that this would be the largest parade since 1880, when the SSJBQ invited its sister organizations from across North America to come to Quebec City for a 'Convention Nationale.' On that occasion, local French-Canadian groups from the city joined with the visitors to form a procession of 10,000 marchers.[87] Though we have to be suspicious of estimates like this, *L'Événement* claimed that there were five times as many people marching in the streets in 1898: 'Never have the streets of our city seen 50,000 people marching in formation. Here was an immense crowd, packed tightly together. We have never seen a more impressive or larger procession of our patriotic societies and mutual benefit associations.' Another newspaper noted that there had also been 'a large crowd along the route ... Has this been a dream? Is it really possible that a city of barely 75,000 people might have put on such a spectacle?'[88] The figure of 50,000 participants may well have been dreamed up by a creative reporter, yet there can be no doubt that the crowds came out in droves, making this the largest parade ever mounted to celebrate *la fête de St-Jean*.

The Language of the *défilé de la St-Jean*

As the crowds watched the marchers pass, they understood that the event had been organized according to certain conventions with roots stretching back to the early nineteenth century. The *défilé de la St-Jean* (the St-Jean-Baptiste parade) spoke a certain language, albeit a very different one from that of the other mainstay of the French-Canadian marching season, *la procession de la Fête-Dieu*, which had been central to Laval's reburial ceremonies. The latter procession was fundamentally religious in character, although not without nationalist undertones. Its roots went back to the Middle Ages, and its form could easily be understood by spectators, and its date, though it changed from year to year, had a fixed relationship to Easter. In contrast, *la fête de Saint-Jean-Baptiste* was a much newer holiday, and its conventions were much more variable; thus, its date was open to negotiation when the Comité du Monument Champlain suggested moving it to September.

John the Baptist is typically seen as the patron saint of French Canadians, yet he did not officially acquire that status until 1908, on the occasion of the large-scale celebrations to honour both founding fathers.[89] Till then, St Joseph had held the formal status of patron saint. His fate as an important figure in French-Canadian culture was probably sealed by the fact that his day fell on 19 March, in the middle of both winter and Lent. Pamphile LeMay observed in 1898 that 'the last large-scale celebration of St-Joseph as the patron saint of French Canadians was in 1661.' According to LeMay, St Joseph still occupied a place on the French-Canadian calendar, but solely in terms of a religious holiday. In the late nineteenth century, Benjamin Sulte distinguished between 'the celebration of our patron saint, la St-Joseph, and our national holiday, la St-Jean-Baptiste.'[90]

John the Baptist's feast day fell near the end of June. Thus the religious dimension of *la St-Jean* competed from the start with its 'popular' dimension. It fell, after all, near the summer solstice, which had been treated as a holiday since pre-Christian times. In New France, the burning of bonfires quickly became a standard form of celebration; this bothered the priests, who feared it would be 'very difficult to transform a fete with a long tradition of wild and noisy frolicking into a solemn religious occasion.'[91] In the end, the priests joined in on the festivities, adding a religious element to the lighting of bonfires.[92]

Although *la St-Jean-Baptiste* fared better than *la St-Joseph* as a significant cultural event during the French regime, even the former was celebrated rather inconsistently. It was observed regularly mainly in parishes that bore the name of the saint.[93] This changed in the nineteenth century, with the creation of an organization committed to politicizing French Canada's *fête nationale*. La St-Jean began to assume its modern form with the founding of the Société St-Jean-Baptiste de Montréal in 1834. In the years leading up to the rebellions of 1837–8, the SSJB set about mobilizing popular support for the Patriotes, a group that was hardly viewed positively by the Catholic hierarchy. In the aftermath of the rebellions, the SSJB – both in Montreal and in Quebec City, where it had just started a new chapter – was led by individuals with closer ties to the church, which was more than willing to cooperate with these organizations in order to strengthen its grip on French-Canadian society.[94] At this point, St-Jean-Baptiste processions became reasonably regular events, beginning in Quebec City in 1842 and in Montreal the following year.[95]

In its early years, Quebec City's St-Jean-Baptiste procession reflected certain aspects of the Fête-Dieu procession, which already had two hundred years of tradition in French-Canadian culture. During the 1842 procession the marchers stopped along the way for mass, in much the same way that Fête-Dieu participants stopped at *reposoirs*.[96] In later years, in both Quebec City and Montreal, most processions ended with a mass, reflecting the Fête-Dieu tradition of having the marchers end up at a church.[97] The decorations along the routes of these early processions were also reminiscent of those for the Fête-Dieu. Typically, there were *arcs de triomphe* along the route, and small maple trees lining it.[98] Also, it had become commonplace by the 1850s for small children to march in the parade, dressed in sheepskins and accompanied by a young lamb. The child was meant to represent 'John the Baptist in his youth; it was believed that his protection would be extended to all those who had joined in on an event in his honour.' This tradition, however, did not begin in Quebec, but rather in France, where it had been a part of Fête-Dieu processions.[99] Somehow, the French precedent was reborn in Quebec, but in St-Jean-Baptiste processions.

Yet there were also fundamental differences between the two events. Some of these can be understood by drawing on Roberto Da Matta's comparison of religious processions and more secular parades. In religious processions, there is no real barrier between those who are marching and those on the sidelines. As Da Matta explains: 'Here the streets are transformed and the frontiers between street and houses are weakened ... We have the sacred entering and being received into the houses.' In contrast, in more secular parades the intent is to impress an audience with the power of those who have been allowed to march, so it is important to raise barriers between participants and spectators. As Da Matta puts it: 'In this kind of event there are only two camps: those who are qualified to be inside the order and the rigid hierarchy of the event and those who are outside the isolating ropes and can only see what goes on in the street.'[100]

The religious term 'procession,' which had long been applied to the Fête-Dieu, was also attached to the *procession de la St-Jean-Baptiste* when it first appeared in Quebec City in the 1840s. Eventually, however, though the term 'procession' continued to be used in connection with *la St-Jean*, the more secular terms *défilé* and *cortège* came to be employed from time to time.[101] This subtle linguistic shift, which moved the St-Jean-Baptiste procession toward Da Matta's parade category, reflected some very real differences between the *procession de la Fête-Dieu*, which was meant to bring spectators and marchers together, and the *défilé de la Saint-Jean*, which sought to separate the two. For instance, when the Fête-Dieu-like procession took Mgr de Laval to his new resting place in the seminary, there were no 'isolating ropes' and participants repeatedly joined and left the ranks of marchers. In contrast, during a St-Jean-Baptiste parade, such as the one held in 1898, marchers were strictly separated from spectators by the marshals, who made sure that no one joined the parade who did not belong to one of the authorized groups. The inclusiveness of the Fête-Dieu procession was reinforced by the presence of women, who would not be seen in either the St-Jean-Baptiste parade of 1898, or the one staged ten years later for the unveiling of the Monument Laval.

The Fête-Dieu procession was more inclusive, but it still conveyed a message about power relations in society. Those at the top of the ladder were placed at the centre of the marching order, near the host. In contrast, the St-Jean-Baptiste procession had no symbol such as the host to anchor it, and was organized in a military fashion, with the various authorized groups separated into divisions arranged in hierarchical order.[102] It was possible for the crowds watching a St-Jean-Baptiste parade to see the marchers as part of a single, continuous line, with each division holding a higher status to the one that had come before. This linear organization was also seen in the route, which typically took marchers from one point to another. In striking contrast, the route of a

Fête-Dieu procession invariably formed a loop to consecrate the territory it encircled.

The two processions also differed in terms of their stability. As Benoît Lacroix has put it, unlike secular fetes, which often reflected a certain 'improvisation ... the religious celebration was the model of stability.'[103] While 24 June marked the day in the Catholic calendar for the celebration of John the Baptist, in fact the *fête nationale* was sometimes celebrated weeks or even months later. Judge Chauveau, as a past president of the SSJBQ, knew there was room to negotiate when he tried to coax the leaders of the society to move the date of the 1898 *fête de St-Jean* to September. Only six years earlier, the fete had been celebrated on 22 August as a compromise between those who wanted to stick to the traditional date and those who wanted to move it to 10 September, the fiftieth anniversary of the ordination of Cardinal Taschereau. Moving the fete to late September would have been the most radical move to date. The point here is that there was a precedent for changing dates.[104]

The unsettled nature of St-Jean-Baptiste celebrations was also reflected in the competition in Quebec City between two different chapters of the society. The Fête-Dieu procession took place under the watchful eye of the Catholic hierarchy; there was no higher authority to impose any particular order on *la St-Jean*. The SSJBQ, which had been organizing annual celebrations since the 1840s, came into conflict with the chapter representing the St-Sauveur district of the city; by the close of the century, each was running its own celebrations. Accordingly, the spectators who watched the 1898 parade would have understood that they were seeing something special: the leaders of the two chapters working together, having designed a route from the Église St-Sauveur to the Église St-Jean-Baptiste, and passing through the territories of both societies.

The tens of thousands of people who lined the streets of Quebec City would also have understood that they were witnessing something special because of the general absence of the *chars allégoriques* (floats), which had become a standard feature of such events. In the early years of the St-Jean-Baptiste parade, most of the floats were prepared by the various lay organizations, which took this opportunity to provide tributes to the French-Canadian experience. Most floats were decorated with large-scale figures, usually lay personalities such as Champlain, less often religious ones such as St-Jean-Baptiste.[105] They also often bore patriotic slogans and the names of the lay organizations responsible for them. Over time, commercialism intervened, and *chars* began to appear with no other goal than to advertise products such as sewing machines and

Commercialization of the St-Jean-Baptiste Parade, Quebec City, n.d. (Archives nationales du Québec à Québec; Livernois Photo, P560, S2, D79312, P1)

pianos. In 1880, in response to this, a committee in charge of 'floats and historical characters' was formed in Quebec City to ensure that 'nothing in the procession might be found offensive in terms of either artistic presentation or good taste.'[106]

In 1898, perhaps to add to the solemnity of the occasion, there was only one float. It belonged to the SSJBQ and bore 'a youngster dressed up as John the Baptist, who was accompanied by a detachment of the Garde Champlain.'[107] Founded in 1894, this was one of a number of *gardes militaires* formed in the late nineteenth century. Most of them were named after heroes from French Canada's past and were committed to the defence of a French-Catholic civilization; thus, Archbishop Bégin referred to the Garde Champlain as 'a home for civic and Christian values.'[108] Quite aside from its ideological orientation, the Garde Champlain contributed something special to the 1898 St-Jean-Baptiste parade: its striking uniforms, which included 'high boots, à la Napoléon and their tight fitting pants which were as white as snow [in striking contrast] with the navy blue of their jackets.'[109] The Garde Champlain added colour to the parade, yet strangely enough, it would not participate in the unveiling of the statue of its hero.

Two Celebrations

There were various characteristics of the 1898 St-Jean-Baptiste parade that emphasized the exceptional character of the event. Nevertheless, a great deal about this *défile de la St-Jean* was consistent with past parades. When it started out from the St-Sauveur district early in the morning, the marchers were placed in the hierarchical order typical of such affairs. The grand marshal and his assistants made sure no one was allowed to march who did not belong to an authorized organization; and each of those organizations was ushered into one of seven military-inspired divisions. Toward the start of the marching order, in the first divisions, were representatives of such working-class organizations as the Association des Bouchers (the butchers), the Union des Tailleurs de Cuir (the leather cutters), and the Conseil Central des Métiers et du Travail (Central Council of Trades and Labour). Bringing up the rear would be the leaders of the SSJBQ, invariably members of the professional classes.[110]

For three hours the tens of thousands of marchers followed a winding six-kilometre route, which took them through the working-class districts of St-Sauveur and St-Roch before climbing to the upper town and eventually to the Église St-Jean-Baptiste, where the journey ended. When they arrived at the church, where mass would be celebrated, the dignitaries in the ranks (from the final divisions) entered. There they were joined by various officials, including Prime Minister Laurier and the governor general, Lord Aberdeen. After the mass, there were speeches outside the church by Aberdeen and by Judge Routhier in his capacity as president of the SSJBQ. Then the crowds dispersed, to make their way at their own pace to the Monument Champlain for the unveiling later in the afternoon.

One of the more striking aspects of the day was the separation of the parade from the main event. The SSJBQ's organizers had been asked to delay their most important activity of the year so as to participate in the unveiling; yet the parade was sharply separated from the official ceremonies. We can only wonder why the Comité du Monument Champlain had not drawn the SSJBQ into the unveiling by continuing the parade to the monument, much as the last leg of Mgr de Laval's ceremony in 1878 had taken dignitaries, Catholic and Protestant alike, to the Basilica.

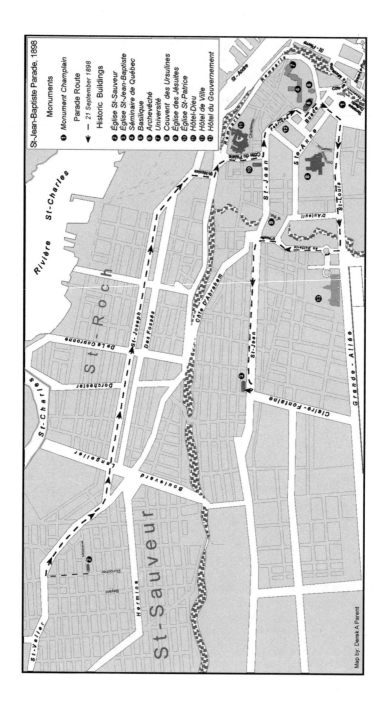

St-Jean-Baptiste Parade, 1898

Monuments

❶ Monument Champlain

Parade Route

→ 21 September 1898

Historic Buildings

❷ Église St-Sauveur
❸ Église St-Jean-Baptiste
❹ Séminaire de Québec
❺ Basilique
❻ Archevêché
❼ Université
❽ Couvent des Ursulines
❾ Église des Jésuites
❿ Église St-Patrice
⓫ Hôtel-Dieu
⓬ Hôtel de Ville
⓭ Hôtel du Gouvernement

Map by: Derek A Parent

Perhaps Judge Chauveau and his colleagues on the committee thought that the St-Jean-Baptiste parade was too exclusively French Canadian for a celebration of Champlain, who was being feted as a founder for both English and French. In fact, there was a precedent close at hand for integrating 'outsiders' into the St-Jean-Baptiste parade: members of the St Andrew, St George, and St Patrick societies had participated in the 1897 event, which had been arranged to help celebrate Queen Victoria's Diamond Jubilee.

For whatever reasons, the leaders of the committee, whose record when it came to celebrating Champlain's Catholic legacy was less than impeccable, had arranged for the parade to be a separate show from the day's main event. Newspapers announced that 21 September 1898 would see the staging of two celebrations, both *la fête nationale et l'inauguration du monument*. Precisely the same terminology was employed by Alfred Paré, a young history professor at the seminary, who kept a watchful eye on the commemorative events that would take place over the next decade and record his observations in a diary.[111] For its part, the Conseil Central des Métiers et du Travail called on all workers to participate in a celebration that, as far as its appeal went, ended with the celebration of a mass. The Union typographique no. 302 called out its members with the following tug at the heartstrings: 'We hardly need to appeal to the patriotism of the workers who will naturally take their place in the ranks of the procession; they will show their patriotic feelings tomorrow by marching as men, as patriots, holding their banners along the way.'[112]

As for the SSJBQ, it had published appeals for a big turnout in *Le Soleil* on the two days preceding the parade. The first observed that 'the national holiday of French Canadians ... will coincide this year with the unveiling'; the second was even more to the point, noting that Quebec City was on the eve of 'two celebrations' rather than a single event with two parts.[113] For better or worse, the organizers from the SSJBQ had been left to organize their own celebration, and they used the opportunity to draw an immense crowd for an event that unabashedly celebrated a French-Catholic heritage – something that would receive rather short shrift later in the day.

Free to chart its own course, the society organized a celebration that began in the early hours of the morning, long before the official start of the parade: 'Upper town awoke to the roll of drums. It saw the Papal Zouaves, a treasure of French Canada and of the temporal power of the pope, on their way to the museum of the university to pick up *le drapeau de Carillon*, another treasure from the French heritage in North

America.'[114] This flag had been a regular part of such parades for fifty years, ever since it was brought to public attention by Louis de Gonzague Baillargé, a Quebec City lawyer who had come across it in a vault in the possession of Frère Bonami, the last surviving member of the Recollet Order in the town. The Recollet told Baillargé that the flag had been carried by Canadien soldiers at a battle fought in 1758 at Fort Carillon, now Fort Ticonderoga, in upstate New York. Though badly outnumbered, the French forces under Montcalm had won a victory – the last major one that they would achieve.

Frère Bonami explained that the soldiers had been aided by the intervention of the Virgin, who hovered over the French troops to ward off English firepower. Accordingly, one side of the flag depicted the Virgin holding the infant Jesus and surrounded by four fleurs de lys. In the twentieth century, this flag – minus the Virgin – would form the basis for the official flag of Quebec. The other side was emblazoned with the French crown.[115] This flag, which combined images of the French and Catholic roots of the French-Canadian identity, offered a very different message from the one that had been chiselled onto the Monument Champlain. The Papal Zouaves, who would become the permanent bearers of the flag in the early twentieth century, reinforced this Catholic message: they marched near the end of the line, just ahead of the member of the SSJBQ who was dressed as Champlain.

The close ties between nationality and religion were similarly on display as the parade made two stops along the way in a manner reminiscent of the interruption of a Fête-Dieu procession at *reposoirs*. It paused first at a site of civil power and then at one of ecclesiastical power. As the parade stopped in front of the newly built city hall, Routhier hailed it as *un palais* (a palace), thus imbuing those whose offices were inside with the sort of civil power that Champlain had once exercised as governor. Mayor S.-N. Parent seemed slightly embarrassed by this exaggeration, but he accepted the compliment in his own brief speech before joining the parade, along with members of city council; in much the same way, certain dignitaries had joined the procession that took Laval's remains to the seminary twenty years earlier.[116]

With its new marchers in tow, the parade approached the nearby archbishop's palace, where Routhier again made a short speech, this time to Mgr C.-A. Marois, the assistant to Archbishop Bégin, who was absent that day for reasons far from clear. The superior of the seminary, Mgr Laflamme, recorded in his journal that Mgr Bégin had refused 'the invitation of the Comité du Monument Champlain, to speak at the unveiling of the monument in question.'[117] It seems that Bégin was only invited as an afterthought, in the same way that Routhier had been added to the program at only the last moment. By the time this 'oversight' had been corrected, the archbishop had already made plans to go to the Maritimes for health reasons. In the end, Bégin claimed he had had no choice but to turn down the invitation to speak at the unveiling. We will never know whether he would have accepted the rather tardy invitation even had he been available. No one was asked to take his place; thus the church was not represented among the speakers at the unveiling. This turned the affair into 'an entirely secular celebration.'[118]

Mgr Marois would be on the platform later in the day, but he would not speak. This means his address to the tens of thousands assembled before the archbishop's residence was the only public statement made that day by a representative of the archdiocese. He did not miss the opportunity to turn Champlain into a Catholic figure, quite unlike the hero to be unveiled that afternoon. He observed that Champlain 'never separated his love for France or for Canada from the love that a child born into the Church owes to his mother. In fact, he placed this second form of love above the first; for he understood that we all belong to God before we belong to kingdoms or owe allegiance to the ephemeral powers of this world.' He called on French Canadians to practise 'the true patriotism ... which far from excluding God and his church, draws upon its noble sentiments and its considerable power.' He closed by holding up as twin models of the perfect patriot, François de Laval and Samuel de Champlain, men who had shown their loyalty both to their people and to their religion.[119]

After Marois' remarks, the parade continued, finally arriving at the Église St-Jean-Baptiste, where most of the officials lucky enough to have been invited to speak that afternoon were waiting for mass to be celebrated. The sermon delivered by Abbé Corbeil, the curé of Ste-Thérèse, just north of Montreal, provided the final opportunity of the day to raise Catholic themes. Corbeil recognized that the afternoon would dwell on 'Champlain's legacy to civil society. As for me, I will dwell on his religious legacy.' He presented the Champlain depicted by writers such as Dionne, who saw the founder of Quebec as inspired by religious zeal. Corbeil praised Champlain not simply as the founder of the first permanent settlement, but also as a key participant in its sanctification. In particular, Corbeil noted the ties that developed between Champlain and the Jesuits, who established a standard for religious devotion that would provide fertile ground for 'the father of French-Canadian christianity, the holy and immortal bishop, Montmorency-Laval' (whose name would not be invoked again on this day). Corbeil closed by reinforcing Marois's message that love for the church and love for the nation were inseparable: 'There is a clear lesson to be derived from Champlain's life, which was so productive because of its grounding in Christianity. Champlain loved his country and his Catholic faith. He had the dream of adding to the glory of each at the same time ... In the image of Champlain, let us try to make our days meaningful for both our church and our country.'[120]

With the end of Corbeil's speech, control over the day's festivities quickly passed from the hands of men who saw themselves rather self-consciously as French Catholic leaders. This passing of the baton was symbolized by a brief event outside the church following mass. Routhier made one final address, this time to the governor general, Lord Aberdeen. From the perspective of the English speakers who had been involved in raising the statue, which was about to be unveiled, Champlain had been above all else the first governor on Canadian soil – a position that Aberdeen now occupied. The governor general thanked Routhier for the parade that had just come to a close, without trying to link it in any way with the unveiling that was just hours ahead. One celebration was finished, and another was about to begin.

Aberdeen as Successor to Champlain

Even though the morning's parade did not channel people to the afternoon's festivities, and even though the unveiling did not always have the enthusiastic support of the local French press, the people still came out in droves for the first public viewing of the Monument Champlain. The newspaper that had estimated the number of participants in the St-Jean-Baptiste parade at 50,000 probably was exaggerating again when it claimed that 'there were at least 100,000 people, men, women and children, crowded upon the Terrace, in front of the Terrace, and in the adjoining streets ... There can be no doubt that Quebec has never seen a crowd as large as this one.' Even if the alternative estimate of 35,000 was closer to the mark, this was still the largest crowd that Quebec City had ever witnessed for an unveiling ceremony.[121]

Those who attended probably heard little of what the various orators had to say, although some undoubtedly read the texts of the speeches in the local press the next day. That being said, the crowds would have noted soon enough that this event was celebrating three different countries, each of which had different reasons for involving itself. Even before the big day, Quebec City residents had been encouraged to fly the English, French, and American flags from the windows of their homes. They were asked to fly the English flag to honour 'our country of adoption,' as well as '*le tricolore* which reminds us of our country of origin.' As for the American flag, it represented 'the nation which provides work and sustenance to a million of our brothers.'[122] The message sent by the flags was reinforced during the unveiling ceremonies. One simply needed to look at the podium: the first row included representatives of the three countries, alongside local representatives of church and state, including Mgr Marois and Prime Minister Laurier. As the afternoon progressed, a clear message was being communicated by the failure of Marois – who had played such a central role that morning – to rise from his chair. But what messages were being sent by the presence of leaders from England, France, and the United States?

The presence of the Queen's representative, Lord Aberdeen, raised the fewest eyebrows. Even within the SSJBQ, it was common to end events dedicated to the celebration of a French Catholic legacy with the singing of 'God Save the Queen.' Only a year earlier, the society had played a key role in the celebration of Queen Victoria's Diamond Jubilee, sending a telegram in the name of French Canadians to their 'illustrious and much-loved Sovereign, in the language dear to their forbears.' The telegram amounted to an expression by French speakers 'of their respect, their loyalty, and their admiration for the great queen who has managed to win the love of her subjects in all the countries of the empire regardless of their language or religion.'[123]

In this spirit, no one questioned why Lord Aberdeen had been chosen to perform the actual unveiling. Quite aside from his vice-regal status, he was the logical choice because he occupied the position that had first been held by Champlain. This conception of Canadian history – that the passage of New France from French to English control had been achieved with little difficulty – was expressed from the podium by Judge Chauveau, who introduced Aberdeen at the very start of the formal ceremonies as the most recent occupant of Champlain's office: 'Providence has decreed that after 290 years of existence, our beloved city should host a spectacle in which our most recent English governor is unveiling the statue of our first French governor. What can be more inspiring than this merging of the past and the present?'[124]

After these remarks, Aberdeen took centre stage and pulled the cord, which almost managed to remove the veil over the statue. According to

Unveiling of the Monument Champlain, 1898 (Archives nationales du Québec à Québec; Livernois Photo, P560, S2 [GH 1070-22])

Alfred Paré, the cloth did not easily lift from Champlain, and as a result there was a 'tearing of the cover, more than the unveiling of the statue.'[125] Be that as it may, at the very moment Aberdeen was doing his job, cannons were fired both from the Citadel and the British and American warships moored in the port. For fifteen minutes 'there was cannon fire which brought back memories of battles from an earlier time.'[126] This reference to such battles as the one fought on the Plains of Abraham might have offended French Canadians. However, the unveiling was suffused with a spirit of *bonne entente* between French Canada and England that prevented anyone from being reminded of what they had lost. When it was his turn to speak, Aberdeen reinforced the day's good will by speaking exclusively in French, even though he usually addressed crowds on these occasions in both of Canada's languages.[127]

In the end, no one had a word of criticism about the role assigned to Aberdeen or the way in which he handled it. The governor general was given the benefit of the doubt in 1898, two years after the election of the first French-Canadian prime minister and a year before the outbreak of the Boer War. For French Canadians, the latter event would be their first encounter with British imperial adventures in faraway places. In 1908, on the tercentenary of Champlain's founding of Quebec, and in the lead-up to the First World War, the precise role of the governor general, Earl Grey, would be hotly contested among French speakers. But in 1898, Aberdeen was universally praised for playing the role of the late-nineteenth-century incarnation of a secularized and bureaucratized Champlain.

'Un bijou de discours'

In the aftermath of the unveiling, Aberdeen received polite approval in the local press, but the French representative, who took the podium immediately after the governor general, was praised to the hilt. One newspaper described the speech of the French consul-general Alfred Kleczkowski as 'a masterpiece' (*un chef-d'œuvre*), while Abbé Paré referred to it as 'a gem of a speech' (*un bijou de discours*).[128] This praise for an official of the French state was especially impressive in light of the rather ambivalent feelings of French Catholics toward the Third Republic, which for some time had been making efforts to limit the influence of Catholicism. Accordingly, for many French Canadians in the final decades of the century, there were really 'two Frances: Catholic France which was either supported or reviled depending upon the circumstances, and the official France, republican and anticlerical, which one either deplored or tolerated with a certain coolness.'[129] Although the image of *la France officielle* improved marginally in 1892, when the Vatican encouraged Catholics to support the Third Republic, enough animosity remained that Kleczkowski, on his arrival in 1894, expressed puzzlement over the point of view of 'our Canadian friends who distinguished between an older [Catholic] France and the one that exists today ... I only know of one France and it is immortal.'[130]

Kleczkowski did not want to lend credibility to the *deux Frances* perspective. Nevertheless, that point of view continued to surface from time to time in the years leading up to the unveiling of the Monument Champlain. In fact, only weeks before the big event there had been heavy coverage in the local press about the latest developments in the Dreyfus affair, which had reached a critical stage with the revelation that the documents which had led to Dreyfus's conviction in 1894 had been forgeries. This only widened the gulf between what many Quebecers saw as two very different Frances: the one was trying to free an innocent man who had been victimized by individuals closely tied to both the military and elements of the Catholic church, and the other saw Dreyfus as representating an impure element in French society that needed to be removed.

In light of French Canadians' conflicting views regarding their *pays d'origine*, Kleczkowski did very well indeed to emerge as one of the stars of the unveiling ceremonies. By and large, he accomplished this by acting as the representative of a secular state that was sympathetic to its largely Catholic population. Thus, on the morning of the unveiling ceremonies he made a point of decorating his friend Mgr Laflamme, rector of the university and superior of the seminary, making him a chevalier of the Legion of Honour on the orders of the French president.[131] In his speech later in the day, it would have been easy for Kleczkowski simply to reinforce the secular French message that was front and centre in Chevré's design for the monument; instead he went out of his way to remind the audience that France had also had a religious mission during its years as an imperial power in the St. Lawrence Valley:

The particular gift of France is that it had twin armies at its disposal, from its military camps and from its Church. From the camps came intrepid soldiers, whose names are still remembered, who served Canada in its adolescence. The Catholic church provided apostles, martyrs and saints. As it turned out, when the military disappeared from Canada, the soldiers of the Church stayed behind. It was as if destiny had decreed that France, having brought the worship of Jesus Christ to Canadian soil, should leave behind, as a legacy of its presence, a certain idealism and the promise of eternity.[132]

Kleczkowski's speech was so well received in clerical circles that it was published twice by *La semaine religieuse de Montréal*, which described it as 'a perfect and delicate piece of eloquence.'[133] Even more impressive was the praise heaped on it by Jules-Paul Tardivel, the ultramontane editor of *La Vérité*. Tardivel might not have been expected to approve of a speech by a representative of the Third Republic; even so, he praised the consul, in particular contrast with Laurier, who spoke from the same podium later in the afternoon. Even though this was a celebration of Champlain, Laurier had few kind words about the France from which the founder of Quebec had emerged. As the prime minister put it: 'It was unfortunate for Champlain that the colony that he founded was subjected to an arbitrary government. Never was New France able to develop as it might have liked, nor did it ever have its own administration. It was always under the control of the ministers and their advisors who, subject to royal authority, were ruling France. This structure was one of the causes for the ultimate destruction of the work of Champlain.' For his efforts Laurier received a letter of praise from a Toronto resident, who asked for a copy of his speech about 'the decadence of French rule.'[134] Abbé Paré was much less positive; he recorded in his diary that Laurier had 'made a long and improvised speech ... presented in a French that was often incorrect!' likewise, Tardivel was shocked by Laurier's lack of tact, given the nature of the occasion. In contrast, Kleczkowski, 'the official representative of the French Republic, did not say a word against monarchical France.'[135]

From Tardivel's perspective, however, what really distinguished Kleczkowski from all the other speakers that day, including Laurier, was that the consul had referred directly to Christ – no small matter, given the general purging of Champlain's Catholic legacy from the occasion: 'M. Kleczkowski was the only speaker to have pronounced the name of Our Lord! The others referred to the Creator, the God of nations, Providence, or Christian civilization; but only the official representative of France had the idea, rather let us say the courage to name the divine who was Crucified, the Saviour of man. Let us honour and thank the consul!' Tardivel combined praise for Kleczkowski with condemnation for the organizers of the ceremony, who had failed to secure a single representative of the church to speak that afternoon: 'We observed with regret that among the speakers called to the podium on this memorable occasion, there was no one representing the Church ... The British, French, Canadian and Quebec governments, along with the Société St-Jean-Baptiste all had representatives on the programme. Why was the Church not invited, so that it might have made its voice heard to celebrate the glory of one of its faithful children?'[136]

The only smudge on Kleczkowski's performance was the rumour that he had blocked the participation of French warships. On the same day that three British warships arrived at Quebec City, Abbé Paré confided to his diary: 'Rumour has it that due to the behind the scenes actions of the French consul, the official representative of the French president at the unveiling, the frigate which was supposed to come to Quebec will not be arriving. It would appear that the consul, wishing to be the only representative of the French republic, did not want to have to share the spotlight with the admiral of this vessel.' It was probably a reflection of the high esteem that Kleczkowski enjoyed that Paré did not automatically accept the theory that the consul had acted out of vanity. The professor from the seminary observed. 'The real reason for the frigate's failure to appear is unknown and will probably remain so for a very long time to come.'[137]

In fact, Kleczkowski's masters in Paris had decided against participating because the only ship that was available was more than twenty years old and was 'ill-equipped to take part in a battle.'[138] They wanted to avoid the inevitable comparison that would be made with the modern warships sent by the British. Though there was not the slightest sign of friction between the French and British officials on hand for the unveiling, the fact remains that the two countries were presently engaged in a stand-off at Fashoda in the Sudan. Kleczkowski observed: 'The absence of French sailors was the only missing element in the wonderful fete in which the memory of France occupied a central role.'[139] Nevertheless, France was not about to let itself look like a weaker global power than the British. In this regard, the fete transcended local matters of identity and touched on larger questions of empire.

The Heroes of the Marblehead

The French did not send a warship to Quebec City; the Americans did, and with considerable effect. In early September the organizers of the unveiling celebration wrote to the U.S. consul asking if his country could 'send one or two vessels ... to add to the brilliance of the inauguration. Champlain's work was not confined to what is now Canadian territory; he explored part of the United States, and gave his name to one of the finest lakes adjoining your country and ours.'[140] In the end, however, neither the Americans' willingness to participate nor the enthusiastic response to the presence of one of their warships had much to do with Champlain's legacy. Rather, the American appearance had everything to do with relations between Canada, Britain, and the United States. The

Americans were just emerging on the world scene as an imperial power in their own right.

When the U.S. consul wrote to his masters in Washington in support of the request from the local organizers, he said nothing about Champlain's exploits, focusing instead on the fact that the presence of such a warship would 'please the United States Commissioners very much.'[141] The commissioners in question were delegates to a Joint High Commission, with British, Canadian and American representatives, that had been meeting in Quebec City since late August with the mandate of resolving a series of problems plaguing Canadian–American relations. Though the commission was considering matters ranging from free trade (or reciprocity as it was called at the time) to fisheries regulation, the issue that had brought the various parties to the table in the first place was the Alaska boundary. This boundary had been in dispute for some time, but establishing its precise location had become more urgent in 1896, when gold was found in the Yukon, in a place that was most easily accessible from American territory in Alaska. Canadian officials wanted the border drawn so that people could enter and leave the gold fields without passing through U.S. customs. This idea found little sympathy among American commercial interests, which were making a killing by supplying goods and services to the Klondike gold fields.[142]

For all the many irritants troubling Canadian–American relations, the American delegates who came to Quebec City in 1898 were hardly perceived as enemies. At least at the start, the tone of the conference was greatly influenced by the Spanish-American War, which had begun earlier in that year and which was already over by the time of the unveiling. The war, which resulted in the American takeover of Cuba and the Philippines, was largely seen in positive terms in Canada, largely because the British had supported the Americans. Most European countries had condemned the Americans' entry into the imperialist sweepstakes; the British had not, seeing the Americans as liberators who had freed the Cubans and Filipinos from Spanish oppression. Moreover, having few friends of its own, Britain intended to take advantage of the gratitude it expected in return for its support of American expansionism.[143]

With the goal of strengthening the friendly ties between Britain and the United States, the organizers of the unveiling festivities delayed their celebration until after the delegates returned from a brief recess on 20 September. The unveiling had first been set for 15 September, to allow time for the statue and the figures that would surround it to be shipped from France. By the start of August, the statue have already been placed on its base. However, by the beginning of September the figures had still not arrived; this forced a delay in the unveiling until 21 September. Even this date almost turned out to be overly optimistic; the surrounding figures were only installed on the eve of the big day. Though there had been some very legitimate reasons for delaying the fete, the officials associated with the event made no reference to them in their public pronouncements. The secretary of the Comité du Monument Champlain made the cryptic remark that it had been delayed 'due to circumstances beyond its control.' However, the reason repeated most often in the local press was 'to allow the attendance of the delegates to the American conference.'[144]

The Americans had been wined and dined from the day in August they arrived in Quebec City. As one commentator observed: 'The evenings and holidays were filled with an unending round of festivities as Quebec's hostesses vied with one another in lavish and exotic entertainments ... One hostess had the feudal idea of staging a "living chess" game for the amusement of the delegates, but an untimely rain storm came up and the colourfully costumed chess pieces broke ranks and scurried for shelter.' For her part, Lady Aberdeen could not understand 'how those poor Commissioners were to get any time for their work with all the social entertainments they were expected to get through.'[145] At the unveiling the Americans sat prominently in the first row of dignitaries, and after the speeches and the unveiling of the monument, they were the guests of honour at a ball held at the city hall. While the French disappeared from view, American and British flags were flown outside the hall; inside were two large banners: God Save the King and Long Live the President.[146]

Although this final event of the day was referred to as 'the grand citizens' ball,' ordinary people were not admitted. While the elite were inside wining and dining, those outside celebrated the American presence in a completely different way: the British and American warships that had come to Quebec were putting on a light show for the occasion. And the American ship was not just any vessel, but one that had fought in Cuba during the recent war with Spain.

The USS *Marblehead* had played a vital role in the recent war, cutting cables crucial to communications back to Spain and helping seize Guantanamo Bay. In sending this particular ship the Americans were also sending a message – one that was likely to be well received not only by the British, who had supported the Americans in the war, but also by French-Canadians, who saw the Americans as the liberators of peoples struggling against Spanish oppression. There was little evidence in Quebec of sympathy for Spain, a Catholic country, but considerable support for a country where 'almost half of the French Canadian family' lived. In fact, there was activity within the United States among 'former Zouaves [in order to] organize French-Canadian battalions ready to come to the aid of their adopted country.' Abbé Paré confided to his diary: 'The Americans are not Savages, as one likes to call them in Europe, but some very civilized gentlemen.'[147]

The *Marblehead* only arrived in Quebec City on the morning of the unveiling. Thus, while French Canadians were marching through the streets of the city, the British ships were firing cannons to welcome the arrival of the war heroes, who then paraded to the ceremonies at the Monument Champlain. The *New York Times* reported: 'When the marines with their colours and band, marched up through the streets and gate of the old city they were greeted with one continuous chorus of cheers. Their uniforms were not so new nor so attractive as those of the British soldiers. They were still wearing their old brown leggings and the blue jackets with which they went through hard fighting, but the Canadians did not criticise these things, and the well-fed, well-dressed British warriors joined in the general hearty welcome to the Americans.'[148] Once the sailors arrived at the monument, their commanding officer, Captain McCalla, in spite of his rather modest rank, was placed in the second row of dignitaries, where he rubbed shoulders with Premier Hardy of Ontario, whose government had contributed to the statue, and various federal cabinet ministers.

McCalla's sailors were seated in places of honour directly in front of the podium, alongside the members of the Comité du Monument Champlain. According to the *New York Times*, the sailors 'had all the time the lion's share of the crowd's admiration.' One of the Canadian delegates to the Joint High Commission remarked that 'the Marblehead mariners attracted a good deal of attention.'[149] When the ceremony was over, they marched away, providing the subject for Paré's final entry of the day: 'It was 4:30; the time had passed quickly ... The American volunteers who arrived from Santiago de Cuba were cheered by the crowds which followed as they marched away. Here was the end of this solemn event: an immense and impressive ceremony in which four peoples had participated officially.'[150]

Whose Champlain?

Though Abbé Paré counted four peoples celebrating in front of the Monument Champlain (presumably the British, French, American, and

Canadian peoples), in fact there were really five. From the start of the project, local English and French speakers had often held conflicting views of it. Even so, there was no particular evidence of tension on the day of the unveiling and this enabled Paré to 'forget' the divisions between Quebec City's two linguistic groups. Many francophones, such as Judge Chauveau, were willing to work with their English-speaking counterparts; but there were also French Canadians who showed little interest in contributing financially to the raising of the monument, who were miffed by the marginalization of Champlain's Catholic heritage, and who saw the St-Jean-Baptiste parade as the most meaningful event of the day.

One indication of this quiet ambivalence was that Mgr Marois never rose from his seat on the dignitaries' platform during the unveiling. Jules-Paul Tardivel complained in *La Vérité* that Champlain's fete had been transformed into a sideshow for the Joint High Commission, little more than a celebration of

the union of the two great English-speaking nations ... This really holds no interest for us. We must constantly remember that although we live under the British flag, we are and ought to remain a distinct people. We are and ought to remain the representatives and the perpetuators of French civilization in North America. We must maintain the French presence on this continent. That is our providential mission, and we should have no other. There is no problem in expressing political loyalty to the English crown; nor is there any problem in being good neighbours to the Americans. But nothing more than that ... We must remain vigilant and not reduce our support for French-Canadian patriotism. No matter what the circumstances might be, we must remain ourselves.[151]

In the end, Tardivel's plea was one of the few sour notes recorded in the aftermath of the unveiling. French Canadians came out in droves, even though the bronze monument made almost no reference to the founder's Catholic legacy, and even though the Saint-Jean-Baptiste parade, which had been shifted from June, was kept apart from the formal unveiling ceremonies, at which no official of the Catholic church spoke. Throughout the 1890s certain French-speaking leaders had expressed concern about immortalizing a secularized version of Champlain; but when the time came for a public celebration, they were able to find just enough religious symbolism to allow their participation. The St-Jean-Baptiste parade may have been cut off from the unveiling, but its inclusion on the program made it difficult for the leaders of the SSJBQ to complain too loudly. As for the ceremony itself, the presence of the French consul referring to Christ by name made it easier for church leaders to accept their own marginalization. A variety of messages were communicated in September 1898, and as a result most French speakers were able to find at least one to which they could respond positively. Ten years later, when an even larger celebration of Champlain was held, many of the same issues would arise. But the context then would be very different, and the story would unfold much less smoothly.

chapter three

Immortalizing Laval, 1878–1908

Laval Returns to the Streets

In the decades following the reburial of Mgr de Laval, clerical leaders, with considerable help from lay allies, mounted two further public celebrations of the bishop. Both were intended to shore up the power of Catholicism in Quebec society. Catholic institutions continued to control education and social services and had even expanded their influence by creating new institutions such as the *caisses populaires*; that being said, the days of the 1870s, when clerics might have confidently tried to influence public affairs, had passed. This change was perhaps best symbolized by the rise to power of Wilfrid Laurier, who was just beginning his career at the time of Laval's reinterment in 1878, who became the leader of the Liberal Party in the 1880s, and who was elected prime minister in 1896. He won the prime ministership even though Quebec's bishops had advised their flock to vote against the former *rouge* because he had been willing to compromise on Catholic educational rights in Manitoba. In the years following his election, Laurier disillusioned Catholic leaders – not only clerics but also laypeople such as Henri Bourassa, who viewed the prime minister as far too willing to make concessions in matters that were important to the survival of a people that defined itself in terms of both religion and national origin. To make matters even worse, Laurier's influence extended to the provincial level, where the Liberals, who took control of the Quebec government in 1897, used their newfound power in an attempt, albeit a failed one, to impose government control over the church-run educational system.

In this context, Mgr de Laval, who had combined ecclesiastical and civil responsibilities, was a potent symbol of how church and state could work together to defend a distinctive French-Canadian identity. This blending of the secular and religious roots of identity contrasted starkly with the highly secularized version of the French-Canadian past embodied by Champlain's statue – a version that would return to the streets of Quebec City in 1908, on the tercentenary of Champlain's founding of the town.

Laval was fêted publicly for the first time since his reburial when his promoters, both lay and clerical, organized a celebration in 1891 on the occasion of the Vatican's decision to allow the case for Laval's canonization – which had been under consideration since 1878 – to pass beyond its preliminary phase. There were strict rules forbidding public celebrations of a candidate for sainthood, but Laval's supporters were not about to miss a chance to place the bishop's legacy before the public. Nor, for that matter, were they about to miss other opportunities that the canonization process provided for encouraging reverence for Laval's memory.

By the early 1900s, however, Laval's journey to sainthood had stalled, whereas Champlain was daily before the public eye now that his monument had been erected. Moreover, discussions were underway for staging a great public spectacle in honour of the founder of Quebec City on the tercentenary of that event. As it happened, 1908 was also the bicentenary of Laval's death, and those who were promoting the bishop's memory were not about to be outflanked by those, such as the governorgeneral Earl Grey, who wanted to celebrate Champlain in order to strengthen Canada's identity as an active member of the British Empire, then engaged in an arms race with Germany. Imperialist talk had always bred insecurity among Catholic leaders in Quebec, who quite understandably were troubled by references to Canada's obligation to aid its Protestant brethren, almost as if the Catholic population did not exist. In this context, the Quebec archdiocese placed its considerable resources behind a campaign to immortalize Laval by raising a monument to him. A monument to Laval would give the bishop a permanent presence in the streets of Quebec City. Just as importantly, its unveiling would offer the pretext for a public festival that would make the 1878 celebration of the first bishop look paltry by comparison.

The Public Celebration of the Venerable François de Laval

During the years of the drive to erect a monument to Champlain, efforts to keep alive Laval's memory continued, though in a very different manner. The campaign for the Monument Champlain focused on such concrete matters as fundraising; efforts to perpetuate Laval's memory focused on having him declared a saint. The local ecclesiastical establishment viewed his reburial ceremonies as an opportunity to launch a drive toward precisely that. Indeed, the final act of the 1878 spectacle was a declaration by Quebec's bishops that they supported the beginning of the formal process that might allow Laval's public veneration.

When Laval's case began making its way through the ecclesiastical bureaucracy, no other male candidate with a connection to Quebec had yet been promoted for sainthood.[1] Marie de l'Incarnation, Marguerite Bourgeoys, and Marguerite d'Youville had already passed the first stage in the process, having been declared 'venerable,' before Laval's case had even begun its journey. Thus Laval's candidacy provided an opportunity to add lustre to the image of someone who, unlike the women candidates, had played a role in both the ecclesiastical and the civil administration of Quebec.

By and large, the drive for canonization took place behind closed doors. The procedures, established in the seventeenth century and still in effect more than two hundred years later, forbade the public veneration of candidates for sainthood. In the wake of the Reformation, the papacy imposed its control over a process that had long permitted local officials to confer sainthood – a practice that resulted in the Catholic calendar being 'drenched in saints.' Such proliferation made any single saint seem less miraculous than might have been the case if a more selective process had been adopted. Moreover, the apparently effortless road for some to sainthood provided an easy target for Martin Luther, who 'rejected the mediation of saints just as he rejected the mediation of the priests.'[2]

In reaction to these criticisms, stringent rules were adopted that centralized decision making. This change increased the cost of any campaign for canonization, since it put in place a complicated procedure involving frequent communications with Rome. These costs would have to be borne by local authorities interested in advancing a particular candidate, so only those who had the support of well-financed backers had a chance of acceding to sainthood. In the Quebec context, this favoured someone such as Laval, who had many strong supporters in the seminary. Within days of the bishop's reinterment, they committed themselves to defraying 'the expenses that will be incurred by the canonization trial of Mgr de Laval.' In case this support was not enough, the archbishop ordered his priests to take up collections to augment the funds invested by the seminary. This system worked against one of Laval's contemporaries, Jeanne Mance, who lacked well-financed sponsors.[3]

As part of its campaign to impose central control, the papacy also sought to prevent local officials from encouraging public celebration of the holiness of candidates. Rome feared that such veneration might skew the process by manufacturing devotion to the candidate instead of allowing that devotion to reflect the candidate's saintly qualities. As Kenneth Woodward put it in his study of the saint-making process, 'Henceforth, any unauthorized display of public cult toward a person prior to beatification or canonization would automatically disqualify the candidate. The faithful could still gather at the tomb of the deceased and pray for divine favours. They could offer private devotions in their homes as well. But they could not invoke or venerate the deceased in a church without jeopardizing his or her chances for canonization.'[4] The organizers of Laval's reburial ceremony worried about damaging the bishop's prospects for canonization, yet it is difficult to examine the 1878 fête without seeing it as a self-conscious effort to promote a certain reverence for Laval's legacy.

After Laval's reburial, there was considerable activity to forward his candidacy for sainthood, although little of this would have been seen by the general public. Laval's dossier was entrusted to Abbé Thomas Hamel, the superior of the seminary, who had also been in charge of the reburial festivities. As the lawyer, or *postulateur*, in charge of moving the case forward, Hamel lined up the witnesses who testified between 1880 and 1883 regarding Laval's reputation for sanctity and between 1898 and 1902 regarding his capacity for working miracles. None of this testimony ever became public, since each witness was required to swear 'an intimidating oath not to reveal either the questions asked or the answers given.'[5]

Laval's candidacy received visible support in 1890 when the findings from the first round of testimony were published. Though the precise testimony of the witnesses remained a secret, letters were published that had been sent to Rome by various parties. The predictable correspondents included representatives of the seminary and the Ursuline nuns; these two groups had also played a central role in the 1878 reburial festivities. There was also a letter from the Catholic judges of the highest courts in Quebec, who separated themselves as a group from their Protestant colleagues and joined forces with the ecclesiastical leaders in support of Laval's canonization. There was also the lieutenant-governor of Quebec, Auguste-Réal Angers, who hailed Laval as 'the true founder of the Catholic church in Canada, and via this church, of the French-Catholic race which has developed here, under the protection of its faith ... In my capacity as head of state of the Province of Quebec, I feel that I have a duty to join with many others to ask Your Holiness ... to see to it that as soon as possible ... the order be given for the introduction of the case for the Beatification of a Great Servant of God.'[6]

These letters were released because Laval had successfully passed through the first stage in the process – in 1890, Rome had declared him 'venerable.' However, his case stalled after that, which precluded any further release of information until after his beatification in 1980. This explains why Laval's journey toward sainthood largely disappeared from public view after 1890, with the notable exception of a fête held the following year to mark the bishop's new status.[7] The staging of public celebrations to honour candidates who had been declared venerable was widespread in the late nineteenth and early twentieth centuries, so much so that Rome felt it necessary to issue a decree in 1913 that explicitly banned these threats to the integrity of the canonization process.[8] Nevertheless, in May 1891 the local ecclesiastical leaders did not hesitate to throw a party, although they were careful to hold it within the walls of the university, not on the streets of the city.

This celebration might have been held the previous fall, at the moment that official word arrived in Quebec City that Laval had been made venerable. Nevertheless, as had been the case in the fall of 1877 when Laval's remains were found, leaders delayed celebrating until the following May; this gave them time to prepare an event elaborate enough to counteract the public's apparent apathy toward Laval's legacy. Only a week before the decision to delay the celebration, Hamel recorded in the seminary's journal: 'There has been little interest among the clergy in responding to the request for donations by Cardinal Taschereau so that the chapel of the seminary might be completed in order to house the remains of Mgr de Laval.'[9] Ultimately, holding the celebration in May 1891 allowed it to coincide with a meeting of the bishops and – perhaps more importantly – with a spectacle in the streets of the city to honour three seventeenth-century Jesuit missionaries.

Jean de Quen, François de Peron, and Jean Liégeois, unlike the Jesuit martyrs honoured in the late nineteenth century alongside Jacques Cartier, had not died heroically.[10] In normal circumstances they would not have warranted special attention. However, they had secured a certain notoriety when their bones, which had been discovered in 1878, only a year after the discovery of Laval's, were inexplicably 'misplaced.'

They were not found again until 1889, in a cemetery on the outskirts of the city. It then took ecclesiastical leaders two years to stage the ceremony that transported the Jesuits to their final resting place in the chapel of the Ursuline nuns, on what just happened to be the eve of the celebration of 'the venerable François de Laval.' An estimated six thousand marchers accompanied the coffins through carefully decorated streets lined with spectators. Nevertheless, to the trained eyes of those who watched the Jesuits pass by, this was not the lavish Fête-Dieu-type procession that had taken Laval to his new resting place. Though both lay and clerical leaders took part, and though various churches were visited along the way, the route of the procession was linear rather than circular, and the order of the marchers did not place the most powerful closest to the coffins. In fact, the coffins of the missionaries were not even at the centre of the marching line, and they were carried by Hurons, not the elite of Quebec Catholicism as had been the case for Mgr de Laval.

Even so, the reburial of the missionaries served as an opening act for the celebration of the bishop, which followed the next day. Since the two events were linked, they communicated similar messages about the unity of church and state – a message that captured the essence of Laval's legacy. In this context, the crypt in which the Jesuits were buried was paid for by the provincial government, and representatives of the Quebec government marched alongside members of the Papal Zouaves. As one newspaper put it, this event distinguished itself as 'a glorious religious and national celebration.'[11]

The reburial of the Jesuits did not conclude before seven p.m., so only hours remained before the mass that was to mark the beginning of the day celebrating Laval's new status. This mass of thanksgiving was celebrated in the Basilica which had been decorated with great care. Various 'relics of the Holy Martyrs' that had been brought to Quebec by Laval himself but that were normally displayed elsewhere, were visible on the altar. The connection to the *ancien régime* was also evoked by the cloaks, gifts of Louis XIV, worn by the clerics celebrating the mass. Even the chalice used during the mass had its origins 'in the time of the first bishop of Quebec.'[12]

After the mass, the crowds dispersed. The organizers were being careful not to take this celebration to the streets; had they done so, they would clearly have been violating church rules regarding the veneration of candidates for sainthood. Nevertheless, the public reassembled later in the day at the university for an evening of 'music, rhetorical eloquence and poetry.' Many of the same dignitaries who had participated in the reinterment of the Jesuits were on hand at what was described in the press as 'a great outpouring of national sentiment' attended by 'His Eminence Cardinal Taschereau, His Worship the lieutenant-governor ... and the elite of Quebec society.'[13] In a manner reminiscent of Laval's reburial, the hall was decked out in flowers, but the centre of attention was the candidate for sainthood: 'A portrait of Mgr de Laval was hung above the stage beneath a canopy of plush material woven with golden thread.' Laval's likeness was front and centre despite rules that forbade the display of such images 'in holy places for public veneration.'[14] The point might be made that the university was not a holy place; even so, the organizers were stretching the rules.

As for the program itself, Mgr Bégin, the future archbishop of Quebec but at the time the bishop of Chicoutimi, was given high marks for delivering 'the most perfect eulogy which has ever been pronounced in honour of the first bishop of Quebec.'[15] Bégin portrayed Laval as the uncompromising prelate whose life had been marked by 'the determination in his soul.' He likened the bishop to a soldier, repeatedly using the words *lutte* (struggle) and *combat*. Laval had done battle with various forces hostile to Catholicism; of these, none had been more dangerous than gallicanism – the idea that the state should play a role in affairs that properly were the concern of the church. As Bégin put it: 'At a time when gallicanism managed to seduce even the greatest minds in France ... it is impressive to see how the first bishop of Quebec managed to resist its attraction, to struggle against false ideas ... and to insulate New France against the invasion of the errors of Gallican thinking.' In the end, thanks to Laval's commitment to maintaining close ties between church and state, French Canadians had survived as a people marked by 'the combined power of religious and national identity.' So that there would be no doubt in anyone's mind about Laval's credentials as not only a religious but also a nationalist icon, Bégin made the point that 'even though he hailed from ancient France, he became the most Canadian of Canadians in terms of his values, his habits, and especially in terms of his heart.'[16]

Two of the program's participants read poems they had composed for the occasion. The first was Abbé Gingras, a curé who had helped plan the event and who felt no hesitation in effectively declaring Laval a saint.[17] He observed that even though Rome had not yet finished its deliberations, French Canadians were already worshipping him as if he were a saint. In this vein, Gingras closed one stanza:

A brilliant, rosy light emanates from his tomb,
And the people say over and over again, 'It is Laval waking from his sleep.
It is the light of a new saint!'

So as not to go too far, Gingras recognized that it was ultimately 'the Church which chooses the holiest of its clergy.' Nevertheless, he was confident that one day *la Patrie* would be able to pay tribute to its first bishop on Rome's recognition of his saintly qualities.[18]

In the spirit of balancing the secular and the sacred, the other poet was the lawyer Jules-Adolphe Poisson, who was no stranger to such celebrations, having composed several poems in 1880 for the massive *convention nationale* of North American French speakers that had been organized by the Société St-Jean-Baptiste.[19] Given his lay background and connections, Poisson avoided any talk of Laval's saintly qualities; instead he described him as the partner of Frontenac, a governor of New France with whom the bishop had quarrelled repeatedly over such matters as the trade in alcohol. Nevertheless, for this occasion he depicted the two seventeenth-century leaders as allies who had worked in harness for the survival of a people who could affirm: 'Indeed, we are still French and Catholic.' In what was reported as an emotional high point of the evening, Poisson linked the past with the present by paying tribute to the late-nineteenth-century successors to Laval and Frontenac, both of whom were in the audience:

As in your case, Frontenac has turned to dust
But after two hundred years of struggles, of dangers,
You are still alive today, the two of you buried under stone;
Laval has returned as Taschereau, Frontenac as Angers.

There was nothing especially noteworthy about associating Laval with the current archbishop, but drawing the connection between Frontenac, a French colonial governor, and Angers, the lieutenant-governor, was another story. By linking these two officials with each other, Poisson was recreating a moment from the reburial of Laval, when the lieutenant-governor of the day was viewed as having inherited the mantle of Vaudreuil, the last French governor. In each case, there was an unambiguously nationalistic message: Quebec, through the person of its head of state, was being spoken of as the successor state to France. A very different story was to be told in 1898; that year, the governor general, Canada's head of state, would be presented as successor to Champlain, the first French colonial governor; this would effectively confirm the transfer of authority from a French Catholic to a predominantly English Protestant state. Needless to say, this message – which would resurface yet again in the 1908 celebration of Champlain – was more popular among English speakers than among French Canadians. However, in 1891 Poisson was celebrating the survival of a French Catholic people. For his efforts he received 'three bursts of applause.' There was a similar reaction to the final item on the evening's program, the 'official' anthem of such events, 'la Cantate en l'honneur de Mgr de Laval,' which prompted further 'applause ... from all parts of the hall as if artillery were being fired. There was electricity in the air.'[20]

With the close of this ceremony, Laval once more vanished from public view. The organizers of this fête had succeeded in walking the very fine line that separated a permissible public celebration of a candidate for sainthood from one that was not. In the end, officials in Rome were satisfied that Laval's case had not been prejudiced by the 1891 fête.[21] However, though Vatican officials may have been content, those in Quebec City must have been disappointed that reverence for the bishop seemed to evaporate once the process potentially leading to his sainthood retreated behind closed doors.

This loss of interest was evident, for instance, in the difficulties experienced by leaders of the seminary who wanted to turn 23 May – the date on which Laval had been reburied – into an occasion on which the hymn of thanks, 'Te Deum,' would be sung so as to 'perpetuate his memory.' By the early twentieth century this practice had been abandoned. On the eve of the unveiling of Laval's statue in 1908, Abbé Paré remarked: 'It was only last year that this tradition was revived, after having been neglected for a number of years.'[22] Perhaps sensing that public reverence was drying up, the seminary arranged for the production in 1904 of '56,000 small pictures of Mgr de Laval.'[23] It is impossible to know exactly what prompted this action, but the pertinent reference is one of the last in the seminary archives to Laval's canonization, which stalled until his beatification (the second step on the road to sainthood) in 1980; as I write these lines, Laval's case has not progressed to the third and final step.

The Monument Hébert

The idea for the Monument Laval first surfaced in 1901 at a meeting of the Société St-Jean-Baptiste de Québec, which had been marginalized during the festivities surrounding the Monument Champlain. The SSJBQ's president, Albert Jobin, noted that the very existence of a statue in honour of Champlain had been the motivation for erecting one for Quebec's other founding father. The society ultimately found 'the project ... a bit premature,' but once it had been suggested, the idea did not go away. In 1902, on the occasion of fêtes to mark the fiftieth anniversary of Université Laval and the sixtieth of the SSJBQ, a consensus emerged among local leaders that an even more elaborate celebration should be held in 1908 to mark the tercentenary of Champlain's founding of Quebec. The journal of the archdiocese was quick to see the possibility of adding Laval to the 1908 agenda: 'The discoverer of Canada [Jacques Cartier] and the founder of civil government [Champlain] having already been honoured with monuments in Quebec City, we hope that it might be possible to celebrate the tercentenary with the erection of a monument to the memory of the Venerable Mgr de Laval.'[24] In 1903, the SSJBQ undertook the preparatory work that ultimately led to the first meeting of the Comité du Monument Laval in March 1904.

By establishing an organization to carry the Monument Laval project through to completion, the SSJBQ was in tune with the 'administrative revolution' that was transforming the affairs of large-scale businesses by creating specialized clerical staffs and complicated organizational diagrams.[25] This revolution transcended the world of business and left its mark on how commemorative events were administered in the last quarter of the nineteenth century. Abbé Hamel had looked after the reburial of Mgr de Laval on his own, much like someone looking after a small family business; in contrast, Champlain's statue was raised and unveiled only after an elaborate series of committees and subcommittees had been created whose structure resembled that of a corporation. The SSJBQ did not seem attuned to these changes when it tried to take charge of the Champlain project in the early 1890s; as a result it had had to turn to 'outsiders' to finish the job. Having a more realistic view of its own limitations this time around, the society helped create a new body that would bring it together with leaders from the university (where the first meeting was held) and the archevêché (the archbishop's palace, where much of the leadership would be found).

In inviting the various leaders to the initial meeting of the committee, Albert Jobin explained that it was important to provide a monument to 'the founder of organized religion ... It is for Catholics and for French Canadians an obligation to provide this honour, this mark of recognition.'[26] In describing the project in this manner, he was communicating the same mixed messages as had been present on Laval's reinterment, when images of the bishop as founder of Catholicism in North America mingled with those of him as father of the French-Canadian people. The first message was reinforced at the initial meeting of the Comité du Monument Laval, when Jobin observed that the project did not belong to 'any one race,' and that he looked forward to the participation of 'Catholics who belong to nationalities other than ours.'[27] In practice, however, the second, overtly French-Canadian orientation won out; English speakers were assigned a marginal role in the committee's organizational structure. Perhaps recognizing the importance of tapping the funds of English-speaking Catholics in Quebec City and beyond, several representatives of that population were assigned to the *comité de souscription* (fundraising committee). However, not a single English speaker could be found either among the officers with overall responsibility for the project or on the *comité de construction*, which was responsible for the actual design of the monument.[28]

In the case of the Comité du Monument Champlain, by the time its formal organizational structure was in place in 1890, French speakers had already shown themselves incapable of raising the required funds. English Canadians had to be courted, with the result that English and French representation on the Comité du Monument Champlain was relatively equal. In terms of the Monument Laval, since the organization was put into place before the work began, French-speaking Catholics did what they could to keep the project under their control. The jobs on the committee were divided between clerics and laymen, nearly all of whom were French speakers; each group represented one facet of Laval's legacy, which was both religious and secular.

With an organization in place, the work began to construct a monument in time for unveiling in 1908, a year that meant different things to different people. In inviting lay and clerical leaders to the first meeting of the committee, Jobin noted that 1908 would mark 'two important dates in the history of our city. It was in 1608 that Champlain founded Quebec, and it was in 1708 that Mgr de Laval died at the seminary.' Pitching the matter somewhat differently, the mayor of Quebec City tried to sell the project to city council by noting that 1908 was 'the 250th anniversary of the consecration of Mgr de Laval as a bishop, on 8 December 1658.' A bit more far-fetched was Mgr Laflamme's hope that 'this date might coincide with the beatification of Mgr de Laval whose case is now before the court in Rome.'[29]

Even though the deadline was four years away, the committee began work on the design of the statue within weeks of being constituted and even before fundraising activities had started in earnest. To facilitate the process – or so they thought – the project leaders dispensed with the sort of competition that had been resorted to for the statue of Champlain. In early April of 1904 they awarded the commission to Louis-Philippe Hébert, the Canadian sculptor who had designed such monuments as the one to Maisonneuve in Montreal, but who had lost out in the Champlain competition – much to the chagrin of Mgr Laflamme, who now sat on the *comité de construction*.[30] Perhaps fearing that he would be passed over yet again, Hébert had made his position clear: '*I will not take part in any public competition* in which foreign artists will be invited to present maquettes.'[31] It was agreed after some discussion that Hébert would be allowed to submit a maquette, and that a competition would be held later only if his design was totally unacceptable.[32] One suspects that Hébert's supporters were acting defensively, to ensure that there would be no repeat of the situation in the 1890s, when a French sculptor received the commission for the Monument Champlain. This fear was especially strong in 1904, when France was about to sever the ties between church and state.

By the end of April, only a few weeks after he had been contacted about the project, Hébert delivered a maquette along with a 'légende' to explain the story he was trying to tell. The sculptor was able to produce a model this quickly by employing various elements from one of his designs that had lost the Champlain competition. At the very top of the monument, standing atop a column, was Laval, simply dressed and bareheaded, with one hand resting on a Bible and the other brandishing a cross, 'the mystical sword of righteous struggle and divine conquest.' Just below Laval was 'a Winged Glory ... symbolic of both fame and peace,' who resembled the figure of Fame on the Monument Champlain, but without the trumpet. Finishing the maquette were three allegorical figures at the base of the column. At the centre of the trio was a female figure, almost identical to one he had proposed for the Monument Champlain, representing *la vaillance chrétienne* (Christian valour). Much like Laval, who had exercised both civil and religious authority, she was a figure 'partly secular and partly monastic'; she held the shield of a warrior yet she was dressed like a nun. Standing to her left was 'the sturdy nomad' whom *la vaillance* was trying to lead into a chapel, the sign 'of a new society which was attached to the land and likely to survive.' This figure, presumably representing a *coureur de bois*, was clutching oars, which suggested that the attractions of life in the wilderness might be more powerful than those of Catholicism. Hébert was trying to show that

First maquette of the Monument Laval, 1904 (Archives de l'Archidiocèse de Québec, 40A, vol 2–2; reproduced from *Daily Telegraph*, Christmas 1904)

'old habits and the power of nature will resist for a long time before giving way to a complete conversion.' To the right of the woman was 'the antithesis' of the nomad, a young man who was listening to her every word and who represented the French-Canadian youth who had attended the seminary founded by Laval.[33]

The monument also had three bas-reliefs designed 'to summarize the political and religious life of Mgr de Laval.' Two of these, one showing Laval baptising the native chief Garakontié and the other the confirmation of a group of natives at Tadoussac, told the same story of Laval's missionary career. The third had the bishop welcoming the Marquis de Tracy, the viceroy in charge of France's North American possessions, to show 'the cordial ties so necessary to unite ... the two powers.'[34]

If Hébert's supporters had hoped this design would be approved quickly, they were in for a surprise. After various complaints raised by members of the *comité de construction*, a three-member panel was chosen to provide a coherent report on the maquette. The panel, which included Eugène-Étienne Taché, best known for coining Quebec's motto 'Je me souviens' and for designing many historical statues in Quebec City, had few kind words for Hébert's work. The committee felt that the statue of Laval was too small, the cross he was holding far too large, and the winged figure too mundane. As for the three figures below the bishop, the panel did not like *la vaillance*, and wanted it replaced with a character who was unambiguously religious. Similarly, it wanted to replace the French-Canadian nomad with a native figure. In terms of the bas-reliefs, the panel wanted to eliminate the redundant conversion scene at Tadoussac and replace it with 'a group of religious figures who were collaborators with Mgr de Laval: Jesuits, Recollets, Ursulines, Augustines, and secular priests [not belonging to a religious order], or any other group preferred by the Committee.'[35]

In the original version of their report, Taché and his colleagues suggested that Hébert's maquette might still form the basis for the Monument Laval, but only 'with the modifications that were proposed.'[36] Curiously, in the copy of the report in the archdiocese archives these words were crossed out and new ones inserted so that the panel now concluded, without any reservations, that 'this project ... appears to us to be very striking, and certainly ranks among the most beautiful works of M Hébert.' Recognizing that the original text had been altered, someone later appended to the copy in the seminary archives the observation that 'pressure had been exerted upon the experts.'[37] We will never know who wrote these words or who if anyone was trying to twist the panel's collective arm, but such pressure would have been consistent with the efforts made from the beginning of the project to approve Hébert as the sculptor as quickly as possible. Whatever actually happened, the panel's report was sufficiently damning that Hébert was forced back to the drawing board. Over the summer of 1904 he worked on a second maquette, with Paul Chevré, the French sculptor of the Monument Champlain, waiting in the wings in case Hébert was not up to the task.[38]

The second maquette incorporated some but not all of the concrete suggestions offered by Taché's panel. Although the figure of Laval remained much the same, Hébert made the suggested changes both to *la vaillance*, now unambiguously religious, and to the nomad, now transformed into a native figure. As for the bas-reliefs, Hébert introduced a scene of Laval in the presence of Louis xiv, and another of the bishop in the company of the religious orders with which he had worked, to complement the one of the baptism of Garakontié.

The response to the second maquette was even more emphatically negative. It seems that within days of viewing the new maquette, Hébert's most loyal supporter, Mgr Marois – the same assistant to Archbishop Bégin who had sat quietly throughout the unveiling of the Monument Champlain – had lost confidence in the sculptor. According to Mgr Mathieu, the superior of the seminary, Marois 'seems to have come to the conclusion that one cannot expect anything satisfactory from M Hébert. [Marois] regrets that the Committee has gone so far down the road in its dealings with the sculptor. If the Committee were to start from scratch, it would probably proceed in a very different manner and would probably insist upon a competition.'[39] Only a few days later, Mathieu returned to the same subject in his journal: 'The Monument Laval has become the nightmare of the committee responsible for it.' Soon after, Abbé Paré confided to his diary: 'I heard it said today that the second maquette is even worse than the first.' He noted that clerical disenchantment with the Monument Champlain had not entirely evaporated, and concluded: 'It is becoming obvious that it is necessary to have a competition among artists and to choose the best maquette; only, it would be necessary to choose more wisely that was the case in terms of the Monument Champlain.'[40]

When it appeared that the whole project was about to go down the drain, the committee turned to Judge Chauveau, who had headed the Monument Champlain project during the 1890s. Chauveau contacted European sculptors for specific suggestions that might allow the project to be saved. In October 1904 he sent a copy of the second maquette to

the French sculptor Maurice Lefebvre, who replied that he could find
nothing positive about a project that lacked 'two indispensable qualities:
style and inspiration.' He further complained that Laval was 'too belli-
cose for a Christian pastor ... As for the allegorical figures, they were
unbelievably banal.' He concluded that no matter where this monument
might be placed, 'the project would have the effect of cluttering up the
location.'[41]

After receiving several other assessments that echoed Lefebvre's, Marois
and his colleagues seemed ready to give up on Hébert. They probably
would have done so had they not believed – wrongly as it turned out –
that they had a legal obligation to continue with him.[42] Not knowing
quite what to do, the committee turned once more to Chauveau, this
time sending him off to Europe, photographs in hand. These he showed
to artists in Paris and Rome, who sent their universally negative assessments back to Quebec. In one of these reports, A. Bonnet, a Parisian
architect, wrote that Hébert's design was 'a work of little value. It lacks
simplicity, it lacks architectural interest, it lacks everything. It would be
better to do nothing than to go ahead with this mistake.' Near the end of
his trip, early in the new year, Chauveau wrote to Mgr Laflamme, the
former superior of the seminary: 'Everyone agrees that the monument
proposed by Hébert is a *monstrosity*, a horrendous piece of work from any
point of view. I am not exaggerating these reactions ... It is absolutely
necessary to have a competition.' The judge was certain that 'there was
no contract obliging the Committee to give the monument project to M
Hébert.'[43]

Back in Quebec City, Hébert was confronted early in 1905 with the
evidence that had been collected and was given one final chance to
prepare a satisfactory design. To clarify the contractual relationship
between the sculptor and the committee, a document was drafted that
required the submission of a third maquette by the fall. It was understood that this maquette would have to receive 'the approval of a committee of French artists.' However, true to the francophobia that had
marked this affair from the start, this obligation was not placed in the
contract; rather, it was stated in a letter, a codicil, that Hébert was forced
to sign.[44]

Although Hébert's detractors were not completely silenced, the new
design received the approval of the committee, which could now turn its
attention to other matters. Though some elements of the monument
had been dramatically altered, the bas-reliefs were largely unchanged
from the second maquette. In the first scene, Laval was shown arriving in

Monument Laval, bas-relief: Mgr de Laval's term as bishop (author's photo)

Quebec City in the company of the priests and nuns who were to serve him. Given that two intricately choreographed processions were to be the highlights of the unveiling ceremonies, it was appropriate for Laval to be shown taking part in a cortège proceeding from the town into the countryside. As in a Fête-Dieu procession, Laval, 'dressed in his pontifical attire,' was at the centre of the line, with priests marching both before and after him. One critic thought it strange that the Jesuits and Recollets at the front of the line had their backs to the bishop, but this is what one would have expected in such a parade.[45] Besides the priests, the group bringing up the rear included nuns and civil officials; this reflected the inclusiveness of a Fête-Dieu-inspired affair.

The second bas-relief reinforced the message of cooperation between church and state by depicting Laval at the court of Louis XIV. This scene included a number of characters from the late seventeenth century, including Colbert, the king's Minister of Marine, who stood just behind the monarch.[46] One wonders why, if Hébert was seeking historical accuracy, Laval and the other clerics were shown in full ecclesiastical garb. One commentator observed at the time of the unveiling: 'No bishop, neither Mgr de Laval nor anyone else, would appear before the Great King dressed in anything other than the normal courtly attire worn by all.' This same observer assumed that Hébert dressed Laval in such a manner only because 'it would have been difficult to recognize the bishops, if they were dressed in lay clothing.' However, this assumption

Monument Laval, bas-relief: audience with Louis XIV (author's photo)

removes the project from the context in which it was produced. This was a monument not only to Laval, but also to the unity of church and state. So both the king and the bishop were dressed as persons of authority; in effect, they were being shown as near equals.[47]

The final scene around the base of the monument showed Laval baptising the Onondaga chief Garakontié. Once again, Hébert brought characters from Laval's life into the picture. The group surrounding the chief included the governor of the time and the daughter of the intendant. It is believed that representatives of tribes other than Garakontié's were present at the actual event; however, the other natives depicted were shown ignoring the baptism. Much like the nomad from the first maquette, who was not sure if he wanted to enter the chapel, so too were these native figures unsure whether they were ready for conversion.

The image of the ambivalent native was also evident among the allegorical figures at the base of the monument. Like the bas-reliefs, these figures had not been dramatically changed from the previous maquette, so some of the criticisms levelled against that version also applied to the final one. The native was still just to the left of the woman representing religion, who was encouraging him to go to the church toward which she was pointing. However, the native was posed leaning backwards away from her. This led one critic to remark: 'If he was listening, why is he not leaning towards the Statue ... in an attentive pose?' A more generous observer interpreted the posture of the native as symbolic of the difficulties faced by the missionaries. In the end, if there were relatively few

Monument Laval, bas-relief: baptism of Garakontié (author's photo)

conversions, this was because of 'the immorality of certain whites and to the greed of the merchants,' against whom Laval had struggled.[48] On the other side of the religious figure was a young schoolboy, who had also been present in Hébert's first maquette. However, new to the final version was the winged figure, identified by one observer as 'the Angel of the [French]-Canadian nation,' who had previously been floating above the image of the church, but who now formed part of the allegorical group, with an outstretched arm offering Laval a palm leaf in recognition of his triumphs.[49]

In the end, the most radical change in the final version was to the figure of Mgr de Laval himself. None of the critics had liked the plainly dressed, cross-brandishing bishop: some had called him too aggressive, while others could not understand exactly what message Hébert was trying to convey. There were still some critics of the new Laval, but most of those contacted by the *comité de construction* seemed highly pleased. One of the foreign experts who had panned the second maquette was greatly impressed by 'the substitution of the bishop with his cross and mitre for the rather private bishop of the first maquette, who would have seemed better suited in a seminary classroom.'[50] Dressed in full episcopal garb, Laval was now presented as a figure of authority, with his right arm 'extended in order to call to his flock, to encourage and to bless them.' The other hand held his staff, 'which is placed upon the ground, as if to make the point that he was responsible for planting the banner of the faith upon Canadian soil.' As for the general demeanour of the

Monument Laval (author's photo)

bishop, he had his head slightly bowed, not looking straight ahead as in the previous versions. Laval was no longer the overly proud figure described by Garneau and Casgrain, but rather a more compassionate one concerned mainly about 'his pastoral responsibilities and the denial of self-gratification.'[51]

The statue of Laval was the most significantly changed element in Hébert's final version, and this is probably what allowed him to keep the commission. Even so, some observers were still unconvinced. Abbé Alfred Paré, watching the whole affair from his perch in the seminary, was not especially impressed by the third maquette when it was produced in the fall of 1905, referring to the new Laval as 'a windmill at rest.' In the spring of 1908, when Laval was placed on top of the column that rose from the base of the monument, Paré observed that it was covered by the Drapeau du Sacré-Cœur, the same mystical flag that had been used in the Saint-Jean-Baptiste parade just before the unveiling of the Monument Champlain. When the wind blew the flag, the statue was revealed to the public for the first time, and the consensus that emerged was highly negative: 'The poor statue of Laval! How it is mocked by nearly everyone. Seen from either rue Buade or the Côte de la Montagne, there is a general sentiment that it is simply horrible. No newspaper has said anything positive about it.'[52]

Although he had never had a kind word for Hébert's efforts, Paré recognized that it was a bit unfair to judge the monument before all the pieces were in place. In the last weeks of May, roughly a month before the unveiling ceremonies, the bas-reliefs and the allegorical figures were positioned below the bishop, at which point the usually acerbic Paré had to admit: 'Each day the monument is looking better and the number of admirers, very limited at the start, is growing all the time.' Nevertheless, Paré concluded on a negative note: 'The monument is going to be beautiful, but its location is awful.'[53]

A Monument Positioned in Whose Honour?

Louis-Philippe Hébert was responsible for the monument itself, but it was the members of the Comité du Monument Laval – more specifically, the clerical leaders associated with the archbishop – who determined where it would be placed. In the case of Champlain, there was never any serious alternative to Dufferin Terrace, which was then being developed as a tourist attraction. For Laval, the issue was not as straightforward. In 1901, at roughly the same moment that the Société St-Jean-Baptiste was beginning to ponder the Laval project, Mgr Henri Têtu, the *procureur* in the *archevêché* in charge of temporal matters of concern to the archbishop, was already before city council trying to secure a parcel of land between the archbishop's palace and the post office. The land in question was occupied by what the project's promoters referred to derisively as 'an isolated block of old houses' (*un pâté de vieilles maisons*). Têtu wanted the city to demolish the houses to create an open space for the Monument Laval.

Though Têtu's petition was supported by various leaders of Quebec City, lay and clerical alike, it also raised questions of historical preservation in the minds of some residents. One of them wrote to the *Quebec Chronicle*: 'Would it not be well to go slow and think this matter out before taking action?' More specifically, the anonymous writer explained that these houses had, going back to the French regime, been across the street from a hotel known as the 'Chien d'or.' A stone with a 'golden dog' had been preserved when that hotel was demolished, and inserted into the wall of the post office, which stood where the hotel had been. 'If this block is removed, the little street known as Port Dauphin with all the historical souvenirs of old France which cling to such a name will no longer exist.' J.M. Lemoine, an early promoter of the Monument Champlain, wrote to the same newspaper that he had little sympathy for saving the block of houses for historic reasons. Even so, he wondered whether this was the 'proper time to ask for its acquisition by the City Council, at an outlay of $10,000 or $50,000, when other projects of city ornamentation and embellishment, perhaps more pressing, engage the attention of the public.'[54]

We cannot say whether these objections slowed the process. We do know that nothing had been done about the *pâté de maisons* by the fall of 1902, at which time Têtu returned to the city council with a further demand, signed by sixty-five local leaders, that *ces masures* (these terrible little houses) be removed to make way for a statue of Laval. There would be no formal committee to promote the project for another two years; even so, Têtu supported this request with an architect's conception of what the site would look like; this rendering included a monument to Laval that had the bishop, positioned in the midst of a green space, looking toward the St. Lawrence and away from the *archevêché*. Têtu's new appeal was supported by a page one editorial in *Le Soleil* intended to strike out against those who were still 'under the impression that by demolishing *le pâté de maisons* ... the city will somehow be losing one of its most precious monuments.' This counterattack was supported by the long-time city engineer, Charles Baillairgé, who considered the houses little more than 'a jumble of old wooden buildings, of crumbling balconies, of out-houses ... This is what visitors see as they come up the Côte de la Montagne ... With good reason, they see them as an absolute disgrace for the city.'

Although *Le Soleil*'s editorial writer was confident that 'the *pâté de maisons* would not find a large number of defenders,' the city did not acquire the contested land until 1903 and did not clear it until the summer of 1904. A few months later it turned the land over to the Comité du Monument Laval. The city did not rush to accommodate Têtu's request; perhaps this reflects the sometimes strained relations between clerical authorities and Simon-Napoléon Parent. The mayor of the city was also the premier of the Liberal government of Quebec, which had tried to strip the church of its control over Catholic schools. Parent responded rather coolly to Têtu, noting that 'there were various points of view that had to be taken into consideration.'55

In particular, there were financial implications for the city, which would have to compensate the owners of the property (losing the tax dollars of the occupants in the process) and then pay the costs for demolishing the houses. Têtu tried to calm Parent's fears about the cost – which would run to more than $50,000 – by pointing to the tourism possibilities of the project. He argued that the city would receive a return on its investment through 'indirect financial considerations' generated by the 'crowds of visitors who would not otherwise have come here.' The mayor wanted something more concrete than this and asked the seminary to cede a small strip of land to allow the city to expand one of the streets in that part of town. The seminary grudgingly complied, but this did not end the obstacles to the city's acquisition of the site.56 Though the historical preservationists had disappeared from the scene, Têtu's proposal still had to overcome the 'recriminations and the protests from those who were being evicted.' These tenants were described – rather dismissively in the volume commemorating the unveiling (not a typical place for invective) – as people clinging to their homes 'as if they were parasitic plants!'57

Têtu and his colleagues succeeded in overcoming all opposition to their acquisition of the site; they found it more difficult to dodge complaints that other, more appropriate sites had been available. At one of its first meetings, the Comité du Monument Laval gave its formal blessing to the *pâté de maisons* site, a decision that elicited criticism from Abbé Paré, who observed in his diary:

This site which is very cramped will not receive universal approval. Many
would prefer to see the monument erected upon the Place de la Basilique
in front of both the Basilica and the seminary. But the leaders at the
archevêché wish to see it in front of their building, so that the monument
would serve as an embellishment for the new façade that they are about to
add! So, they are going to force this ridiculous location upon everyone else,
on the pretext that the *archevêché* is bound by a promise to the city to place
the monument there if the city were to demolish the *pâté de maisons* ... The
truth of the matter is that the *archevêché* wants the Monument Laval as an
ornamentation for its new façade ... In the meantime, there are two beautiful public places, the Jardin Montmorency and the Place de la Basilique
which will have to wait a while longer to have monuments of their own.

Paré's theory was born out by the fact that the day after it had been
decided to go ahead with the *pâté de maisons* site, work began on the
archevêché, which was already being prepared for Laval's return to the
neighbourhood.[58]

The two alternative sites suggested by Paré were both public spaces on
which it would have been much easier to construct a monument. Both
were large, level expanses of land with considerable historical significance. The Jardin Montmorency – Mgr Laflamme's preferred location
for the Monument Champlain – had been the site of the bishop's palace
during much of the French regime and of legislative buildings thereafter.[59] As for the Place de la Basilique – which later became the site of a
monument to Cardinal Taschereau, the bishop at the time of the discovery of Laval's remains – it would have symbolized Laval's religious and
secular legacies, situated as it was between the Cathedral and the city
hall.

The chosen site provided considerable challenges to the monument's
architects and builders. It fell off by twenty feet from one side to the
other, perched as it was atop the Côte de la Montagne, which connected
the upper and lower towns.[60] The committee took possession of the site
in the fall of 1904. The following year was occupied with preparatory
work for the construction of an immense base for the monument. By the
spring of 1906 the end was not yet in sight and word now leaked out that
Louis-Philippe Hébert was unhappy that the foundation was becoming
as substantial as his sculpture. The superior of the seminary reported on
a subsequent meeting of the committee dealing with '[the question] of
the base of the monument and of the architectural landscaping of the
site ... Everyone agrees that the work to date is unsatisfactory ... Some

radical thinkers believe that it would be better to start from scratch and to replace this massive stone foundation with a grassy slope.'[61]

In the end, there really was no turning back on the original design, which by the spring of 1906 had generated financial problems to go along with its aesthetic ones. The base had already cost $12,000 out of what would be a total budget for the monument of roughly $45,000, and the end of the preparatory work was still nowhere in sight. In this context, the nominal head of the committee, the notary L.P. Sirois, who usually took a back seat to colleagues of the archbishop such as Mgr Têtu, was thrust into the limelight to seek funds from laypeople, who so far had contributed relatively little to the effort. In April 1906, Sirois wrote an unprecedented letter to potential lay contributors in which he discussed the cost 'of the considerable preliminary work.' At the moment, the committee was still far short of its final goal of $50,000, which was to cover both the monument's construction costs and an appropriately spectacular unveiling ceremony. However, Sirois was not thinking that far ahead when he observed: 'At this point in the project, it is important to know whether we can really count upon the $17,000 that still has to be collected.'[62]

Eventually, the needed funds were raised. Meanwhile the work continued. The base was completed in 1907, the pedestal atop which Mgr de Laval would stand was finished the following spring, and the bishop was lifted into place in time for the long-anticipated unveiling in 1908. Most people had come to admire Hébert's sculpture, but many doubted that this site had been worth the costs incurred along the way. The space was sandwiched between the *archevêché* and the post office, so it was all but impossible for anyone to appreciate the monument by standing back from it. Also, the monument faced the *archevêché*, the one place from which it could easily be viewed.[63] Ordinary people looking up at Laval would have been staring at the post office. This led one of the Europeans called on to assess Hébert's maquettes to remark sardonically that the location seemed to have been chosen 'as a tribute to the Canadian Postal Service ... The nearby Jardin [Montmorency] would make an infinitely more desirable location.'[64]

Abbé Paré observed that the monument had been placed 'on a thoroughfare on an incline,' thus making it almost 'impossible to look at. However, the *archevêché*, and in particular Mgr Marois and, even more so, Mgr Têtu, wanted the monument in front of the *archevêché* ... The committee had no choice but to give in to the decrees coming from there. [Laval] is visible to the public, but he is not on display to celebrate the artistic achievement of those responsible for the project.' Paré saw the statue as a monument to the archbishop and his staff, going so far as to quip: 'There are some mean-spirited people who have been saying that Mgr Marois managed to erect a bronzed likeness of himself.' In the end, it was only possible for Marois and Têtu to impose their will because of their ability to raise large amounts of money. Without these funds the project might never have seen the light of day, or it might have been positioned on some other, less costly and perhaps more appropriate site.[65]

Fundraising

The SSJBQ had launched the project of a monument to Laval, just as it had launched, in the 1890s, the project of a monument to Champlain. In each case, however, it ended up being marginalized by its inability to raise the required funds. With the Champlain project, it was squeezed out by English speakers; with the Laval project, it was pushed aside by the leaders of the archdiocese. Though a layman and a cleric were appointed co-treasurers with responsibility for fundraising, only the latter, the indefatigable Mgr Têtu, was heard from during the four-year campaign, which began early in 1904. In the years he led the drive to pull down the *pâté de maisons*, he showed himself to be someone who did not take no for an answer. This quality served him well in his efforts to raise $50,000 – far more than the $30,000 raised, with considerable difficulty, for the construction of the Monument Champlain.

Within weeks of his appointment, Têtu was on the job. He acted like a modern-day fundraiser, preparing custom-made appeals for the different constituencies that might support the project. At first he concentrated on reaching Catholics across North America. He sent specially tailored letters to bishops and members of religious communities beyond Quebec whose territories had been within Laval's jurisdiction in the seventeenth century. Têtu admitted himself that these appeals had little success. After the unveiling ceremonies, he observed: 'If the celebrations were beautiful and spectacular, this was not because of the American bishops, only five of whom bothered to make donations and none of whom attended our fêtes.' Têtu's gloomy assessment was borne out by his accounts, which showed a total contribution of $1700 from the American clergy – a figure roughly matched by the Canadian clergy outside Quebec.[66]

Given the lukewarm support for the project beyond his own province,

Têtu concentrated on the various elements of the Quebec church. He sent carefully crafted appeals to members of religious orders, bishops, and curés, always careful to emphasize the nationalist element of the Laval celebrations. This lent his message an emotional connection to the bishop that was missing in those sent to English-speaking North Americans. For instance, in the letter be prepared for Quebec's religious communities, he observed that Laval's life had symbolized for French Canadians 'the close ties that have always existed between Church and State.'[67] Perhaps this reference to the role of church and state in early twentieth-century Quebec mobilized French-Canadian communities; it would have been meaningless to English speakers outside the province.

Catholic institutions within Quebec were the most significant contributors to Têtu's war chest between 1904 and 1906. This is reflected in the lists of supporters he published from time to time in the local newspapers.[68] These lists – undoubtedly designed to embarrass those who had not yet given – showed that nearly all the contributions, totalling $33,000 by the spring of 1906, had come from bishops, curés, religious orders, and *fabriques* (the lay-run boards that administered the assets of each parish). Têtu's campaign benefited in these years from the support of the archbishop, who sent a letter to all his clergy at the start of the drive, and another in 1905 to keep it rolling. In the second letter, Mgr Bégin made it clear he was watching carefully who was contributing and who was not: 'Of the roughly 200 parishes in the diocese with resident curés, only 44 have responded to my appeal. I am encouraging the others once again to fulfil their obligation ... In addition, I would like to see that all of the students at our seminaries, colleges, convents and schools make their contributions, however small they might be. Accordingly, I am asking all curés, superiors, directors and chaplains to aid the members of the committee.'[69]

To the same extent that he succeeded in raising funds among the clergy, Têtu failed among laypeople. Late in 1904 the ever-observant Abbé Paré noted that a certain disaffection among laymen had made them reluctant to contribute:

The way in which the deliberations were handled in terms of the erection of the monument seems to have left the citizens of Quebec City cold, if not hostile. Some residents view the actions of the members of the different committees as having created problems. In particular, there is resentment towards the dictatorial behaviour on the part of the ecclesiastical authorities. Moreover, some laymen complain that they were left on their own to finance the construction of the Monument Champlain. They spent the money then that the clergy would like to see provided today for the Monument Laval.[70]

By early 1906, faced with spiralling costs for the base of the monument, Têtu set about overcoming the antipathy of ordinary Quebecers. Throughout the spring, many meetings of the fundraising subcommittee were held. These first targeted judges, civil servants, and politicians; then plans were made to recruit the curés of the various Quebec City parishes to raise support among the general public.[71] The decision to go directly to Quebecers was supported by a widely circulated letter in April 1906 from L.P. Sirois, the committee president. To strengthen the impact of this message, it was distributed to the clergy as part of another letter from Mgr Bégin, who thus lent his hand to the campaign to raise funds from the people.[72]

This shift in Mgr Têtu's strategy was reflected in the subscription lists that regularly appeared in the local newspapers. Only 2 per cent of the first 845 contributions came from laymen; but between April and August 1906, 85 per cent of the 645 donations came from residents of Quebec City without any obvious connections to the church. Most of these contributions, however, were small. Up until the spring of 1906, contributors were offering an average of nearly $40. This figure fell to $11 for the ordinary residents of Quebec City, many of whom gave only $1 to the canvassers who had fanned out into the working-class neighbourhoods. Têtu was referring to these canvassers when he observed, during the drive to tap the modest savings of Quebecers, that they might send in their contributions 'without waiting for someone to come knocking on their door.'[73]

Mgr Têtu was extremely grateful for the $6,400 that ordinary people had provided at a time when the costs for the project were mounting and the pool of potential institutional subscribers was drying up.[74] However, he also understood that the benefits from drawing these people into the project were more than financial. Just as the production of crowns had drawn the public into the celebration of Mgr de Laval's reburial, these one-dollar contributions made hundreds of Quebecers feel part of the fete to come. As Têtu put it at one point in the campaign, it did not really matter how much someone paid; what did matter was that they had joined in the effort: 'We are not very demanding, even the most modest gift will earn the donor the honour of a place [on the subscription list].'

He was dogmatic when it came to the question of whether someone could contribute without having his name on the list; he understood the impact of each single contribution on those who had not yet contributed: 'Some of our donors are incredibly modest and do not want to have their names published. Nevertheless, it is important and sometimes advantageous to make their identities known. Providing an example is a very practical and meaningful form of preaching.'[75]

By a certain point, all ordinary Quebecers who were willing to contribute had already done so. The institutional donors had dried up long before. As a result, the fundraising drive reached a dead end in the late summer of 1906. After August, subscriptions fell off dramatically. Over the next two years there were only 227 subscribers, roughly evenly divided between lay and church-related contributors. In fact, no lists were published between August 1907 and April 1908, after Têtu established a policy of going public only after he had collected a further $200. Nevertheless, the drive continued so that the Comité du Monument Laval might meet its projected expenses, which now included the staging of lavish unveiling ceremonies to rival those of the Champlain tercentenary, which by the spring of 1907 was slated to be held as an event quite distinct from the Laval celebration.

The Champlain festivities obviously annoyed Têtu, who by early 1908 was blaming them for his fundraising difficulties. Instead of recognizing that he had already bled the rock dry, he accused the tercentenary of draining dollars away, and he said as much in the comments he published along with his lists. In particular, he pointed to the efforts to raise public funds to turn the Plains of Abraham, where the French had been defeated in 1759, into a national park. Even though French Canadians contributed relatively little to this drive (see chapter 4), it annoyed him just the same. In March 1908, while he was trying to raise the final $2,000 required to reach his goal of $50,000, he spoke bitterly about Quebecers who were wealthy enough that they 'ought to be contributing thousands of dollars.' Unfortunately, they 'seem to have limited their contributions to the hundreds. They are saving their money in order to buy the Plains of Abraham.' In the end, Têtu was content that his cause was just, if not well endowed: 'After all, Mgr de Laval, the founder of our church, is more valuable than Wolfe, Montcalm, Lévis and Murray.' These were, of course, the military heroes of 1759–60, who would be fêted during the tercentenary celebrations on the plains.[76]

Only a month later, sounding more strident than ever, Têtu emphasized the need to raise the final dollars, not to build the statue but rather to stage the unveiling ceremonies:

> No one appreciates the cost of the celebrations of June 21, 22, and 23. We do not have access to the hundreds of thousands of dollars available for the fêtes of the tercentenary which will follow ours. We are rather insignificant, humiliated, poor, almost annihilated, in the face of such riches ... The funds at our disposable are pathetically small, but without them it would be impossible for us to have the beautiful Fête-Dieu procession, or the lovely music, or the illumination of the city, or special seating for our special guests and most generous donors. We would not even have the beautifully decorated altar that will be constructed for the mass to be celebrated at the foot of the statue of the first bishop of Quebec.[77]

This was not the first time that Têtu had referred to French speakers as a humiliated people who felt dwarfed by the funds available to the 'other' celebration. In 1905 he had written in very similar terms to Prime Minister Laurier, to whom he had appealed for public funds. Ultimately, the federal government contributed $5,000 to the cause, thus making it the single largest contributor by far to Têtu's war chest.[78] In spite of this support, Têtu was offended when he heard that Laurier had described this contribution as one, not to celebrate Laval, but rather 'upon the occasion of the tercentenary of the founding of Quebec City.' Têtu said that the prime minister's comments had resulted in his 'humiliation' and had made him feel 'ridiculous.' For his part, Laurier expressed puzzlement at Têtu's rather odd way of offering thanks: 'I simply do not understand the tone [of your letter].'[79]

Talks had been underway for some time to connect the construction of the Monument Laval with the celebration of Champlain's tercentenary, so it was hardly surprising that Laurier had linked the two events. Clearly, the chief fundraiser had a large chip on his shoulder. His sense of grievance is perhaps what gave him the energy to run a long and sometimes frustrating fundraising campaign, but it probably also made him the wrong man to reach out for funds beyond his own community. In the end, the Monument Laval was paid for almost entirely by French Canadians; this only reinforced the inclination of Mgr Bégin and colleagues such as Têtu to present Mgr de Laval as a local hero. In 1878 he had been promoted as a figure who spoke to Catholics beyond Quebec; in 1908 he was ascribed a much narrower appeal, in part so that he might serve as a counterweight to the pan-Canadian figure of Champlain, who was to be so lavishly promoted by the federal government in association with the governor general, Earl Grey.

A Celebration of Church and State

From the first mention of raising a statue in honour of Laval, the project had been viewed by its clerical supporters as part of a larger celebration that would take place in 1908, which besides being the bicentenary of the bishop's death was the tercentenary of Champlain's founding of Quebec City. Notwithstanding his rather shrill reply to Laurier a year later, Têtu expressed support in 1904 for equal billing of the founding fathers in a common celebration that would speak to 'the very close ties that have always existed between Church and State.'[80] By the fall of 1906, several draft programs were being circulated for a joint Champlain–Laval fete, which would take place between 28 June and 3 July 1908. The latter date was of historical significance since it would mark the anniversary of Champlain's arrival at Quebec City.

These programs had been produced by a committee established early in 1906 to coordinate the 1908 celebrations. The Comité du Centenaire, headed by Mayor George Garneau, adhered to the same organizational model of committees and subcommittees that had already been adopted by the Comité du Monument Laval. The project was overseen by a sixty-member executive committee on which Mgrs Marois and Mathieu were the only clerics – a rather ominous development for those who had been hoping that Laval and Champlain might receive equal billing.[81] The actual program was the responsibility of a subcommittee, of which Marois was a member. In October it produced a draft that made the unveiling of the Monument Laval a relatively insignificant affair to be dispensed with early in the celebration, on 30 June. The main event of the celebration was to be a *grande parade historique* held on 3 July, the final day of the fete, 'which would bring together in a single procession: all the national societies, floats, and groups of marchers dressed up so as to represent some of the great moments from our past.'[82]

Within days of the first meeting of Mayor Garneau's program subcommittee, the Comité du Monument Laval had struck a group of its own to draft an alternative program. It is telling that Mgr Marois himself headed this latter group – an indication of his discomfort with the direction the 'official' tercentenary committee was taking. In this alternative version, every effort was made to downplay the multinational aspects of the celebration. In this vein, the parade of the national societies was eliminated from the day marking Champlain's arrival. Instead, the major event of 3 July would be a celebration of modern technology, 'the official opening of the Quebec Bridge, which will be the Monument of our tercentenary.' The Marois group shifted the parade to 1 July, placing it at the start of a day with a heavily loaded schedule. There was still no room in the event for the national societies – only a display of their coats of arms (along with that of France) around the Monument Champlain, where the parade would end. After speeches and the singing of 'O Canada,' the crowds would move the short distance to the Monument Laval, which was given the lion's share of attention in this French Catholic version of the program. As Marois put it: 'The unveiling will take place to the firing of cannons and of artillery, as well as the chiming of the bells of the Basilica. French frigates, if they are on hand, will be invited to add the powerful and solemn voices of their cannons.' If this were not enough, Marois also envisioned the continuation of this narrowly French-Canadian celebration on 2 July with the staging of the always moveable Fête de St-Jean, complete with a procession to the Monument Laval where mass would be celebrated.[83]

Here were two irreconcilable versions of the joint Champlain–Laval fête. Each gave pride of place to one founding father at the expense of the other. These conflicting drafts anticipated the disintegration of the joint celebration of the two heroes and the emergence of two entirely separate ones. There were hints of this separation early in 1907, triggered by reports that the fete might be delayed until 1909 because Laurier wanted it to coincide with the opening of the Quebec Bridge, which could not be completed by the summer of 1908. Although still a rumour, the Comité du Monument Laval had resolved to go ahead on its own if need be, 'without concern for any delay in the celebration of the tercentenary of the founding of Quebec.' Though the clerical leaders of the Laval project were unanimous in sticking to their date, a dissenting voice was raised by H.J.J.B. Chouinard, a long-time leader of the SSJBQ, who was also a significant figure in the emerging tercentenary organization. Chouinard opposed 'the idea of separating the unveiling of the Monument Laval from the fetes of the three-hundredth anniversary of the founding of Quebec.'[84]

Having already anticipated this turn of events, it is hardly surprising how the Laval committee reacted when Laurier decided in April 1907 to put off the Champlain celebration until 1909. Only a few members favoured going along with the delay; the vast majority wanted to hold the line so as to honour not only the anniversary of Laval's death but also the precise date of Champlain's arrival. The committee observed that 'the fete for the unveiling of the Statue Laval will mark the precise date upon which Quebec was founded, a date that should not be allowed to pass by without any celebration.'[85] However, even this determination to somehow keep the joint celebration of Laval and Champlain intact had faded away by the end of 1907, as clerical leaders recognized the advantages of freeing themselves from the precise date on which Quebec had been founded. In announcing their decision to abandon 3 July, the leaders at the *archevêché* sounded a bit guilty as they expressed the hope that their celebration, now scheduled for late June, would draw attention to 'the unforgettable date marking the foundation of the city of Quebec.'[86] In the end, this guilt did not restrain Mgr Bégin and his colleagues, who recognized that they now had the opportunity to set off on their own to create a spectacle without precedent.[87]

The leaders of the archdiocese calculated that the unveiling could be moved back to late June, to sandwich it between the two high points of the French-Canadian marching season: the Fête-Dieu, which in 1908 had to be celebrated on 21 June, and the Fête de St-Jean-Baptiste, which would be celebrated two days later. In the final months of 1907, the tercentenary organizers went from fearing that their fête might be cancelled altogether after the collapse of the Quebec Bridge, to the final decision that it would be held in the summer of 1908, precisely because the collapse of the Quebec Bridge had eliminated the justification for its delay until 1909. Earl Grey, who had pushed Laurier to return the Champlain celebration to either July or August 1908, now saw the possibility of bringing Laval back into the fold. However, he was told in no uncertain terms by Mgr Mathieu, the superior of the seminary, that this was impossible because 'the first day of these fetes [in honour of Laval] will be dedicated to an immense procession which will be held on Sunday, 21 June ... The Fête-Dieu procession can only be held on this day, and not on any other day of the year.'[88]

At it turned out, the tercentenary would be celebrated in late July in order to accommodate the calendar of the Prince of Wales, who would emerge as the star of the show. As a result of this scheduling, the actual date on which Champlain had arrived at Quebec was abandoned, thus making the tercentenary seem somewhat artificial. In contrast, the Laval celebration, although hardly spontaneous, seemed more natural, falling as it did between the two main holidays of the summer calendar. One of these had a date that was unchangeable; the other only missed the feast day of French Canada's recently proclaimed patron saint by a day – a far cry from the three-month delay in 1898.[89]

By positioning the unveiling between these two holidays – one run by the clergy and the other by laymen – the organizers of the unveiling were able to reinforce the message of church–state unity that had been embodied by Mgr de Laval, and that would be engraved on the front of the monument. In the early months of 1907, while the Comité du Monument Laval was debating whether to go along with the shift of the tercentenary to 1909, it was also busy discussing the issue of the inscription. This matter had raised many difficulties for the promoters of the Monument Champlain, who were divided over the use of Latin. Ten years later the clerical leaders responsible for the Monument Laval, who might have been expected to look favourably on the language of their church, never seriously considered the use of a Latin inscription. Perhaps this reflected the growing importance of raising monuments that tourists could understand.

The role of tourism was underscored by the advertisements for the retailer La Compagnie Paquet that were published in a number of Quebec City newspapers on the eve of the Laval celebration. Below a large sketch of the Monument Laval surrounded by clerics, the advertisement screamed out in bold type: THESE SATURDAY BARGAINS WILL DIVIDE YOUR ATTENTION EQUALLY WITH THE UNVEILING OF THE NEW LAVAL MONUMENT. It went on to note, in gentler tones,

> As everyone knows, Saturday is always Bargain Day at Paquet's. But on the eve of the greatest demonstration Quebec has ever seen, it would be strange indeed if we did not make an extra special effort to present unusually attractive offerings for those who have come from a distance to witness the ceremonies ... Come here on Saturday ... You will find a rare feast of Bargains awaiting you – a feast worthy of the Great Demonstration in honour of which it is presented.[90]

In the end, the importance of tourism helped keep Latin off the Monument Laval. But nothing could prevent the choice of an inscription that unambiguously presented the bishop's legacy as the ultimate expression of the unity of church and state. Without much debate, the leaders of the committee decided to use a French text prepared by Mgr Têtu, which described Laval as

FOUNDER

of the church in New France and of the seminary of Quebec.

STATESMAN

in the organization of the Sovereign Council, in various fruitful missions
to the court of France, in calming souls and peoples.

APOSTLE

of the faith, education, and temperance.

VENERABLE

by his virtues of charity, strong will, and mortification.

An early version of this text had gone so far as to credit Laval with
founding the Sovereign Council, a body that played a significant role in
the administration of late-seventeenth-century New France. Têtu only
reluctantly agreed to soften this passage. Even so, it was obvious that
Laval's secular heritage was being accorded a central place.[91]

None of the versions of the inscription made any reference to the
fact that Laval had been born in France. In contrast, Champlain's
French ancestry was clearly pointed out on his monument, and the
French consul had been a key participant in the celebrations of 1898.
However, the unveiling of the Monument Champlain had been a secular affair, whereas the Laval celebration was a clerical one and was
being held at a time when French Canadians were deeply concerned
about the plight of their Catholic brethren in the Third Republic. The
French government had broken off diplomatic relations with the
Vatican in 1904, definitively separated church and state in 1905, and
declared Alfred Dreyfus innocent in 1906. The clearest indication of
the crisis facing Catholicism in France was the arrival of 1,200 members
of religious orders in Quebec between 1902 and 1904. Many of these
orders had seen their operations compromised by new laws that made
their activities illegal. These men and women, who constituted over
10 per cent of all *religieux* in Quebec, were a constant reminder of
what France was – and what Quebec might become if it relaxed its
vigilance.[92]

As the Monument Laval neared completion, the wariness of Quebec
clerics toward France was expressed by Lionel Groulx, who would go on
to become the most important French-Canadian historian of the first
half of the twentieth century. In his memoirs, Groulx recorded his
painful impressions of a France he could not entirely love:

I could not love its religious waywardness, and I could not love its politics ... In the Paris of 1907 I had more than sufficient opportunity to get a taste of the anticlericalism that was in the air ... I was staying at the Séminaire d'Issy-les-Moulineaux (near Paris) where all of the priests were required to wear the cassock. As a result it was impossible to visit Paris without having to endure insults and hissing both from children and older passers-by, some of whom were well-dressed men. The anticlericalism of early twentieth century Paris deeply hurt me.[93]

For his part, Mgr Bégin wrote to his clergy in 1907 asking them to urge their parishioners to pray for France, which 'is currently passing through the most terrible religious crisis in the annals of history.' The archbishop reminded his flock that 'the misfortunes of France offer us some serious and useful lessons. Let us turn a deaf ear to pernicious men who might seek to spread evil ideas amongst us.'[94] In this political climate, Laval was being presented to the public as if he had not been born in France. In fact, the only reference on the monument to Laval's ties to France was on the bas-relief showing him in the company of Louis XIV – a scene that reinforced the message of church–state unity.

This same message was to be communicated to the public during the three-day celebration of the bishop's legacy. One day had been enough to unveil Champlain's monument; it would take three to unveil Laval's. This was partly because the public was becoming blasé about the raising of monuments, so that celebrations had to be ever more sumptuous in order to bring people into the streets. On another level, Mgr Bégin and his colleagues felt that national pride required their event to celebrate Laval to be as spectacular as the one being prepared – under the watchful eye of Earl Grey – to celebrate Champlain.

In late June, Quebec City ground to a halt for *le triduum* (the three-day fete) in honour of Laval. Each day was intended to communicate a particular aspect of the bishop's legacy. The first day, the Fête-Dieu holiday, was called *la journée de Dieu*, since the body of Christ would be carried through the streets. The second day, when the monument would be unveiled, was called *la journée de l'Église* in recognition of Laval's status as the founder of institutional Catholicism in North America. The third was called *la journée de la patrie* since it coincided with the celebration of the Fête de St-Jean-Baptiste. As Adjutor Rivard, a professor from Université Laval, put it: 'It is only fitting that the Laval fete be celebrated between *la Fête-Dieu* and *la Saint-Jean*, between the fete of Religion and that of Patriotism.' Rivard was pleased that 'the noble shape of our Bishop will be unveiled between the celebration of the two guiding forces for strong nations, love of Church and love of Country.'[95]

La journée de Dieu: The Fête-Dieu Procession

The organizers at the *archevêché* were counting on the two most important processions of the French-Canadian calendar to draw the public into Laval's celebration.[96] To that end, the Fête-Dieu procession of 1908 was celebrated in a way never before seen. This ceremony was deeply rooted in certain conventions stretching back to medieval times. This meant that any departure from the norm was easily recognizable – Quebecers were well versed in processions. In particular, the public would have been struck by the fact that the organizers had decided 'there shall be only one procession of all the parishes of the city.'[97]

For more than two centuries the parish had been the basic unit around which Fête-Dieu processions had been organized; this reflected the widely held view of lay and clerical leaders alike that the parish was the fundamental institution for protecting French Catholic culture. In the early twentieth century, a time when Quebecers were struggling to respond to the challenges posed by urbanization, immigration, and imperialism, the parish was still generally seen as the natural unit of organization. For example, Alphonse Desjardins used parishes when creating a form of credit union, the *caisse populaire*, that French speakers might call their own. As Desjardins put it: 'The *caisse populaire* is a strictly parish-based institution: it is born, grows, develops and prospers in the midst of the extended family within the parish.'[98]

Desjardins opened the first *caisse populaire* in 1900. He eventually recognized that his parish-based credit unions could not compete with the banks if they did not borrow some of the centralizing business techniques of their competitors. The head offices of the banks moved funds from place to place as investment opportunities dictated; in their early years, the *caisses* were prohibited by their own rules from employing funds outside the parish. By the 1910s, Desjardins had concluded that the *caisses populaires* needed to be able to move surplus funds beyond the boundaries of individual parishes if they were to remain viable. In the end, he made the necessary adjustments to allow them to compete with much larger competitors.[99]

Much like Desjardins (whose efforts they strongly endorsed), the leaders of the archdiocese concluded in 1908 that this special Fête-Dieu procession would have to transcend parish boundaries if it was to com-

Conclusion of Fête-Dieu Procession at the Basilica, 1908 (Musée de la Civilisation, fonds d'archives du Séminaire de Québec, Fête de Mgr à la Cathédral de Québec, Jules-Ernest Livernois, 1908, N° Ph1987-0796)

pete with the Champlain celebrations later in the summer. They also recognized that the proprietary instincts of the parishes might be offended, so they appointed the relevant curés to a special committee with responsibility for the procession. No doubt this action was meant to soften opposition to the archbishop's demand that each parish contribute $500 to the costs of the affair.[100] A further concession to parish loyalties was evident in the design of the closing ceremony of the procession. To celebrate the return of the host, the marchers would be assembled on the square in front of the Basilica. This was to be 'divided into as many rectangles as there are parishes within the city; so there will be eight rectangles, starting from the Basilica and extending to the limits of the square in front of it. Each rectangle will be assigned to one of the parishes, and it will be occupied exclusively by representatives of that parish.'[101]

These allowances for local identities aside, the procession was organized to present Catholicism as something larger than parish life and not simply part of it. In an early version of the procession, the marchers were to have gone past various parish churches, with *reposoirs* in place. In the end, Mgr Bégin and his colleagues rejected this route, because it would have focussed on identities too trivial for the occasion. Instead the procession would start and end at the Basilica, the archbishop's church, and pass through the main streets of the city in order to maximize the number of spectators and participants. The only *reposoir* would be at a major intersection, to underscore the separation of the event from the neighbourhoods.[102]

The centralized control of the procession was also reflected in the decorations along the route. Months before the big day, officials of the archdiocese divided the route into twenty-two sections, in the process again sidestepping the parishes. Each section was supervised by *un zélateur laïque* (a zealous layman), who was supposed to encourage people to decorate their houses, especially with banners. This decoration was to be done without 'too much repetition of the same banners and ornaments.'[103] Having appointed the *zélateurs* to encourage aesthetic variety, the *archevêché* retained control over the inscriptions on the banners, working closely with the female religious orders, which would produce them for sale 'at reasonable prices to citizens who want to acquire them so as to decorate the fronts of their homes.' Citizens who planned to avail themselves of this service were advised, in the fall of 1907, to order immediately whatever materials they required 'so as to avoid the rush in the following spring.'[104]

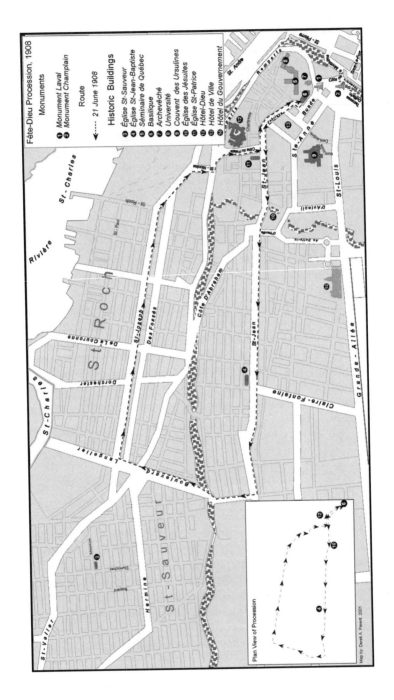

Fête-Dieu Procession, 1908

Monuments
① Monument Laval
② Monument Champlain

Route
---- 21 June 1908

Historic Buildings
③ Église St-Sauveur
④ Église St-Jean-Baptiste
⑤ Séminaire de Québec
⑥ Basilique
⑦ Archevêché
⑧ Université
⑨ Couvent des Ursulines
⑩ Église des Jésuites
⑪ Église St-Patrice
⑫ Hôtel-Dieu
⑬ Hôtel de Ville
⑭ Hôtel du Gouvernement

Plan View of Procession

Map by: Derek A. Pasant 2001

On top of this, the *archevêché* conscripted the religious orders to decorate the public spaces along the route, in particular to construct seventeen *arcs de triomphe* along the procession route. Some of these *arcs* were paid for by religious communities – for example, the one designed, built and financed by the Sœurs de la Charité de Québec. Their annalist was obviously proud of the 'beautiful *arc de triomphe* at the corner of rue St-Jean and rue d'Youville,' which was illuminated and bore 'the insignia of our order upon its facade.' The Sœurs de la Charité were also responsible for producing many other decorations along the route; this had required them to work 'without respite over a period of several months.'[105] The sisters provided the labour, but the materials costs (when not absorbed by religious orders) fell on the parishes, which were instructed by the *archevêché* to take up 'a special collection ... for this purpose.' Having already contributed directly to Têtu's fundraising campaign and indirectly through the special levy on the parishes, seventy residents of one parish cobbled together $236 for the construction of their *arc de triomphe*.[106]

In accordance with centuries of tradition, the organizers of the Fête-Dieu procession tried to build a feast for all the senses. Incense burners were placed at various points along the route, and twenty-five choirs and another twenty-five brass bands were positioned along it, in an alternating pattern.[107] Mgr Têtu somehow found the time to serve on the *comité de la musique*, which was organizing the choir that would perform after the procession returned to the Basilica. Along with the final list of contributors to his war chest, Têtu published an appeal to 'all the singers to persevere and to sing together in the immense chorus at the final blessing of the host which will take place from the monumental arch being constructed in front of the Basilica.'[108]

The most attention of all was paid to the order of marchers. In the earliest version of the *ordre de la procession*, prepared by Mgr Bégin and his associates in the fall of 1907, the line began with various groups of laymen in ascending order of importance, starting with representatives of various associations of craftsmen and ending with the members of the Privy Council. This hierarchical arrangement of the various elements of civil society was typical of St-Jean-Baptiste processions, and the organizers of the Fête-Dieu proposed to appropriate it for this occasion. After the laymen came church-related participants, who were also arranged in ascending order, starting with the members of female religious orders and finishing with members of the hierarchy, who would accompany the host. Bringing up the rear were members of male religious communities, the clergy of the various parishes, and finally – as in all Fête-Dieu processions – *les fidèles,* the ordinary folk among the faithful.[109]

Little of this survived the negotiations that must have taken place before the event. When the procession finally took place, the various artisanal groups no longer led the procession; however, they would be seen two days later leading the St-Jean-Baptiste parade. Instead, the *procession du St-Sacrement* began with various groups of laymen organized along parish lines. This was an attempt to retain something of the traditional parish-based design of the event. Newspapers commented on the activity early on the morning of the procession as representatives of the various parishes assembled at marshalling points before setting off, one parish after another.[110]

Bégin's 1907 design was transformed to lend it the symmetry that was typical of Fête-Dieu processions. By placing nearly all of the lay elements at the front of the line (in ascending order), followed by the religious elements (once again in ascending order), the original design had missed one of the central goals of a Fête-Dieu procession – namely, to present society as a single body by arranging its various elements in ascending order of importance before the appearance of the host, and then in descending order of importance thereafter.

The problem of symmetry was resolved by placing the parade of parishes first, with the religious orders to follow, then the secular priests, then the bishops who accompanied the host. Along the route, various members of the hierarchy were given the honour of carrying the *ostensoir* (the receptacle holding the host), starting with Mgr Bégin and concluding with Mgr Sbarretti, the papal delegate to Canada. To help the spectators sort out the gradations of status among the clergy, the Sœurs de la Charité prepared special garments for the occasion, including 'three Roman-style cloaks made of silk for the highest ranking priests, as well as three short cloaks, two sashes, five white cloaks to be worn over the cassock, four cloaks to wear around the shoulders, and four short cassocks made of satin.'[111]

The only exception to this hierarchical arrangement was that the sole French representative was positioned at the head of 'the delegation of bishops.' Even though his status would not ordinarily have placed him so close to the host, 'l'abbé de la Trappe de Bonnecombe (Aveyron, France), dressed in his white robe, covered with a cloak of the same colour, and wearing both a mitre upon his head and a cross upon his chest,' was promoted into the ranks of the bishops to show the sympathy felt by the Quebec hierarchy for its embattled French counterparts.[112]

Fête-Dieu procession, 1908 (Musée de la Civilisation, fonds d'archives du Séminaire de Québec, Procession de la Fête-Dieu Lors de l'Inauguration du Monument Laval, Léon Roussel, 1908, N° Ph1986-1188)

The civil dignitaries were then placed right behind the host, with Sir Wilfrid Laurier leading the way, followed by other members of the lay elite in descending order of importance. Bringing up the rear was an undifferentiated group of people described in most accounts as *le peuple*.[113] It is impossible to know exactly who constituted 'the people,' but it seems reasonable to assume that some were individuals unaffiliated with any particular group who wanted to take part and not simply watch the event. This certainly would have been in keeping with the Fête-Dieu's tradition of inclusiveness.

The sense that all were welcome was evident in other ways. Several observers commented on the participation of Protestants, who clearly were not made to feel excluded from this event. Abbé Paré remarked that during the closing ceremonies in front of the Basilica, there were both 'Catholics and Protestants. I saw Protestants on their knees, crying tears of deep emotion.'[114] The organizers' commitment to inclusivity was also reflected in the participation of several orders of cloistered nuns: the Sœurs Augustines, responsible for nursing care at the Hôtel-Dieu de Québec, and the Sœurs Ursulines, a teaching order. Both orders had roots reaching back to Laval's time. In fact, the procession that took Laval's remains to their new home in 1878 had made a point of visiting the two orders, in recognition of their connection with the bishop. The inclusion of these two orders, much like the obliteration of parish boundaries, reinforced the point that the unveiling of the Monument Laval was a very special occasion.

Some nuns were reluctant to participate because of the physical effort demanded by the roughly 3-kilometre route, which included a steep uphill climb toward the end. As the chronicler of the Ursulines noted, they feared such a long walk 'under the intense rays of the June sun.'[115] But Mgr Bégin was not about to take no for an answer – the nuns were meant to provide a dramatic element to the procession, and their presence would be appreciated by nearly everyone who later commented on the event. In the end, the nuns were encouraged to march only the first 600 metres of the route; after that, carriages would take them home. Thus, they spent relatively little time in the outside world. The Augustines' chronicler observed that their day had begun with a trip 'to the Parlour of the Seminary; there they met the Mères Ursulines whom they were pleased to see once again and with whom they joined the procession as far as the curé's residence next to the Église St-Jean-Baptiste; there they boarded carriages which took them back home at 10:30.'[116] Even this brief appearance was significant, since it indicated that the Fête-Dieu procession was open to all and that its route had no barriers to prevent anyone from joining or leaving the celebration.

Every detail of the Fête-Dieu procession was carefully considered in order to deliver a message. Though one observer remarked that 'everything was symbolic,' it is impossible to know what the 100,000 people in attendance drew from the experience.[117] It seems likely, however, that most would have understood that this event was violating certain conventions in order to celebrate the different aspects of Laval's legacy. While the parade had been designed to display the power of Catholicism, it also drew attention to the survival of a people. The procession's organizers encouraged the participation of Catholics who were not French Canadians; in contrast, Bishop Bourget had made Montreal's Irish Catholics feel that they did not quite belong in such celebrations.[118] That being said, almost everyone who marched in 1908 was French Canadian, with the result that the procession became a celebration of both a religion and a people. L'Événement viewed the event as a demonstration of faith on the part of la nation canadienne-française. In a similar fashion, the chronicler for the Sœurs Augustines remarked that this had been 'an unforgettable day filled with sweet and holy joy as well as a deep sense of national pride.'[119]

A similar version of Laval's legacy was communicated at the end of the day. Not about to waste a minute of the time at their disposal, Mgr Bégin and his advisors took advantage of the first evening to schedule the ceremony marking the end of the academic year at the university bearing Laval's name. The dignitaries in town – including Earl Grey who had been absent during the Fête-Dieu procession – showed up to hear various speeches, including one by Mgr Mathieu. The rector spoke about Laval's role in inspiring the generations of priests who had been trained at the seminary. As Mathieu put it, these priests still looked to 'the saintly bishop as a model ... Each day they ask him to keep them under his protection, to help them to remain capable of merging together, in his image, the interests of Church and State, their two guiding lights.'[120]

La journée de l'Église: The Unveiling of the Monument Laval

The middle day of the fête did not require another procession to attract the public's attention, but it began with one just the same. Early in the morning a cortège of bishops, priests, professors, and civil leaders marched from the *archevêché* the short distance to the chapel of the seminary, where mass was celebrated. This route was strikingly similar to the one that had been followed in 1878 during the *translation intime* that took Laval's bones to the same chapel, beneath which the bishop's remains now rested. Following mass, there was a sermon by Camille Roy, a professor at both the seminary and the university. Returning to the theme of church and state that had been heard only hours earlier at the end of the first day of the fête, Roy observed: 'The Church that was founded in New France ought to be involved today, both here and elsewhere, in public affairs. It should perhaps be even more involved here than elsewhere so as to follow the courageous example of our first bishop.' Because of his initiatives, Laval had possessed 'religious and political power that we can scarcely imagine today.'[121]

The day's main event came much later in the afternoon. By 3:00 p.m. everything was in place for the long-awaited unveiling of the Monument Laval. As the crowds approached, some were perhaps reminded of certain aspects of Laval's reburial ceremonies thirty years earlier. Crowns were again in evidence, and though there were fewer of them than in 1878, they were much larger. One enormous crown had been placed prominently over the statue, another at the base. Also around the base were a number of Hurons, who had not participated in the Fête-Dieu procession but were here now – as they had been in 1878 – to reinforce the native images on the monument. The lay and clerical dignitaries were seated on several stands that had been built for the occasion in the tight space surrounding the monument. The mass of spectators, estimated anywhere between 50,000 and 100,000, stood wherever they could for a view of the event to come. Some positioned themselves atop telegraph poles. Still others found places on Dufferin Terrace, close to the Monument Champlain but too far from the Laval monument to see or hear what was taking place.[122]

What those lucky enough to have a good view then saw was the final version of an unveiling ceremony that, like every other aspect of the celebration, had gone through many drafts. One of the earliest had called for the participation 'of all the national societies: St-George, St-Patrick, St-Andrew and St-Jean-Baptiste' and the decoration of the terrace around the monument 'with the coats of arms of the English, Irish, Scottish and French-Canadian national societies.' The organizers of the unveiling literally pencilled out all but the 'Catholic national societies,' thereby countenancing the involvement of Irish Catholics. When the big day finally arrived, even the Irish had been shunted aside. In the same spirit, an early version of the speaker list was edited to eliminate a special slot for an Irish Catholic leader. This narrowing of focus was similarly evident when the idea of giving a central role to 'the regular troops passing through Quebec' was crossed out. The only troops now would be French Canada's 'own' soldiers, the Papal Zouaves.[123]

This editing was done at precisely the same time a program was being shaped for a celebration of Canada, in all its diversity, at the tercentenary. Clearly, the organizers of the Laval unveiling had decided to focus sharply on a celebration of French-Canadian identity. This preoccupation did not, however, preclude the participation of the governor general, who was the engine driving Champlain's fête. Since the Laval celebration was designed to show the unity of church and state, there was plenty of logic in having the head of state stand alongside the church leaders at the main event. Grey's thinking on the matter was similarly straightforward: he wanted to draw church officials into accepting, if not enthusiastically supporting, the grand celebration he was preparing. He recognized that Bégin and his advisers would probably look askance on both the consecration of the battlefield on which the French had been defeated in 1759 and, perhaps even more importantly, the involvement of representatives of the much hated French republic. In light of these various concerns, Grey was willing to participate at the unveiling, provided that Begin tolerated the tercentenary.

Grey and the *archevêché* worked out an arrangement whereby the governor general would lift the veil from the Monument Laval.[124] Nevertheless, Grey made no secret to his confidants that he had little respect for Bégin and his colleagues. In a letter to the colonial secretary drafted at roughly the same time that negotiations were concluding, he observed: 'The position in Quebec province is not satisfactory. The priests are stimulating the growth of a Nationalist sentiment. They are capturing the clever young men in the Universities ... At present the priests are heading in a direction which Laurier thinks will eventually lead to another abortive Papineau trouble!' In the same letter, Grey recognized that heavy ammunition might be required later in the summer if the clergy had not been brought under control, and indicated that he intended to invite Lord Norfolk, the highest-ranking Catholic peer in England, to attend the tercentenary: 'He might be useful. It is in the interests of the Roman Catholics of Canada that they should be emancipated from the clutch of the retrograde ambitious ultramontane French hierarchy now in power.'[125]

Whatever Grey and the leaders at the *archevêché* thought of each other, they participated in a show that officially began with the governor general's arrival at the site of the monument. This moment was marked by the sounding of bugles. Then, after some welcoming remarks by L.P. Sirois, the notary who had served as the nominal head of the Comité du Monument Laval, Grey took up his position to unveil the statue. This carefully choreographed street theatre began with six children – all great-nephews and nieces of archbishops of Quebec – handing him ribbons connected to the monument. At the same moment a mechanical device was set in motion that raised the covering over the statue up into the large crown that had been placed above the monument. Simultaneously, doves were released, each of which had a message tied to its leg with the words: 'We are coming from the Laval fetes; tell the newspapers.' If this were not enough, the mechanism triggered several small angels in the crown, which cast flowers upon the statue and spectators alike. The official account of the day's events noted that the angels were so lifelike that 'more than one woman in the crowd trembled with terror in thinking about the precarious positioning of these adorable cherubs.'[126]

Grey concluded his participation with a speech, delivered in French,

Unveiling of the Monument Laval, 1908 (Musée de la Civilisation, fonds d'archives du Séminaire de Québec, Cérémonie au Monument Laval à l'Occasion du 2e Centenaire de Mgr de Laval, 1908, PH1987-0845)

in which he touted the blessings of British rule that had allowed the creation of a country where 'Catholics and Protestants are on an equal footing.' More audaciously, he went on to observe that the theme of racial harmony would be at the heart of the tercentenary, for which the unveiling served as 'a convenient prelude.' The archbishop and his associates, who had decided to detach their fête from the tercentenary, could not have been pleased with Grey's suggestion that their celebration was little more than an opening act for his own. Grey did not mind telling his superiors in London that he had 'rubbed it in' by making reference 'to the advantages [French Canadians] enjoy under British rule.' He even flattered himself that 'both prelates and laity' were so taken in by his performance that they did not quite grasp the political statement he was making.[127]

There were various perspectives regarding who had 'won' as a result of the governor general's involvement in the unveiling. As H.V. Nelles has put it, the officials in the *archevêché* could feel that they had prevailed by manoeuvring Grey 'to be posed within a picture framed by the ultramontane church.' Yet another point of view was offered by Abbé Paré, who watched the festivities with the other clerics lined up alongside the *archevêché*. Paré conceded no victory to the governor general, all but mocking him for having been upstaged by the fancy mechanism, which he called *une boîte à surprises* (box full of surprises), that had actually unveiled the statue: 'So, it wasn't really the governor-general who, in pulling upon the ribbons, started the work of the *boîte à surprises*, but rather two men hidden behind an attic window of the Post Office, who by means of strings were able to set the mechanism in motion.'[128]

Grey's 'victory' was also tempered by the messages communicated by the speakers who followed him to the podium. First came the papal delegate, Mgr Sbarretti, followed by Mgr Bégin. Both made the obligatory references to Laval's legacy of church–state unity, which probably contributed to Grey's sense that he had been at an 'ultramontane debauch.'[129] Then came a less prestigious but no less interesting group of speakers, who shifted the focus to France, Laval's country of birth, which had been left off the monument just unveiled. The French connection was first raised by Père Henri Hage, whose sole qualification for speaking on that day was that he could add to the festivities 'the accent of a Frenchmen from the old motherland.' Hage understood that he had not been thrust before tens of thousands of people because of his status. Even though he had been in Canada for a number of years, he was there to represent Catholic France, much like the Trappist monk who had marched in the Fête-Dieu procession. He began his address: 'Honour and Glory to our Catholic faith. Let us remember with appreciation our old motherland of France!' Near the close of his speech he drew attention to the 'cloud of false doctrines' that had fallen on the land that had sent out Laval.[130]

Hage's message was reinforced by the final speaker of the afternoon, who had not even been on the program. Pierre Gerlier was vice-president of the Association catholique de la jeunesse française (ACJC), the sister organization of a similarly named body that had been founded in Quebec in 1903.[131] The ACJC was committed to the idea that 'the French-Canadian people have a special mission to fulfil on this continent and that they ought, to achieve that end, keep their unique character that distinguishes them from others.'[132] Given this mandate, the ACJC distinguished itself in the years leading up to 1908 by its energetic support of the efforts of Armand Lavergne to have the federal government commit itself to the greater use of French. When this proposal was going nowhere, the ACJC started to circulate a petition, which had gathered nearly 500,000 signatures by the time of the unveiling of the Monument Laval.[133]

At the same time they were collecting signatures, the association's leaders were watching carefully over the planning of the events of 1908, ever on the lookout for opportunities to insert themselves into the celebration so as to prevent any dilution of the French Catholic message. When the organizers of the Laval and Champlain celebrations decided to go their separate ways early in 1908, the association resolved to become a part of the unveiling by holding a convention immediately after the ceremonies; it tried to secure a place on the tercentenary program by staging a celebration at the Monument Champlain the day before the 'official' events were scheduled to begin.

Gerlier was in Quebec City to represent his organization at the ACJC's convention, and was pressed into service to add one final element to the celebration of 'la France Catholique.' That this was a last-minute change to the program was evident in the description of Gerlier's performance as that of an *improviste* (someone improvising). So as not to tax the patience of the audience, which thought that the end of the program had come, Gerlier offered only 'a few brief remarks.' Nevertheless, the spontaneous way in which he emerged on the scene emphasized a point raised throughout the last part of the program. Gerlier paid tribute to Laval, the embodiment of what France had once been, and he promised that 'the great Catholic nation would reappear' one day soon.[134]

Gerlier's message was reinforced by the music performed that afternoon in the breaks between the speeches. Most spectators probably heard little of the speeches, which would be reprinted verbatim in the press the next day. They probably heard more of the music, all of which harkened back to an older and more admirable France. Immediately after Grey's speech, the choir and brass band performed the official anthem of these events, the 'Cantate en l'honneur de Mgr de Laval,' with words by Octave Crémazie, which fêted Laval and Champlain as 'two French heroes.' The spectators also heard Crémazie's words in 'O Carillon,' an ode to the French flag that had made such an impact during the unveiling of the Monument Champlain. The choir alone performed the only piece with music written by a French composer and words by a French lyricist. 'France! France!' had been composed in 1860 for l'Orphéon de Paris, a French choir recruited from the working class to sing pieces with religious themes. The chorus of 'France! France!' repeatedly called on God's protection for France – a refrain that in 1908 could only have been interpreted as a criticism of the regime in place in Paris.[135] Earl Grey had come to Quebec City in June in order to clear away clerical opposition to the involvement of the leaders of the Third Republic in the tercentenary celebrations in July. He had probably not expected the unveiling ceremonies to conclude with an attack on those men.

La journée de la patrie: La St-Jean

In May 1908, only weeks before Laval's fête, Pope Pius X declared St-Jean-Baptiste the patron saint of French Canadians, even though he had long been celebrated as if he already filled that role. The events that led to the pope's pronouncement had begun the previous fall, within days of the decision to hold a three-day spectacle in honour of Laval. Mgr Bégin was about to leave for a trip to Rome, and the Société St-Jean-Baptiste lobbied him to speak to the pope to secure 'a special favour worthy of these glorious anniversaries' about to be celebrated in 1908. The announcement from Rome was timed perfectly to add lustre to the first celebration of St-Jean-Baptiste in his new capacity – an event that would close out the fete of Laval.[136]

This declaration was a small step toward stabilizing a celebration that was not steeped in the centuries of tradition that marked the Fête-Dieu. Even though Saint John the Baptist's feast day was 24 June, it had been celebrated in September in conjunction with the unveiling of the Monument Champlain. During the planning of the 1908 festivities, when it had appeared that there might be a joint Champlain–Laval fête in early July, the Fête de St-Jean was scheduled at one point for 2 July. In the end, it only wound up on 23 June so that it could take place two days after the date on which the Fête-Dieu holiday had to be held.

Quite aside from its timing, there had long been other elements of instability in the mounting of Quebec City's St-Jean-Baptiste celebrations. Until the turn of the century, two events had been staged each year, one by the Société St-Jean-Baptiste de Québec, and the other by the chapter of the society representing the St-Sauveur district of the city. In 1898 a temporary truce between the two had allowed a single celebration on the morning of the unveiling of the Monument Champlain. It was only in 1900 that the two chapters signed an agreement guaranteeing a single St-Jean-Baptiste celebration, with control passing back and forth from year to year. However, this agreement perpetuated a certain instability by rotating the place at which the St-Jean-Baptiste mass would be celebrated among five different churches and by making no effort to regularize the route to be followed by the procession.[137]

Moreover, though the agreement referred to both the procession and the celebration of mass as part of the St-Jean-Baptiste celebration, it said nothing about the relationship between the two. In fact, over the years the mass had been shifted from the end of the procession to the start, perhaps to guarantee that the marchers would not disperse at the end of the parade, skipping the mass altogether and going on to other, more secular forms of celebration. This separation of the secular and religious aspects of these festivities was especially evident in 1906 and 1907, when the mass was celebrated on 23 June, with the procession to be held on the 24th, immediately followed by an afternoon of outdoor entertainment. By the turn of the century, even when the mass and the procession were held on the same day, the mass invariably came first, followed by the procession, the day then closing with games and other forms of entertainment.

The St-Jean-Baptiste celebrations may have been more malleable than those surrounding the Fête-Dieu, but the organizers in the SSJBQ were still able to communicate a message to the people who either participated in or observed the procession as it passed through the streets of Quebec City each year.[138] Here was an event that was organized by the lay leaders of the city, almost invariably professionals or owners of small businesses. These members of the petite bourgeoisie cooperated with clerical officials, but they still saw the St-Jean-Baptiste celebration as an opportunity to draw attention to the existence of a people defined along national as much as religious lines. The Fête-Dieu was a religious event with secular overtones; the St-Jean-Baptiste procession was a secular event with religious overtones. Thus, when Mgr Bégin asked that the Fête de St-Jean-Baptiste be integrated into the Laval celebrations for 1908, the SSJBQ's leaders immediately agreed to participate. Unfettered by any strong sense that there was a precise date on which their event had to take place, and mobilized by the growing sense that the Champlain celebrations were going to deny the existence of a French-Canadian nation, they only asked when to show up.[139]

Once they had agreed to celebrate 'la St-Jean' on the day following the unveiling of the Monument Laval, the leaders of the SSJBQ began negotiating with the clerical authorities regarding the form this special St-Jean-Baptiste procession would take. Although it had become customary by 1908 to celebrate mass before the procession, the *archevêché* wanted to return to the earlier tradition of having the marchers proceed toward the religious celebration, as was the case in the Fête-Dieu. The SSJBQ organizers agreed to this, but wanted mass to be celebrated on the Esplanade, a large (and secular) green space outside the old walls of the city, perhaps to facilitate the movement of the crowds to the games that were scheduled for later in the day. In the end, however, they complied with clerical demands that the procession lead to the Monument Laval, so as to focus attention on the hero of the moment.[140]

There were similarly complicated negotiations regarding the route to be followed. The officials at the *archevêché* wanted the two processions connected with the Laval celebrations to follow the same route so that the decorations could be used twice. This would keep down costs and create 'a twin exhibition of religion and patriotism.'[141] Although the SSJBQ had agreed to go along with the date selected by Bégin and his advisors, some of its leaders resented the loss of any remaining control over 'their' event; they felt that they were being forced to follow the route of '*la procession du St-Sacrement* ... We prefer to continue our job of organizing the procession so as to create a true demonstration of our nation.'[142]

In the end, the St-Jean-Baptiste procession of 1908 followed some but not all of the route that had been traversed by the Fête-Dieu marchers two days earlier. Thus, much remained that distinguished the one event from the other. The Fête-Dieu procession followed its traditional 'loop'; the St-Jean-Baptiste participants started at one point and finished at another, as was the norm. More specifically, the latter began on a number of streets in the St-Roch section of the city before following a section of the Fête-Dieu route. It then passed through a number of side streets in the St-Sauveur district before following a section of the Fête-Dieu route to the Monument Laval. The clerical organizers of the *procession du St-Sacrement* had consciously altered the 'normal' parish-based route in order to build an event that spoke to the glory of the church. By taking their procession through several neighbourhoods, the SSJBQ organizers were distinguishing their event as one that was closer to the people.

On another level, the Fête-Dieu procession of 1908 distinguished itself as much more 'popular' than the one associated with 'la St-Jean.' At least in theory, no one was excluded from participating in the former; in contrast, the St-Jean-Baptiste procession was even more explicitly exclusionary than in previous years. As in the past, the 1908 procession was divided into military-style divisions. This time there were twenty-five of them. The first nine included various trade unions and groups of tradesmen. These were followed by divisions that included groups of small businessmen. The notaries, doctors, and lawyers – the sorts of men who led the SSJBQ – appeared only in the final two divisions.[143] As usual, women were not present. Though children had been specially included for the occasion, only boys 'of French origin on at least one or the other side of their family' were allowed to participate.[144] Concerned that only authorized marchers should take part and that these should occupy their rightful places in the hierarchy, the organizers provided appropriately prestigious uniforms to the constables, who had watched over the event since its inception.[145]

Scattered between the divisions were a number of floats bearing individuals dressed as figures from the French-Canadian past. In previous St-Jean-Baptiste parades, some of the *chars allégoriques* had had more to do with commercial advertising than with the celebration of a people. In planning the 1908 parade, the SSJBQ had at first decided to bar floats altogether, presumably to add to the solemnity of the occasion. Soon, however, various members of the society began calling for floats that would celebrate heroes of the past such as Jacques Cartier, Montcalm, de Salaberry (the French-Canadian military hero of the War of 1812), and of course Champlain. Each was to be 'escorted by the Knights of Columbus as well as the various *Gardes* [such as the Garde Champlain discussed in the previous chapter] bearing the names of the individuals [on the floats].' To reinforce the new status of the 'official' saint, there were two *chars* carrying *un petit St-Jean-Baptiste*, not just one, as had been typical of past parades.[146]

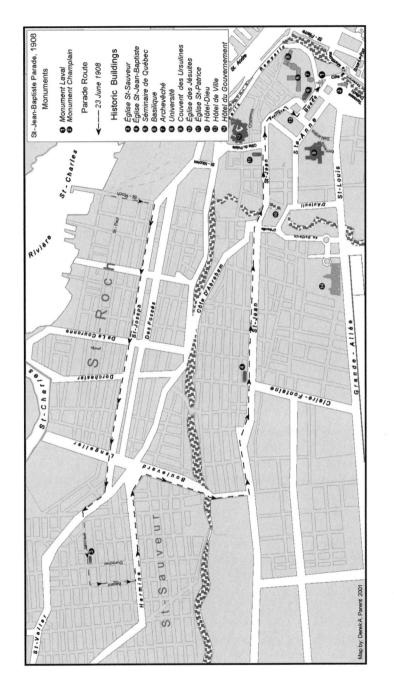

St-Jean-Baptiste Parade, 1908

Monuments

① Monument Laval
② Monument Champlain

Parade Route

←— 23 June 1908

Historic Buildings

③ Église St-Sauveur
④ Église St-Jean-Baptiste
⑤ Séminaire de Québec
⑥ Basilique
⑦ Archevêché
⑧ Université
⑨ Couvent des Ursulines
⑩ Église des Jésuites
⑪ Église St-Patrice
⑫ Hôtel-Dieu
⑬ Hôtel de Ville
⑭ Hôtel du Gouvernement

Map by: Derek A. Parent 2001

The procession set off shortly after eight a.m. and reached its destination, the Monument Laval, three hours later. As at the end of the Fête-Dieu procession, mass was celebrated by the Papal Delegate before a crowd estimated once again at 100,000. With the end of the mass, the bugles sounded, as they had the previous day, to announce the arrival of the governor general. In 1898, Lord Aberdeen had attended the mass at the close of the St-Jean-Baptiste parade that formed part of the ceremonies for the unveiling of the Monument Champlain; this year, Grey stayed away from the religious part of the day's festivities, perhaps to express his disdain for matters Catholic. The governor general was seated on the same speakers' platform that had been used for the unveiling. Then Mgr Paul-Eugène Roy, the auxiliary bishop of Quebec, took the podium to deliver the main speech of the day. Before beginning his remarks, Roy called for the ropes restraining the crowds to be dropped. This impressed Alfred Paré, who had also been struck by the efforts to keep the masses away from the speakers during the previous day's unveiling ceremonies, presumably to guarantee Grey's safety.[147]

Paré had little to say about Roy's speech. However, he described the drawing of the people toward the podium in some detail: 'Mgr Roy looked at the space before him, kept vacant by a line of police and soldiers, and then at the crowd which was anxious to move forward: towards the podium, to be able to hear the speaker.' Roy then asked that the crowd be allowed to come forward. 'Finding that the job was being looked after rather slowly, Mgr Roy cried out, "Would someone let the crowds come forward." Applause erupted from everywhere, the crowds broke through the line of police, and the area was occupied in the wink of an eye.'[148] Roy's dramatic effort to bring the speakers closer to the masses paralleled the efforts of the SSJBQ's leaders earlier in the day to take their procession into the neighbourhoods of the lower town.

The Fête Continues

The official account of *le triduum Laval* declared that it ended with the close of the St-Jean-Baptiste ceremonies at the bishop's monument. For many residents of and visitors to Quebec City, however, the day had just begun. Immediately after the formal ceremonies, many attended the games sponsored by the SSJBQ. This event reinforced certain of the exclusionary aspects of the procession from earlier in the day. Throughout the afternoon, various athletic events were held in which 'only French Canadians were able to compete for prizes.' This masculine activity confirmed the society's view that the entire Laval fête had been a celebration of 'our religious faith and the virility of our race.'[149]

Throughout the day, through such means as arranging a 'private' police force to supervise its procession and invoking 'laws' to bar outsiders from its games, the society had made it possible for Quebec's lay leaders to flex their muscles, most notably by taking control of the city's streets on a weekday, bringing normal business activities to a grinding halt. The Catholic hierarchy had a certain legitimacy in its own right that was supported, in the case of the Fête-Dieu procession, by centuries of tradition. In contrast, the secular leaders of the SSJBQ had to work with an event that had had no fixed form and that the clerical leaders tried to influence as much as possible so as to impose a certain unity on the celebrations surrounding the unveiling of Laval's monument. Mgr Bégin and his colleagues succeeded to a degree in imposing their will; even so, there remained significant aspects of the St-Jean-Baptiste procession and the games that followed which sent a message, to both participants and spectators, about the power of French-Canadian secular leaders.

The games ended late in the afternoon, but for many people it was still too early to go home. What remained for the evening were two very different types of events that in some ways reflected the cleavages within the local French-Canadian population over the tercentenary, which was only weeks away. One of these events was a fireworks show sponsored by the SSJBQ, which attracted several thousand spectators to Parc Victoria. Included in the extravaganza were fireworks creating 'portraits of Mayor Garneau, of Champlain, and especially the emblem of the SSJBQ and [the likeness] of the Honourable M [Adélard] Turgeon,' the president of the society. When the show ended at 10:00 p.m., 'the happy spectators and strollers returned to their homes.'[150]

Laval's image had been inescapable during the three-day celebration, yet he had faded from the scene within hours of the official close of the ceremonies. He was replaced by Champlain and, even more significantly, by the mayor. Though Garneau had played a rather insignificant role in the Laval celebration, he had been from the start a key player in the planning for the tercentenary. The appearance of his likeness in the company of Champlain's suggested that this was not really the final event of the Laval celebration, but rather a prelude to the tercentenary, in which the SSJBQ, uneasy about the affair from its inception, still hoped to play a main role.

The fireworks show may have been the most popular event in Quebec City, but it was not the only one scheduled for the final night of Laval's fête. Across town, at the university, the ACJC was beginning its *premier congrès général* (first general assembly), which would continue for three days. In the months leading up to Quebec's summer of celebrations, the leaders of the ACJC had been working diligently to assemble as many French Catholic leaders as possible in order to extend the Laval fete and to provide a forum for those who were unhappy about the much too Protestant tercentenary to come. In that context, the archbishop of St-Boniface, Mgr Langevin, was pleased to participate in order to send a message to both 'the good English-speakers' and 'our free-thinkers' who wished to 'push us out of the celebrations of the tercentenary.' In contrast, Mayor Garneau was able to find other things to do; he and all the lay organizers of the tercentenary were conspicuous by their absence.[151]

On the first night of the ACJC convention, the speakers included many who had been seen during the Laval celebrations, including Pierre Gerlier, the representative of the sister organization from France, who had been enthusiastically received at the close of the unveiling ceremonies and who would leave his mark once again. But the most dramatic moment came with the speech delivered by Hermas Lalande, a Jesuit priest from Montreal, who had long had a reputation within the ACJC as an *intégraliste* – that is, someone committed to the purity of the French Catholic race. Given this, it was hardly surprising, as Abbé Paré observed, that Lalande 'presented a powerful diatribe against Freemasons, liberals, the apathetic. He touched upon questions of present-day politics with the subtlety of a bull in a china shop, pestering the federal and provincial governments, the bishop of Montreal, the rector of Université Laval. He presented his speech with a strong dose of a nationalism of the most recent vintage.' Lalande's views had been contested within the ACJC by other, more moderate figures who considered themselves *conciliatoristes*. This faction was represented on the last night of the fête by Mgr Bruchési of Montreal, a confidant of Prime Minister Laurier, who 'gave the appearance of someone who was seeking, at the time he was talking, to find a thought, a phrase that might counteract the vehemence of the language used by Lalande, the Jesuit.'[152]

The fireworks show looked like the start of the celebration of Champlain. In contrast, the ACJC convention allowed the French Catholic spirit of the Laval fete to last a few more days. Several weeks later, on the eve of the tercentenary, the ACJC would take to the streets to advance its point of view once again. It was supported in this by elements within the SSJBQ, an organization that had helped hatch the idea of the tercentenary but was feeling increasingly out of the loop as Champlain's celebration approached. To be sure, some leaders of the French-Canadian community – including officers of the SSJBQ and members of the Catholic hierarchy – would participate enthusiastically in the celebration. But they would find themselves divided from those French Catholics who viewed the events of July 1908 with a jaundiced eye.

chapter four

Champlain's Tercentenary?

Visitors and Residents

Only four weeks after the close of the Laval fête, the streets of Quebec City came alive once again, this time for the celebration of the tercentenary of Champlain's founding of the town.[1] By any standard the tercentenary extravaganza held in the last two weeks of July was the largest commemorative event ever staged in Canada. It was more expensive and had a longer run than all past celebrations of the founding fathers combined. Moreover, the tercentenary drew more people to Quebec City than any of the earlier fêtes. Over its two weeks a city of 70,000 became home to as many as 150,000 visitors, including hundreds of dignitaries, more than 5,000 sailors from the British, French, and American battleships moored in the port, and over 10,000 Canadian militiamen.[2]

So great was the anticipated flood of visitors that organizers had to scramble to accommodate them. By the time the fête was four months away, Mayor Garneau and his colleagues recognized that there was going to be a housing crisis; they calculated that hotels, rooming houses, religious institutions, and private homes would be able to absorb only half the expected visitors. Desperate times called for desperate measures: a 'Great White City' of 740 tents, complete with stoves, beds, water, and electric lighting, was built on the Plains of Abraham to shelter some of the anticipated visitors.[3]

While French-speaking Catholics constituted 85 per cent of the local population, most of the visitors would be English-speaking Protestants, the great majority from other parts of Canada. This meant that the tercentenary organizers were going to have to put on a spectacle that would entertain these visitors without alienating local people. This was going to be hard, since the two groups did not always agree on the significance of the events of July 1908. Tourists had become an important part of the economy of Quebec City, which from the late nineteenth century had been providing North American visitors with a cheap and easily reachable glimpse of Europe. One turn-of-the-century travel guide to the city was subtitled 'A Quaint Medieval French City in America.' At the same time, the celebrations would be attracting English speakers who wished 'to honour the ground where the foundation of Greater Britain was laid,' and to witness the British Empire's military and naval might.[4]

For the local French Canadians, the presence of so many outsiders would transform the tercentenary into an event unlike any of the previous celebrations of the founding fathers, especially those designed to celebrate Laval's legacy. The bishop's fêtes had been relatively uncomplicated affairs, since there was no question that he belonged to French Canadians. There had been arguments about the precise meaning of his legacy, but those debates took place within the French-Canadian family, with outsiders such as Earl Grey making only cameo appearances. In the end, the disagreements over Laval's legacy did not prevent the participation of Protestants such as Henri-Gustave Joly or Catholics with chequered pasts such as Wilfrid Laurier alongside ultramontane clerics such as Mgr Bégin. These men disagreed passionately about the relative power of church and state – a theme that was unavoidable in any celebration of Laval. Even so, they had been able to set aside their differences and pay tribute to a French-Canadian hero, and invariably ended the celebrations with the singing of 'God Save the King.'

In these celebrations of the survival of the French-Canadian people, this heartfelt tribute to the empire had provided the grounds for a rapprochement between men who had very different ideas about the future. For Bégin, as for many lay and clerical leaders, the arrival of the British in the late eighteenth century had amounted to a 'providential' deliverance of French Canadians from revolutionary France; in the British Empire, Catholicism would be able to flourish. In contrast, according to Joly, Laurier, and their kind the British had brought French Canadians the advantages of parliamentary democracy.

Because Laval belonged to French Canadians, his legacy could be celebrated without defensiveness, without the sense that outsiders were somehow foisting their views on a conquered people. This meant in turn that the various elements of French-Canadian society could trumpet their British connection in their own distinctive ways. The celebration of

Champlain was much more complicated because his legacy could be appropriated by any number of groups outside the French-Canadian community. English-speaking Protestants could identify with Champlain because he was a secular hero, the founder of a European civilization in North America. As the first colonial governor on Canadian soil, governors general saw him as the first of their line.

The raising of the Monument Champlain brought a diverse cast of characters together, and at times there were bruised feelings, especially among French speakers, who felt they were being marginalized in the celebration of one of their founding fathers. Yet the grumbling never became too loud, and figures as diverse as the governor general the French consul general, the president of the Société St-Jean-Baptiste, the representative of the archbishop of Quebec, and leaders of the local English-speaking population were able to come together for the unveiling in the fall of 1898. Just as they had during Laval's reburial twenty years earlier, French speakers enthusiastically joined in the singing of 'God Save the Queen' at the close of the festivities. In doing so they were reaffirming the loyalty they had expressed only a year earlier, when they celebrated the Queen's Diamond Jubilee.

The unveiling of the Monument Champlain might not have worked out quite so well had it taken place even a year later, after the Boer War broke out, transforming the French-Canadian image of the empire. In the decade between the two celebrations of Champlain, English Canadians – some of whom would come to Quebec in 1908 – began to view the empire's strength as synonymous with Canada's strength. At the same time, some French Canadians began to doubt the good will of their English-speaking counterparts, who had been all too willing to divert Canadian resources toward imperial adventures. This perspective was advanced most energetically by Henri Bourassa, who had been elected to Parliament when Laurier swept into power in 1896. After Laurier decided to allow Canadian volunteers to fight in the South African war, Bourassa resigned his seat so that his constituents could express their views on the matter in a by-election. He figured correctly that they would rebuke Laurier. In his letter of resignation to the prime minister, he wrote that he still saw himself as a 'British citizen, proud of his rights and jealous of his liberty, loyal to England and its august sovereign.' At the same time, however, he was not prepared to see Canadian resources squandered on irrelevant overseas adventures because he was 'loyal above and beyond everything else and forever to Canada.'[5]

Early in the new century, Bourassa inspired the formation of several nationalist groups whose purpose was to defend French-Canadian interests from those of outsiders. In 1903 two groups were established: the Ligue nationaliste, which focused on the threat posed by British imperialism; and the Association catholique de la jeunesse canadienne-française (ACJC), whose convention would close the Laval celebrations in June 1908. Although the two groups were fairly small, they were well represented among the clergy and the province's petite bourgeoisie.

Groups like these demonstrated their ability to mobilize Quebecers in the provincial election of 1908, in which Henri Bourassa challenged Lomer Gouin, the premier of Quebec and a staunch Laurier supporter, in his own Montreal riding. Questions of imperialism were never openly discussed during this campaign; however, Bourassa's personal popularity was directly related to this broader campaign against the rise of outside influences in the lives of French Canadians. Only weeks before the Laval fête in Quebec City, the streets of Montreal were filled with eager supporters of Bourassa; they attended large rallies for their own candidate and disrupted those organized by Gouin. On the eve of the election there was supposed to have been an *assemblée contradictoire* – a public debate between the two candidates. This was cancelled by Montreal authorities, who worried that violence might erupt. In the end, Bourassa defeated Gouin; he also won a personal victory in a second riding outside the city where he spent election day. On his return to Montreal on the night of his victories, he was met at the train station by a crowd of supporters and was 'hauled homeward in a carriage drawn by students at the head of an impromptu parade which interrupted traffic for several hours.'[6]

The passions that were evident in the streets of Montreal reflected the edginess of many French Canadians. This malaise would find its way onto the streets of Quebec City, especially after the Laval fête was separated from the celebration of Champlain early in 1907. Until then, even loyal followers of the Bourassa-inspired movements had believed the 1908 fêtes might celebrate all the various components of the Canadian population. However, once Laval was out of the way, the tercentenary celebration evolved so as to satisfy the tourists who would be attending the consecration of the Plains of Abraham and the more general celebration of the empire.

This troubled many French Canadians, including Bourassa, who arranged to be out of the country during the tercentenary. Before his departure he commented: 'In my soul, there is not a shadow of a doubt, knowing Earl Grey as I have learned to know him in Ottawa, that he decided from the beginning to transform the celebration of the birth of Quebec and of French Canada into a grand historic reminder of the Conquest in order to show his imperialist friends in London that the new imperial religion has made progress among French Canadians. His second objective consists of affecting the spirit of French Canadians by rubbing their noses in the notion of imperial grandeur.'

Grey was perhaps overstating the case when he referred to developments in Quebec by early 1908 as potentially leading 'to another abortive Papineau trouble.'[7] But he was not that far off the mark in recognizing that there was a limit to which French-Canadian loyalty to the British connection could be taken for granted. Many French speakers would go along with the tercentenary; others would show their disapproval either by attending rallies protesting its imperial dimensions or by offering very limited support for a fete with which they could not entirely identify.

Promoters and Opponents

Bourassa's cynicism about the tercentenary was at odds with the boundless enthusiasm displayed by another French Canadian. H.J.J.B. Chouinard had been involved in commemorative events in Quebec City since the 1870s, when he served on the organizing committee responsible for celebrating the bicentenary of the diocese of Quebec. As both the *greffier* (clerk) of Quebec City and the *annaliste* (recorder of the activities) of the SSJBQ, Chouinard was well placed to contribute to the various celebrations of the founding fathers. Although he played no role in organizing the reburial of Laval, which the church had controlled, he had served as secretary to the committees responsible for the monuments to Champlain and Laval. When the organization for staging the Champlain tercentenary began to take shape in 1906, he was tabbed as secretary once again. He would retain this post after the National Battlefields Commission (NBC) was formed in the spring of 1908. The NBC would be managing the fêtes scheduled for July, and after this, the construction of a park on the Plains of Abraham, which was to be the lasting legacy of the tercentenary.[8]

Chouinard's qualifications for all of this extended beyond his experience in the commemorative industry; if anyone could claim to have first thought of the celebration, it was he. As Chouinard told the story, he was standing with the mayor of Quebec City, Simon-Napoléon Parent, at the celebration in 1902 of both the fiftieth anniversary of Université Laval and the sixtieth of the SSJBQ. Parent asked Chouinard when such crowds might ever return to the streets of Quebec; Chouinard replied that something truly grand might be done to mark Champlain's founding of the town. In 1904 Chouinard fleshed out his ideas in the Christmas edition of the *Quebec Telegraph*, but nothing came of them until early in 1906, when he tried to enlist the support of the SSJBQ, noting that the tercentenary should have 'not only a French-Canadian character, but rather a Canadian one in the largest sense of the term.'[9]

The society blessed Chouinard's project, but found itself where it had been before – supporting a project that was far beyond its means. As before, it called on the mayor of Quebec – now George Garneau – to organize a public meeting of interested parties from both linguistic communities. In 1898 the same formula had resulted in the SSJBQ's virtual exclusion from the unveiling of Champlain's statue. Throughout 1906 and into early 1907, this committee received various drafts for a possible program from Chouinard; all of these reflected his desire to hold an event that a broad cross-section of Canadians would be able to support, and that would include representatives from the French and British governments. He envisioned a celebration in late June and early July 1908; it would celebrate, among other things, Champlain's arrival at Quebec (3 July), the unveiling of the Monument Laval, the opening of a museum of Canadian history, and the creation of a national park incorporating battles from 1759–60 won by both the British and the French. Furthermore, Chouinard imagined 'a national procession, in which there would be all of the elements of the Canadian nation, and which would include an historical parade.' Chouinard's pan-Canadian celebration was immediately condemned by the officials at the *archevêché* responsible for the Monument Laval, who feared the dilution of the French Catholic dimension of the fête. Watching developments from the seminary, Alfred Paré was more generous: 'There is going to be a little bit of everything.'[10]

Chouinard's ideas had the support of the local committee, but they were going to require federal funding if they were ever to be translated into reality. From the start, Laurier proved difficult to pin down; he well recognized the dangers of committing himself to any commemorative scheme that might further antagonize his supporters, especially in Quebec, where Bourassa's movement was gaining strength. The Quebec City committee only managed to meet with Laurier early in 1907, and it received little in the way of concrete support. By April, Laurier was calling for the celebrations to be delayed until 1909. After the collapse of the Quebec Bridge in October, he seemed prepared to put off the tercentenary indefinitely. Later in 1907, when the idea was revived to stage the celebration in the summer of 1908, Laurier dragged his feet in passing the legislation that would provide federal funding. Grey called the prime minister 'the old procrastinator.' Exasperated, he wrote to him: 'We have been waiting, waiting, waiting ...'[11]

While Laurier played for time, the governor general energetically promoted Chouinard's idea, which he hoped might stimulate French-Canadian support for the empire. In 1904, before he left England to take up his Canadian post, Grey had been informed by 'his predecessor and brother-in-law, Lord Minto ... that Canada's reluctance to take part in any imperial scheme was the result of political difficulties created by the presence of the French-Canadian population.'[12] After arriving in Canada, Grey quickly recognized the benefits of staging commemorations to advance the imperial cause. In 1905, on the centenary of the death of Admiral Nelson, he tried to organize a ceremony that would bring French and English speakers together in the name of empire. He abandoned this plan after Laurier pointed out that French Canadians would regard the celebration as indicative 'of a new imperialism of which they are frightened and to which they are opposed.'[13]

A few weeks after dropping the Nelson scheme, Grey visited Quebec City for the first time. Almost immediately, he was captivated by the idea of turning the Plains of Abraham into a symbol of imperial unity. In 1905 a relatively small tract of land bearing the name 'Plains of Abraham' was the property of the federal government, which had acquired it from the Ursuline order four years earlier. Ottawa had immediately leased the parcel to the municipal government for development as a park. Grey recognized that to create a truly impressive commemorative site – a *lieux de mémoire*, to use the expression of twenty-first-century historians – more land than this would have to be acquired. He seized on the idea – originally proposed by Chouinard – of including the nearby Ste-Foy battlefield, where the English had been the losers, so that the message of French defeat might be blunted. To take the edge off the legacy of defeat, by Grey also called for the raising of 'a colossal statue of the Goddess of Peace on the first point of Quebec visible to vessels coming from across the seas.'[14] Grey was proposing a statue slightly taller than the Statue of Liberty, intended to show immigrants coming up the St. Lawrence that this was British territory, on which two former enemies now lived happily together.

Grey imagined visitors being transported by an elevator inside the statue to the goddess's head, where they would look out through a telescope built into her eyes. A list of the names of subscribers to the park project would be inscribed on the walls in 'the chamber of her bosom.' Grey set about raising private donations for the battlefield project. He had no choice, with costs spiralling (they had reached an estimated $2 million by the end of 1907), and with Laurier apparently unable or unwilling to move the tercentenary dossier forward. Grey's fundraising campaign was targeted at donors both in Canada and throughout the empire. Private contributions for the park project eventually brought in around $200,000 – far short of the $1,000,000 he had hoped to receive just from individuals outside Canada.

However one calculates the figures, Grey's appeal was a flop. He had hoped for support from the various governments of the empire, but only secured a token grant from that of New Zealand. Similarly, he had presumed that English Canadians would rally to his project. In this regard, J.M. Courtney, the federal deputy minister of finance, observed from his temporary post as NBC treasurer: 'I do not think that any measure that can be devised could extract money from the pockets of the people of Canada. The plain facts are that the inhabitants of the Dominion are not enthusiastic in this matter. Those who for other objects such as the Patriotic Fund and the India Famine Fund could offer hundreds and sometimes thousands are now giving five and ten dollars, and many are refusing to subscribe at all.' In the end, Grey found himself forced to take part in a scheme – really a scam – masterminded by the publisher of the *Montreal Star*, Hugh Graham, who made a contribution in the guise of an anonymous American businessman in order to shame Canadians into contributing.[15]

English Canadians were reluctant contributors to the battlefields fund; French speakers were even more reserved. Grey naively believed that French Canadians would contribute to his campaign after recognizing that tourist dollars 'would find [their] way into the hands of the Roman Catholic hierarchy, and thus increase their ability to maintain their schools and charities.' Laurier had a much more sanguine view of the situation, cautioning the governor general before he set off on his crusade that it would be wise to avoid collecting from francophone students, because 'subscriptions from the French Canadian schools might compare unfavourably with those from others.'[16] Abbé Paré, from his perch in the seminary, commented on the staging of a gymnastics demonstration: 'a benefit performance to help finance the battlefields park ... There were a number of Québécois who were sympathetic to the student performers, but who stayed away from this event because the receipts would go to the battlefields park, an unpopular project in certain circles which see it as an imperialist invasion on the part of British officials.'[17]

For a variety of reasons, French Canadians showed little interest in supporting the battlefield fund. While the NBC received over $15,000 in direct contributions from individual Canadians, hardly any of the donors' names sounded even vaguely French Canadian. There was no groundswell of support for the fundraising efforts among French speakers, and the NBC's own actions did little to generate one. To attract contributions, the commission sent posters to every bank branch in Canada, calling on local citizens to donate to the battlefields fund. Unfortunately, the posters were in English only, and as a result, Courtney received several complaints, such as this one, from the manager of the Banque Nationale office in Chicoutimi: 'I would ask you to be kind enough to send us a French copy of same as our population here is mostly only French speaking.' Courtney replied that the commission thought it 'unnecessary to print the placards sent to the banks in the two languages.'[18]

Similarly, the NBC sent English-only materials to encourage local governments to contribute to the fund. In the end, the few contributions from Quebec municipalities came mostly from cities with sizeable English-speaking minorities, such as Montreal, or those with English-speaking majorities, such as Westmount. Understandably alienated was the secretary-treasurer of the County Council of Arthabaska, who replied to Courtney: 'I have received your letter and your circular to be read to the County Council of Arthabaska. I must tell you that the county council is composed of Canadian descendants of French with only one English man, so I will be glad if you could send your circular in French.' English-only federal forms were the norm for the time, but they could not have helped fundraising, which would have been a hard sell in the best of circumstances.[19]

To accelerate its fundraising efforts, and to encourage contributions from those who preferred not to contribute directly to Quebec City, early in 1908 the NBC provided seed money to create the Quebec Battlefields Association. A central committee was established in Ottawa, with responsibility for creating local committees across Canada.[20] In the end, only two of the two hundred local organizations formed were in Quebec, one in Montreal and the other in Quebec City. The Montreal branch was a success, raising well over half the $85,000 collected by the association. However, if the linguistic composition of schoolchildren who contributed to the effort is any indication, most of the donors were English speakers.

Children were encouraged to collect funds by filling in books with room to include donations of 10 cents from each of fifty people. Children who took out books, and those who succeeded in raising the $5, had their names printed in local newspapers. These lists spoke volumes about the fundraisers' inability to attract French-speaking donors. The *Montreal Daily Witness* printed one such list, which included the names of 540 children who had acquired collection books; only thirty of these children had names that sounded even vaguely French. The same edition of the newspaper printed the 'honour roll' of those who had returned their books along with the $5. Only seven of the eighty names sounded French.[21] A Montreal journal printed photos of twenty-eight 'Patriotic Montreal Children' who had qualified for the honour roll. All of them seemed to be English speakers, except for the Provencher children, Blanche and Alexis.[22]

In Quebec City, which was 85 per cent francophone, only 10 per cent of the three hundred local donors belonged to the linguistic majority. Several of these French speakers were prominent figures in the tercentenary organization; the biggest contributor was Mayor Garneau himself, who donated $1,000 of the total donations of roughly $7,200.[23] He was joined on the list by various members of the local elite. Lieutenant-Governor Jetté, Henri-Gustave Joly (the former premier), Sheriff Charles Langelier (who would play Champlain in the tercentenary pageants), and J.A. Charlebois, the NBC's notary, who was helping assemble the land for the park. Missing from the list were ordinary French speakers. The ranks of English-speaking contributors were bolstered by children from English-language schools; there were no such collections from the French-speaking community. Mgr Têtu, who had fumed that funds were being diverted from the Monument Laval campaign to the one for the battlefields, really had nothing to complain about.

The failure of Grey's campaign meant that his grandiose schemes for the park had to be cut back dramatically; there would never be a Goddess of Peace. It also meant that the tercentenary would depend on federal funds. In March 1908, after much brow beating from Grey, Laurier finally introduced legislation to create the National Battlefields Commission. The commission was to have a budget of $300,000 to stage the tercentenary (in the short term) and to supervise the construction of the battlefields park (in the long term). Five commissioners would be named by the federal government, but any province or imperial government that contributed $100,000 would be entitled to a seat as well. As it turned out, only Ontario and Quebec – each of which contributed the necessary amount – would be entitled to appoint commissioners. Laurier agonized over the prospect of the British government sitting on the commission, since this would highlight the imperialist dimensions of the project. Grey finally lost his temper with the prime minister, complaining bitterly that Laurier was paying too much attention 'to Ultramontane prejudices against anything in the nature of imperialism ... The unique advantages enjoyed by the French-speaking Catholics in the Province of Quebec are a direct result of its inclusion in the British empire. A refusal, or rather a hesitation on the part of the Dominion government to acknowledge this fact, because of some narrow ultramontane prejudices in the Province of Quebec, which is difficult for a generous mind to understand, much less sympathize with, will not strengthen the hold of the Dominion government on the love and confidence of either Canada or the Empire.' Grey told Laurier that his political demise was imminent unless he could convince Canadians that the government was not under the control of 'the prejudices of the most reactionary section of your people.'[24]

Laurier had launched his political career thirty years earlier by standing up to the Ultramontanes, so he needed no lecture on the subject from Grey, who did not have to worry about getting re-elected. Had the governor general listened closely to the impassioned speeches of two *nationaliste* members of Parliament, he would have understood the pressures facing Laurier. Armand Lavergne had been associated with Bourassa's movement from its inception. By March 1908 he was an independent member, having been expelled from the Liberal Party the previous year. He was no doubt speaking for many Quebecers when he rose in Parliament to object to the incorporation of a memorial to the events of 1759–60 during a celebration of what Champlain had done in 1608. 'It seems that the hero of the feast has been forgotten, that the name of Champlain is placed entirely in the shadows and that another scheme, of an entirely different character, has been brought forward, a scheme which I would favour to the utmost in the year 1959. But we must remember that we are now in 1908; that Quebec was founded in 1608 and that we are not celebrating the second centenary of the battle on the Plains of Abraham, but the third centenary of the founding of the city of Quebec.'[25]

True to the Bourassiste position of supporting Canada in the broadest sense, but not the empire, Lavergne proposed an amendment to Laurier's bill that would have eliminated its most blatantly imperialistic feature – the possibility that foreign leaders would be represented on the NBC. When his amendment was defeated by both Liberals loyal to Laurier and Conservatives – some of whom celebrated the imperialist possibilities of the tercentenary – Lavergne voted for the bill despite his reservations. As it turned out, this was one of his final actions in Parliament; soon afterwards he resigned his seat to run alongside Bourassa in the June provincial election. Lavergne was returned to the Quebec legislature, where his name ultimately became attached to the 'loi Lavergne' – energetically supported by the ACJC – which provided certain guarantees for the use of French at the provincial level.

Laurier's bill was also attacked by Lorenzo Robitaille, who was troubled by the presence of an English-speaking majority on the NBC. He asked the house: 'Shall we permit a foreign majority – a majority of outsiders – less qualified for this special purpose to rule the commission? It is not fair and equitable. Would the city of Toronto permit Quebecers or others than their own to have the last word in the arrangement and planning of a work similar to the one about to be performed in Quebec?'[26] Robitaille's reference to English Canadians as 'foreigners' was a rather extreme point of view that was outside the Bourassiste tradition, and he received no support in the house, not even from Lavergne. In the end, having made his point, Robitaille followed his *nationaliste* colleague in supporting Laurier's bill.

Yet Robitaille's words and his level of support in Ottawa were less important than who he was. He had secured his seat in Parliament in 1906 after Bourassa broke openly with Laurier. Soon after, a by-election was held in a Quebec City riding not far from Laurier's, and the Liberals nominated a local businessman, who was expected to win easily. At Bourassa's urging, Robitaille ran against him, and won. The high point of the by-election campaign came when Bourassa and Lavergne addressed a crowd of 6,000, thus paving the way for Robitaille's David-like victory.

Now that he was a figure of some prominence, Robitaille appeared in public alongside the leaders of the *nationaliste* opposition to the Liberals that was beginning to form at the provincial and federal levels. In the summer of 1907, while Laurier was marking time on the tercentenary issue, Bourassa was heating up his provincial campaign against Gouin, and by extension Laurier. In a rally in the St-Roch district of Quebec City, in Laurier's own federal riding, Bourassa, Lavergne, and Robitaille addressed a crowd of 15,000: 'But the meeting was broken up by a barrage of tomatoes, eggs, and stones from Liberal stalwarts directed by Louis-Alexandre Taschereau,' the future premier of Quebec, who would be the Quebec government's appointee to the NBC only eight months later. By the spring of 1908 the tercentenary's finances were in place, but so too were opponents of the fete, who would have their own story to tell.[27]

The Death of a Parade

It was clear by the start of 1908 that there would be a big celebration in Quebec City later that summer. The peripatetic Chouinard was still drafting proposals for it. He had wanted a celebration of Canada in all its diversity; however, the French Catholic dimension had already been compromised by the hiving off of the Laval fete – an action he had opposed from within the Comité du Monument Laval. In the early months of 1908, still other components would disappear from his original scheme. There would be no museum of national history, and no exhibition touching on the history of Canada.

Early in the negotiations, Laurier had rejected the museum idea, which he saw as prohibitively expensive. He preferred to concentrate on the battlefields project. However, the idea of mounting a historical exhibition was still on the drawing board in 1908. Mgr Mathieu, the superior of the seminary, was contacted by the tercentenary committee about the possible use of his institution as the site of an exhibit of artefacts and documents relating to the history of New France. In early March, Mgr Mathieu responded that this would raise problems; however, he hoped to 'find a solution to these problems in very short order.' In spite of his willingness to engage in further dialogue, the tercentenary organizers shut the door, noting that they had decided 'to drop the project in light of the limited time at their disposal.'[28] The committee continued to pursue highly complicated projects that spoke to more than the French regime, such as the mounting of historical pageants on the Plains of Abraham. Yet it seemed too busy to bother with Chouinard's historical exhibition, which though simpler to stage could not touch on the experience of English-speaking Canadians.

More significant for the ultimate shape of the tercentenary was the deletion from the final program of another Chouinard project, 'an immense procession of all of our national societies, along with groups of figures from the past, officers and soldiers from various periods, who would be interspersed in with floats that would draw attention to some of the most beautiful moments from our history.'[29] In this there was no mistaking Chouinard's SSJBQ roots: he was proposing a procession through the town that would look very much like a *défilé de la St-Jean*. The only difference was that the Irish, English, and Scottish national societies would be included. In the end, this parade was never held – a development that symbolized the transformation of the tercentenary over the course of 1908.

The demise of Chouinard's procession began with the announcement in January 1908 that the men overseeing the tercentenary were considering the incorporation of historical pageants. As the Montreal paper *The Standard* declared in a headline, these pageants were 'England's Recent Craze.' Dramatic recreations of scenes from the past were an almost exclusively English phenomenon; they were as culturally specific – if not as steeped in tradition – as Fête-Dieu and St-Jean-Baptiste processions.[30] These processions brought together large numbers of people, who were arranged in various hierarchical arrangements before being sent off to move through the streets. In contrast, pageants were relatively static presentations of the past staged in outdoor amphitheatres. They were designed to tear down the barriers within society, as individuals from all walks of life dressed in period costume. As the *Standard* put it: '[Pageants] have lowered distinctions between peers and peasants, between mistresses and servants, between capitalists and workmen. Rich and poor, cultured and uncultured, men and women of low and high esteem have all worked together on a common level for the purpose of picturing before the world some of the great and brilliant deeds in the history of the nation.'[31] Of course, the people staging these pageants tended to be members of the ruling classes, who stood to profit by defusing the opposition of the lower orders to their power. This was of no little significance, considering that a severe recession had begun the previous fall.[32]

Louis Napoleon Parker, the father of the early-twentieth-century pageant, was resolutely antimodern, and reconstructed scenes from England's distant past as a means of blurring social distinctions that had been encouraged by the onset of the industrial age. At the same time, his spectacles, which he began staging in 1905, reflected something of a modern spirit, in that they sought historical accuracy and rejected the use of allegory or mythology. This realism made his pageants much more accessible to society at large than spectacles such as the St-Jean-Baptiste procession, which were incomprehensible to anyone unfamiliar with their conventions.[33]

At a different level, the processions through the streets of Quebec City were more accessible than most pageants, which required land, often some distance from the city centre. This land was necessary to erect temporary bleachers, from which spectators watched re-creations of the past on a vast stage. In a sense, pageants privatized public space; they erected barriers that kept out all but those who had paid to see the performance. Pageant organizers chose these spaces carefully, in the hope that a dramatic setting would add to the event's overall impact. In this regard, the Plains of Abraham – already in the news because of the campaign for a battlefield park – were chosen for the tercentenary pageants in order to give them some added punch.

As soon as pageants entered the discussions of tercentenary organizers, Chouinard's 'procession of all of our national societies' began to fade from the deliberations. By early February, he too had jumped on the pageant bandwagon, having concluded that these historical performances would draw larger crowds than his parade. Actually, there was little to support this calculation. In fact, the historian Thomas Chapais, who chaired a subcommittee dealing with the pageants, wondered 'if the population would not be put off and unhappy if it were forced to pay to see these spectacles.'[34] Yet, these reservations could not stop the growing support among organizers for the pageants, which soon became a central feature of the tercentenary. Eager to provide these dramatic representations of the past with as much exposure as possible, even Chouinard began to wonder about the value of displaying the divisions within Canadian society through the participation of the national societies. He eventually concluded that a parade of actors from the past – including Wolfe and Montcalm, who would march together – might provide a much more appealing message to the crowds, especially those who had come from some distance.[35]

With the cancellation of the parade of the national societies, the SSJBQ now had no official role in the celebration it had helped conceive. Soon joining it on the sidelines was another group that did not quite fit into the emerging celebration. The Garde Indépendante Champlain, which had played a key role in the Champlain celebration of 1898, sought a grant of $1,200 from the organizing committee to finance an assembly in Quebec City of its chapters from across French Canada. This association had close ties to the ultramontane wing of Quebec Catholicism. It was turned down flat, and told that 'its role was to participate in the Laval fêtes.' To make it clear that some French-speaking groups were more desirable than others, the same committee only weeks later provided $2,000 to the Association des médecins de langue française de l'Amérique du Nord so that it could hold a convention at the time of the tercentenary.[36]

By mid-March, the national societies – most notably the SSJBQ and the Garde Champlain – had become such conspicuous orphans that organizers decided that something, however cosmetic, had to be done to bring them into the celebration. These groups were eventually offered a marginal place on the tercentenary calendar. In the final program, their parade was scheduled for 30 July, the next to last day of the fete. By then the Prince of Wales, around whose schedule the entire affair was being shaped, would have already left town. Though the SSJBQ was obviously seen as a minor player, its leaders sought funds to put on a proper show. Clearly, they had used up most of their resources for their role in the Laval celebrations. Through their president, Adélard Turgeon, a Laurier loyalist who was one of the prime minister's appointees to the NBC, they asked for $2,000. Despite their strong connections, there is no evidence that funds ever were committed, and this placed the SSJBQ's participation in jeopardy.[37]

The minutes of the society for April testified to the 'existence of a deep bitterness regarding the character of the celebrations for the tercentenary of the founding of Quebec.' Member after member rose to express one grievance or another. J.-E.-A. Pin, a union leader who was also helping organize the SSJBQ procession for the Laval celebration, observed that 'among the workers there is concern that worker organizations are not represented either upon the executive or the different committees.' T. Béland complained that 'the Association of Retail Merchants has been completely ignored in the setting up of the various committees.' There was even a complaint about the imminent passage of control over the Monument des Braves. This had long been looked after by the SSJBQ; it was about to become the property of the NBC.

The members of the society who were intimately involved with the tercentenary tried to fend off these complaints. Turgeon asked members 'to work to dissipate the noticeable malaise which would be so detrimental to the success of the fetes.' Chouinard, who was taking the minutes of an especially rancorous SSJBQ meeting, editorialized by noting that 'the fears that were expressed had no basis in fact.' Perhaps these appeals had some effect; the society continued to hope that it would be permitted to march in the tercentenary, even though they had absolutely no reason for such confidence.[38]

Only weeks before the start of the fête, the society took part in various meetings with the Irish, English, and Scottish national societies to organize the parade for 30 July.[39] One has to wonder whether any of these societies were very interested in a procession that would barely be noticed by the public, which would have understood the celebration as having ended with the departure of the Prince of Wales. At one of the early July meetings, the treasurer of the SSJBQ openly admitted that he could not see the point of the exercise; more generally, there were doubts among society members regarding the enthusiasm of the other national organizations. The death knell for the parade tolled only two days before the start of the tercentenary. At a meeting at city hall attended by the various French-Canadian parties but not the English-speaking societies, it was decided to cancel the parade. No clear explanation for this was ever provided. One newspaper speculated that the cancellation was a result of the preoccupation of many members of these groups with the pageants, and by their failure to get sufficient time off work from bosses, whose 'good will' had already been tested (in the case of French speakers) during the Laval festivities. As for the SSJBQ, it explained in its annual report: 'We would not want to undermine the good impression made by our demonstration of 23 June [during the Laval celebration].' It will never be known whether this meant that the SSJBQ was not up to the task, or whether the society realized that its English-speaking partners were not going to come through, thus leaving it with the opportunity of looking foolish, marching after the party was all but over.[40] In 1908, as in 1898, the society was marginalized during a celebration of Champlain. In each case it was shunted aside after others came forward with the resources to foot the bill.

One Parade Dies and Another Is Born

The SSJBQ was an umbrella organization that brought together such moderate figures as Chouinard and Turgeon, who willingly participated in the transformation of the tercentenary, as well as more nationalist figures, who were troubled by the changes to Chouinard's original design. Even the latter members were not so zealous that they were ready to look foolish by marching in a parade after the party was over. A completely different logic was at work in the minds of the leaders of the ACJC.

For these uncompromising defenders, both lay and clerical, of a French Catholic nation, there was scarcely a break between the closing of the Laval festivities and the start of the tercentenary. Though the

Laval celebrations officially ended on 23 June, the ACJC stayed in Quebec City for another three days to hold its first *congrès général.* Before the convention was over, delegates had been treated to more than fifty speeches on a wide range of subjects of interest to French-speaking Catholics. Most seemed besieged by the dangers lurking around. The last day of the convention was in many ways the most interesting, since it was designed to light a fire under the members to continue their vigilance into July, the month of the tercentenary. Henri Bourassa had been scheduled to speak. In his absence, Armand Lavergne called for the crowd to be faithful to its Catholic and French roots, and to think of Catholicism not only as 'a religion for parades, to be celebrated superficially, but rather a religion that has to be lived, which has to provide a constant and healthy influence.' At the same time, it was essential 'that we remain French in our language, customs and beliefs.'[41]

In this last regard, Lavergne welcomed the presence of Pierre Gerlier, the representative of the ACJC's sister organization in France, who embodied 'the France which was Catholic and traditional.' Gerlier had been a last-minute participant in the Laval celebrations, and had stayed for the ACJC convention. He was asked to address both the opening and closing ceremonies; at the latter, he presented the final speech. This was not by accident, since the question of the participation during the tercentenary of the representatives of godless France, embodied by the Third Republic, had risen from time to time during the convention. Particular aim was taken against Louis Herbette, who had been named to the French delegation and who was already under attack in the local Catholic press for a variety of sins, including his Masonic connections. Gerlier provided the desired contrast with Herbette, and he did not disappoint his hosts. He was leaving Canada shortly after the convention, and he hinted that he was tempted to stay around for the tercentenary to do battle with the enemies of Catholicism. In the end, however, he reminded his audience that though they had challenges to face, France's were more daunting and required the services of *un soldat du Christ* such as himself.[42]

After Camarade Gerlier (as he was referred to in the ACJC's internal documents) had fired up the crowd, the convention closed with the passage of a number of resolutions designed to recommit French-Canadian youth to the defence of their nation by fighting such evils as urban life, alcohol, and Jewish immigration. The chronicler of the meeting closed his account: 'Adieu! Non! ... Quebec is going to see us once again next month in order to celebrate its heroic founder and to begin the series of tercentenary fetes by means of a grandiose demonstration.' There was no mistaking that the ACJC intended to celebrate the memory of Champlain, the French-Catholic hero, who was being marginalized in the organization of the tercentenary. More specifically, the association planned to stage an event at the Monument Champlain for 19 July; this was designed to intrude on the tercentenary, Earl Grey's 'fete tainted by imperialism,' which had been scheduled to begin on the following day.[43]

From the start, the leaders of the association and those organizing the tercentenary were on different wavelengths. The Quebec City chapter of the ACJC, which was responsible for the demonstration, claimed that it had asked the tercentenary organizers for $200 to help stage the event, only to be turned down. For their part, those same officials insisted that the association had asked for nothing more that 'the moral support of the committee' – support that was immediately offered.[44] It seemed that the tercentenary organizers wanted to appear sympathetic toward the ACJC celebration, albeit without providing any visible sign of support that might be viewed negatively by English-speaking Protestants, discomfited by the presentation of Champlain as a Catholic figure. In this spirit, the NBC published programs indicating that the two-week-long celebration was now slated to begin on 19 July – not 20 July as had long been the case – with a demonstration at the Monument Champlain. In spite of this apparent sign of support, the chairman of the NBC and mayor of Quebec, George Garneau, along with the other tercentenary leaders, managed to find something else to do on the day of the ACJC celebration. In the letter indicating he was unavailable, Garneau referred to the event as 'a worthy prologue to the magnificent celebrations about to begin.' This expression was echoed in the official publication issued after the tercentenary, which viewed the events of 19 July as having been *une prélude* – little more than a warm-up act and not really part of the main event. Another publication simply ignored this celebration of a French Catholic nation altogether, presenting 20 July as the real start of the fête.[45]

For their part, the leaders of the ACJC saw their celebration more as the conclusion of the Laval fête than as the start of a new one. In the weeks between the close of their convention and their demonstration at the foot of the Monument Champlain on 19 July, they never really rested, organizing a series of rallies in working-class areas of town where people were already suspicious of the motives of leaders such as Earl Grey.[46] To combat this cynicism, the tercentenary's promoters organized a public meeting in the St-Roch district in early July, at which Garneau –

who would be too busy to attend the ACJC celebration – took a leading role. He tried to connect with his audience by playing the class card, noting that he had come 'much like you, from a long line of workers.' Charles Langelier, who was responsible for recruiting volunteers for the pageants (and who would later play Champlain), tried the same tack, referring to Champlain as 'a talented worker ... who undertook the construction of our beautiful Quebec.'[47]

Garneau and his colleagues received good reviews for their performance at the meeting, even in the Catholic journal *Action sociale*. Perhaps they drew away some support from the ACJC; even so, plenty of people turned out for the association's rallies in the following weeks: 3,000 at the next one, in the St-Sauveur district, and another 1,500 (certainly more than Garneau had attracted) at one in St-Roch.[48] Some of the speakers took parting shots at the tercentenary, but most emphasized the importance of the demonstration on 19 July for those who wanted to present Champlain as a resolutely French Catholic hero. One speaker observed: 'Champlain was one of those who believed that religion has always been the best source of nourishment for patriotism and that nothing better supports a flag than a cross.'[49]

As befit a Catholic event, the ACJC demonstration on the eve of the tercentenary began with a procession. This one bore a certain resemblance to the St-Jean-Baptiste parade that had passed through the streets only a few weeks earlier at the close of the Laval celebrations. The two followed different routes, but each started in a working-class section of the city and ended at a monument to a founding father. The 5,000 who participated in the ACJC procession were not arranged by occupational associations, as had been the case in the larger St-Jean-Baptiste parade. Instead, almost all the marchers were Catholic youth, and they were organized by parishes. As in the St-Jean-Baptiste *défilé*, there was a hierarchy: after the parade of the parishes came the Garde Indépendante Champlain, whose prominence had been magnified by the refusal of tercentenary organizers to encourage its participation in the 'mainstream' celebration. Bringing up the rear were members of the royal family of Catholic organizations, *les Zouaves pontificaux*, accompanied by a last-minute addition to the procession – two groups of young men dressed as Montcalm's soldiers. This suggested that the ACJC rally was not completely detached from the tercentenary; this rearguard would perform again in the weeks to come in both the pageants and the historical procession connected to them.[50]

The procession was watched by an estimated 25,000, people, who so

Demonstration by ACJC at the Monument Champlain on the eve of the tercentenary, 1908 (Archives de la Ville de Québec, negative, 7148)

impeded the marchers that the police had to clear the route for them. After arriving at the Monument Champlain, the senior members, who had brought up the rear, formed an honour guard in front of the monument, which was to serve as the speakers' podium. The papal flag and *le drapeau de Carillon* – a fixture at events like this – were prominently displayed, and the monument was decorated with floral crowns recalling the crowns that had marked the reburial of Mgr de Laval thirty years earlier.

Once everyone and everything was in place, the speakers addressed the crowd that had filled the open area around the statue and two stands constructed for the occasion. First to speak was Maurice Dupré, president of the Quebec City chapter of the ACJC, who had as much to say about Laval as about Champlain, thus reinforcing the sense that this was as much the end of Laval's celebration as the start of Champlain's. He went out of his way to draw parallels between the lives of the two heroes: 'Just as Mgr de Laval had a heart that was French as well as the soul of an apostle, so too was Champlain as interested in being a good Christian as he was in promoting the interests of his adopted land.' The speakers who followed carefully noted Champlain's French and Catholic roots, emphasizing the latter in order to distinguish him from the representatives of the godless France who were beginning to arrive in town. In this vein, Ernest Légaré hoped for the rise 'of a new and Catholic France ... God will not abandon France, his eldest daughter.'[51]

After the speeches, the ACJC rally came to a close. While many in the crowd would go on to watch or participate in the tercentenary events, the ACJC event had been designed to send a strong political message about the continued existence of a French Catholic people. This does much to explain why the tercentenary organizers stayed away. The absence of the leaders of Quebec Catholicism is a bit more difficult to explain. The official account of the youth rally would state that the stands had been packed with 'monseigneurs, priests and members of religious orders,' yet not a single church official was identified by name, which suggests that the leaders may not have been on hand. Furthermore, there is no evidence that any curés preached to their parishioners that they should take part in the event. Contrast this with the considerable clerical support for the rather modest celebrations at the Monument Champlain earlier in the month, on the precise anniversary of Champlain's arrival at Quebec.[52]

Watching all these events unfold was the omnipresent Alfred Paré, just back from a brief rest following the Laval celebrations. Reflecting the suspicions of the hierarchy about this demonstration, Paré viewed it with a jaundiced eye. He complained that the speakers could not be heard over the strong breeze and that the affair went on far too long. One speaker was so long-winded that each time he stopped to take a drink of water, there was a sigh of exasperation from the crowd, which thought that his pause meant the speech was finally finished: 'At the end of his long speech, the square before him was almost empty; spectators had even left the grandstands ... The general feeling was that the demonstration had been a total flop. It was lacking both spirit and organization. Only the procession made an impact ... There was really little enthusiasm for the event.'[53] The photographs left behind provide some support for Paré's observations; they show the stands as at least partially empty. Other photos, perhaps taken earlier in the afternoon, show dense crowds in attendance. In the end, Paré emphasized and probably exaggerated the negative in order to demean an event that had little support within the local ecclesiastical establishment.[54]

The French Connection

The SSJBQ and the Garde Indépendante Champlain having been purged from the 'official' events of the tercentenary, the ACJC rally became one of the few moments in late July for celebrating the Catholic legacy of French Canadians. Certainly, it was the only event in the streets of Quebec in which a Catholic past was celebrated to any great degree. Though the pageants contained pages from that past, the procession of historical actors that had bumped the St-Jean-Baptiste parade from the program contained nothing more than 'a handful of costumed priests [who] appeared in the retinue of Henri IV, the Protestant convert.'[55] In spite of this marginalizing of matters Catholic, Abbé Paré and his superiors were prepared to separate themselves from the ACJC event because besides being a celebration of Catholicism, it was a harsh public rebuke of the regime then ruling France. In light of the considerable hostility toward the Third Republic, one might have expected the Catholic establishment to embrace the tone of the ACJC rally, but it didn't. To understand why, we must look into the complicated relationship between Quebec's ecclesiastical leaders, the British authorities, the Vatican representative in Canada, and the French government.

First let us consider how Paré and his colleagues viewed the Third Republic, at least in private, in the first decade of the new century. As we saw in regard to the unveiling of the Monument Laval, while representatives of *la France catholique* were welcome, those of the French government were *persona non grata*. Their position was hardly softened by reports in the press in the midst of the tercentenary that the conflict between the Catholic hierarchy in France and the French government was heating up.[56] Paré reflected this francophobic attitude on the very morning of the ACJC rally when he observed in his diary that both British and French sailors were in town to take part in the naval manoeuvres that would form part of the tercentenary. While the English sailors

were parading triumphantly through the streets of our town, the poor French sailors received no public sympathy from French Canadians. They

are looked at with indifference, because today the government of the
French Republic is atheist and persecutes the Church in France ... Much
has changed about the popular view of the French. Roughly ten years ago
when French battleships still had chaplains aboard, there was much public
cheering for the sailors ... The English were furious about that ... Today,
sympathy goes automatically to the English, and the French are all but
ignored.'[57]

Paré tended to be fairly temperate in his reactions to the events around
him, yet when it came to the Third Republic, he minced no words in the
years leading up to the tercentenary. In particular, he shared the view of
many in the local Catholic establishment regarding the cause for the
departure of Alfred Kleczkowski, the popular French consul who had
distinguished himself in 1898 during the unveiling of the Monument
Champlain. Paré believed that the consul had been chased from his post
in 1906 as a result of the machinations 'of the Freemasons of Montreal
who demanded that the French government recall him because he was
too clerically-inclined.' The source for this accusation was the ultramontane *La Vérité*, which on the eve of Kleczkowski's departure published
documents which 'proved' that a conspiracy had led to the consul's
transfer to Uruguay. According to this paper, freemasons based in Montreal had contacted their counterparts in Paris to pressure the French
government for Kleczkowski's removal. The consul, according to the
documents, deserved this fate 'because instead of representing the Republic's interests with sincerity and dignity, he used his office to harm
the interests of French republicans, and at the same time to protect the
priests and members of religious orders from France who were coming
to establish themselves in Canada.'[58]

The more liberal newspapers threw cold water on the 'Kleczkowski
Incident,' noting that there was something odd about the consul being
promoted as part of his ouster. To this *La Vérité* replied, in the spirit of all
believers in conspiracies, that this was the beauty of the plot: the consul
had been removed (which was all that the masons had wanted), but the
culprits were not suspected because it looked like a promotion.[59] However tortured the logic, the suspicions surrounding Kleczkowski's departure did not die; they surfaced during the ACJC convention that followed
the unveiling of the Monument Laval.[60] In the aftermath of Kleczkowski's
departure, relations between the clergy and the consul's successors were
cool to say the least. Paré, for instance, thought that the lieutenant-
governor should refuse to have any dealings with Kleczkowski's immedi-

ate replacement until he showed himself to be a real *français catholique*.[61]

All of this helps explain why clerical authorities reacted with horror at the thought that representatives of the French state might be invited to take part in the celebration that Grey was promoting. In 1898, Kleczkowski had represented France; in 1908, it was feared that a higher-ranking official might be sent as a representative to cement the close ties between France and England that had been established in 1904 by the Entente cordiale. Grey felt that this accord had made French representation necessary; he also saw the tercentenary as an occasion for improving relations between French and English speaking Canadians. With England at peace with France, 'we have an opportunity before us, for the first time in the history of Canada, of securing the active co-operation and goodwill of the French Canadians in an attempt to put the famous battlefields of Quebec in a shape worthy of their traditions.'[62]

Perhaps Grey did not understand French Canadians' general antipathy toward France; perhaps he did understand but didn't care. In any event, his support for French participation provoked considerable behind-the-scenes manoeuvring. Beginning in the fall of 1905, the anti-French campaign was watched over from Ottawa by Abbé Alfred Sinnott, the secretary to the apostolic delegate, Mgr Donato Sbarretti. When the unveiling of the Monument Laval was slated to form part of the tercentenary celebrations, Sinnott observed in a letter to Mgr Mathieu, the rector of the university: 'In view of the attitude of the [French] Government towards the church and the cruel war it has made upon religious orders and the Catholic religion, would it not be very strange if representatives of that Government were invited and given places of honour in any festivities held in Catholic Quebec? On the contrary, it would be a nice tribute to old Catholic France and just rebuke to the present Government, if there were present from the mother country some member of the Hierarchy or some distinguished French layman who has been valiant in defence of Catholic rights – but no representative of Official France.'[63] Not much had changed by the beginning of 1907, when Sinnott wrote again to Mgr Mathieu that 'a Catholic city founded by Catholics could not and ought not invite to festivities altogether Catholic a government actually engaged in a most scandalous persecution of religion.'[64]

Mgr Mathieu listened patiently to Sinnott's concerns, but he never seemed eager to get into a public brawl over this issue, recognizing how important it was for his institution – and Quebec Catholicism more generally – to maintain good working relationships with the federal government and the British representative in Canada. The office of the apostolic delegate tended to view matters from a different perspective, preoccupied as it was with the Vatican's broader diplomatic agenda, which in this case focused on relations with France. This was not the first time that the delegate and officials in Quebec had not seen eye to eye. Ever since the position of apostolic delegate had been created in the late nineteenth century, there had been frequent squabbling over French Catholic minority rights, with the delegate showing little interest in fighting with Ottawa to defend the use of French. Moreover, by 1908 Mgr Bégin and Mgr Sbarretti had been arguing for a number of years over the holding of a meeting of all Canadian bishops; each claimed the right to preside: the former because his diocese was the oldest, the latter because he was the representative of Rome.[65]

By the start of 1907, Sinnott was heating up his attack against French participation in the tercentenary. For his part, Mgr Mathieu was preaching calm, especially in light of the imminent separation of the Laval and Champlain festivities. It now seemed likely that the latter would be delayed until 1909. Mgr Mathieu thought the apostolic delegate would be pleased that French representation at the unveiling of the Monument Laval could be avoided: 'This will provide us with the opportunity to stage a beautiful religious and civic celebration.' In fact, Mgr Sbarretti was so sharply focused on the Champlain fête that he never showed any great interest in the Laval celebrations. The apostolic delegate failed to contribute to the construction of the monument until the very last minute; even then, he provided only $30. This slight was not lost on Paré, who remarked in his diary: 'It seems that the Italians receive more readily than they give.'[66]

Now that Laval had been removed from the picture, Mgr Mathieu was philosophical about the tercentenary. He even hoped that with the Champlain celebrations scheduled for 1909, there would be time to use quiet diplomacy to persuade Laurier and his colleagues to 'adopt our way of thinking.'[67] However, if the rector of the university had hoped to dampen Sinnott's thirst for waging war against *la France officielle*, he failed dismally. By the fall of 1907, when it still seemed that the tercentenary would be held in 1909, Mgr Sbarretti's assistant had taken charge of a campaign to plant articles in Catholic newspapers across Canada that would lay out the dangers of allowing French participation in the celebration of the founding of a French Catholic settlement. Sinnott hoped these articles would influence public opinion and, ultimately, force political leaders to do the right thing. In some of the many letters he wrote as part of his campaign, Sinnott encouraged priests to plant articles pointing out 'the impropriety of inviting representatives of an avowedly anti-Catholic government. The only true representative of the France loved by the French Canadians would be a member of the French hierarchy or some distinguished layman.' He advised his correspondents that it was important to 'return again and again to the subject, if necessary, in order to create a correct public opinion upon this important matter.'[68]

Sinnott's campaign had little impact on public opinion. Even so, the question of France's role in the tercentenary remained contentious. The issue heated up in early 1908, when the fête was definitely slated for later that year, with the Prince of Wales scheduled to play the leading role. The presence of the prince increased fears that there would be a French presence, and a prestigious one at that. Recognizing the depth of clerical concerns, Grey skilfully earned some political capital by agreeing to participate in the unveiling of the Monument Laval. As H.V. Nelles put it: 'When Grey asked for [the bishops'] support of the tercentenary, they had a request to make of him. Would he kindly attend a little celebration [in honour of Mgr de Laval] they were planning.' Mgr Bégin and his colleagues may have been displeased with various aspects of the tercentenary, including the French presence, but in the end they kept a diplomatic silence, assuaged by such actions as the inclusion of the Duke of Norfolk, 'the most prominent Catholic layman in Great Britain and said to be a close confidant of the pope.'[69]

As the tercentenary approached, Mgr Sbarretti decided he would boycott all events at which members of the French delegation were present. In the end, he only managed to meet the prince – who was usually in the company of the Frenchmen at public functions – by attending a private luncheon for the heir to the throne held at the seminary's country retreat.[70] Unlike the apostolic delegate, the local ecclesiastical leaders avoided making a show of their displeasure; in this, they were honouring their understanding with the governor general. Mgr Bégin and his colleagues by now recognized that some French representation was inevitable, and they tried to make the best of a bad situation. Yet they must have been pleased when the French government decided to send a delegation far less prestigious than the ones representing England (led by the heir to the throne) and the United States (led by Vice-President Fairbanks, who had also been part of the American delegation in 1898). There is no evidence that the British asked the French to send a delegation headed by a mere vice-admiral; nor do internal

French documents explain why Horace-Anne-Alfred Jauréguiberry was appointed. Most likely, the French realized they were going to receive a rough treatment from the local population and decided to cut their losses by sending a relatively low-ranking delegation.

Though the French had reduced the stakes by sending a kindly (albeit Protestant) military man, other aspects of the mission were meant to provoke clerical authorities. It was almost as if the French government was telegraphing its displeasure at the warm welcome Quebec had extended to members of religious communities seeking a new home.[71] For instance, the French displayed a certain malice when they sent Jauréguiberry to Quebec aboard the warship *Léon Gambetta* – named after one of the founders of the much-hated Third Republic – as a last-minute replacement for the *Montcalm*, whose name might have evoked a far more positive response from French-speaking Catholics in Quebec. Even more provocative, however, was the inclusion of Louis Herbette, a long-time *conseiller d'état*, in the delegation. The French foreign ministry claimed that Herbette had earned his place on the basis of 'the services he has rendered towards the development of Franco-Canadian relations,' but this was only part of the story.[72]

Herbette was no stranger to Quebec, having visited the province several times, often to meet with groups or individuals who were at odds with the Catholic church. Because of his fondness for Quebecers, the poet Louis Fréchette referred to him as 'Oncle Herbette.' However, if Herbette was the uncle of French Canadians, the tie that linked him to this branch of *la famille française* was strictly linguistic. He did not show the least interest in the Catholic dimension of French-Canadian identity, and as a result some were dismayed by his appearance in an official capacity at a celebration of the founding of a French Catholic civilization in North America.[73]

In 1908, Herbette was accused in the Catholic press of various sins: of having links with the Masonic lodges involved in the Kleczkowski affair; of participating in the closing of religious orders in France; and of involvement in la Ligue française de l'Enseignement, a French organization devoted to making schools 'secular, free, and compulsory.' This group had been the inspiration for the Ligue d'enseignement, established in Montreal in 1902. The Montreal-based League was not prepared to go as far as its French counterpart, yet its very existence suggested the infiltration of anticlerical ideas. Accordingly, the Quebec clergy railed against the league, thus precipitating its demise.[74] By the time of the tercentenary it had been dead for five years, but the fact that it had ever existed at all, and its connections with France, fuelled the anger against Herbette. Recognizing how deeply he was hated, Herbette chose not to travel to Canada on one of the French warships, to avoid embarrassing the other members of the delegation, who might be found guilty by association by Catholic leaders in Quebec.[75]

In the months leading up to the tercentenary, the French Catholic press focused sharply on Herbette. Typical of this was the wish published by *La Vérité* that 'our compatriots should remember the exploits of Oncle Herbette and should give the welcome that he deserves in a strongly Catholic land.' Toward the end of the tercentenary, the same journal reported that there had been 'widespread outrage against Oncle Herbette in the French-Canadian press.' By the time it left Quebec City, the French delegation recognized that it had suffered from 'a certain coolness because the newspapers criticized the composition of our mission prior to our arrival.'[76] This animosity was not lost on the Prince of Wales, who asked Mgr Mathieu, the rector of the university: 'Why is there such antipathy towards these people?' Mgr Mathieu pointed the finger at Herbette: 'This gentleman claims to be a Catholic and yet he is a dangerous influence for our French-Canadian Catholic youth. He sees himself as the emancipator of our young people from their religious beliefs, which this old idiot views as outdated and only suited to preserving the ignorance of the young ... There you have it, Your Majesty, this is a man who is dangerous for our youth.'[77]

To be fair, the French delegation was being damned for past sins, real or imagined. That being said, it didn't help itself by behaving the way it did during the tercentenary. In particular, it went out of its way to clash with Mgr Bégin over French participation in a mass that was to be celebrated on the Plains of Abraham halfway into the fête. Only days before the Sunday in question, the French consul, Joseph de Loynes, wrote to the archbishop to inform him that 'the members of the French Delegation are prepared to attend the solemn mass' so that they might 'provide a sign of their respect for the religious sentiments of the French-Canadian people.' There is no reason to believe that the members of the delegation had any particular desire to attend the mass. Rather, they saw this as an opportunity to embarrass the clergy, correctly calculating that Mgr Bégin was not about to issue an invitation that would immediately be brandished by Herbette as evidence of the archbishop's surrender. So the former wrote that such invitations were not his responsibility: 'I have nothing to do with the organization of this item on the program for the fetes.'

Had Mgr Bégin wanted to extend an invitation, he could certainly have done so. When he withheld his blessings, the French were able to play the part of innocent victims. Loynes observed after the fête was over:

> I scarcely need to say that, in spite of the negative attitudes encouraged by the press, the conduct of the clerical leaders received something less than general approval ... The Honourable Lieutenant-Governor, Sir Louis Jetté, declined to accept the seat that had been reserved for him next to the Duke of Norfolk, as a response to our exclusion. It must be noted that from this date there was a remarkable reversal [of the view towards us] among all classes of the population ... If the admiral had been able to prolong his stay, the coolness from the beginning would have given way to sympathy which was growing all the time.[78]

Although Loynes may have been correct in viewing Jetté's absence as a sign of solidarity with Herbette, there is no reason to think that public opinion turned against the archbishop and toward the French delegation as a result of the bickering over the invitation to the mass.[79] In the end, however, accuracy was really beside the point, since the consul's account was for the internal use of his ministry. Nevertheless, the story points to the willingness of the French delegation to embarrass the hierarchy when given the opportunity. Had local ecclesiastical leaders participated in the ACJC rally, during which the French government was loudly criticized, the representatives of *la France officielle* would have had a golden opportunity to present themselves as victims of church intolerance. Better to ignore Herbette and his colleagues as much as possible – a strategy that also suited Earl Grey, who badly wanted Catholic tolerance of (if not enthusiastic support for) the tercentenary. It made sense for Mgr Bégin and his associates to keep quiet about the representatives from France, especially with Grey offering his participation in the unveiling of the Monument Laval as part of the package.

Dressing Up the Town

After the ACJC demonstration at the Monument Champlain – an event that some saw as little more than a prelude to the tercentenary – the 'real' celebration started. Tens of thousands of visitors flooded the city, crowned by the arrival of the most prestigious guest, the Prince of Wales. His appearance three days after the French Catholic celebration kicked off a series of spectacular events, some through the streets of Quebec

City, others on the Plains of Abraham. But even before the program had really begun, there was much for visitors and residents to observe: the city had been transformed by a variety of decorations.

The question of decorations bedevilled the organizers, who wanted to appeal to visitors without alienating French Canadians. Which flags were to be flown? English? French? Canadian? French-Canadian? None of these were 'neutral.' One newspaper reported that the streets had been festooned by 'foreign decorators,' who had hung 'multicolour flags' bearing such markings as suns and moons, 'everything other than the emblems with which we are familiar ... The bizarre flags, whose appearance has been widely deplored, have still not disappeared from our streets.'[80] By the time the tercentenary began in earnest the city had been decked out, through the efforts of local citizens, businesses, and NBC officials, with a wide variety of more conventional decorations – albeit ones that underlined the divisive nature of the event.

Much of the city ended up with decorations reflecting the legacy of France and England, whose newly established friendship was an important element of the tercentenary. The monarchs from Champlain's Canadian career were celebrated along a corridor running from the port up the steep Côte de la Montagne, past the Monument Laval, to the statue honouring Champlain. In the days to come this route would see the first journey through the streets of Quebec by the Prince of Wales, followed by a historical procession of actors who would later perform in the pageants. Henri IV and Louis XIII were celebrated in this district of Quebec City; English monarchs dominated the streets leading to the Plains of Abraham, through which various parades would pass. Reflecting Grey's desire that the plains become a symbol of imperial strength, this part of town – an English-speaking enclave – was decked out with banners in honour of every monarch from William IV (1820–30) to Edward VII. The current king was also saluted by means of a huge flag hanging from the facade of the legislative building facing the Grande-Allée.[81] The only exception to this celebration of the empire was the strategic positioning next to Edward VII of Henri IV; this added to the spirit of *bonne entente* between England and France, which the tercentenary organizers hoped to reinforce.

Just around the corner, the front of the legislative buildings told a very different story through banners celebrating the two founding fathers. Both were presented in assertive poses. Champlain was shown wearing an 'obsidional crown' – a term from antiquity for a crown bestowed on someone having led a siege. Laval was decked out much as he had been on his statue, with his 'mitre, ecclesiastical hat, and cross.'[82] This celebration of Quebec's French legacy, both lay and clerical, continued with the various decorations in front of the legislature that had been commissioned by the Quebec government (i.e., not the tercentenary organizers) and designed by Eugène-Étienne Taché. The architect and long-time civil servant had come up with the original plans for the building over thirty years earlier and had, in the process, authored the province's motto, 'Je me souviens.' For the tercentenary, Taché arranged for the construction of sixteen immense urns filled with flowers; each was crowned by the coat of arms of either a French town (such as Brouage) or a French leader (such as Richelieu) with which Quebec City had had a connection.[83]

But Taché's most spectacular contribution to the tercentenary was his design of a *temple du souvenir* to house a bust of Champlain by the sculptor Louis Jobin. This was the only structure built in Champlain's honour in 1908, and it is perhaps a reflection of Champlain's marginal role that Taché's 'temple' was referred to, in one of the English-language commemorative volumes, as a 'Crowned Arch' or 'Ionic Arch,' without any reference to *le fondateur* by name.[84] These descriptions merely pointed to the physical characteristics of the sixty-four-foot-tall structure, within which rested the rather small bust of Champlain. There was a huge base, on which rested the compartment holding the bust, covered by a roof held up by six Ionic columns. The structure was capped with 'the royal crown of France,' to recall the role of the French state. At the same time, the structure also had religious significance, in that it resembled a *reposoir* as might have been found in Fête-Dieu processions such as the one staged in association with the Laval celebration. A *reposoir* was a huge structure with a raised platform on which a priest stood holding the host before the faithful, who would drop to their knees in prayer. Here, however, Champlain occupied the place of the host.[85] This spectacular monument was removed shortly after the tercentenary, and no trace of it has survived. But even during the celebration of Champlain, it was a marginal part of the show, situated off the beaten path of the major processions through the streets of Quebec.

A few blocks from the legislative buildings, visitors to Quebec City would have seen still other references to Quebec's French Catholic legacy: a series of banners decorating rue St-Jean, where the parades from the Laval celebration had passed in June. Gone were references to the glory of Catholicism, such as the banner that read JESUS, RULE OVER US, PROTECT US, SAVE US. This had been replaced by concrete tributes to

Temple du souvenir, 1908 (Archives nationales du Québec à Québec, P418, S2, D4, P3)

a heritage that had both religious and secular components. There were banners in honour of religious institutions such as the seminary and state ones such as the Sovereign Council. There were also tributes to individuals as diverse as Marguerite Bourgeoys and Jean Talon. Like the decorations in front of the legislative buildings, those on rue St-Jean would not have been seen by spectators of or participants in the major processions, which largely kept either to the Côte de la Montagne or to the roads leading to the plains. This marginalization generated complaints. For example, a prominent merchant was unhappy that the parade of pageant performers was to be routed away from rue St-Jean, 'the most commercial street in Upper Town,' in order to accommodate the comings and goings of the Prince of Wales.[86]

Even in the absence of a procession down the main commercial artery of the upper town, visitors might still have seen the decorations on rue St-Jean as they wandered through the city. They were less likely to see the decorations in the St-Roch and St-Sauveur districts which were perhaps, the most interesting in town. English-speaking tourists rarely ventured into these French-Canadian working-class districts – a point underscored by the experience of Vice-President Fairbanks, who only found himself in them when he became lost.[87] Evidently, the decorations in this part of the city were for local consumption.

These decorations took advantage of the many *arcs de triomphe* left over from the Laval celebrations. As one journal put it: 'The arches, having been cleaned up, looked like new. They received a new coat of paint; they were covered with artificial flowers and with inscriptions which made reference to certain facts worthy of being chiselled into our memory.' There were tributes to the first settlers of New France, to martyrs who had died for the faith, to the governors and intendants of New France, and to the bishops of Quebec from Laval to Bégin. There were also banners overhanging the streets naming the heroes of French-Canadian history, the founders of cities across North America (ranging from Champlain to J.B. Beaulieu, the founder of Chicago), and the premiers of Quebec since Confederation. Nowhere was there the slightest reference to anyone who was English-speaking; presumably this was part of an effort to soften the occasionally loud opposition from this part of town to the tercentenary.[88]

Champlain Day?

Most of the people in town, French and English speaking, residents and visitors, civilians and military personnel, would have recognized that the fête had really begun with the arrival of the Prince of Wales on the fourth day. On this subject, there was little to choose between the *Montreal Star*'s assertion on the day of the landing of the prince that 'all that has occurred hitherto is but a preface to his reception' and the screaming headline in *Action sociale* announcing, now that the prince had arrived, the start of 'Les Grandes Fêtes de Québec.'[89] While English-Canadian enthusiasm was to be expected, tercentenary officials must have breathed a sigh of relief when the prince's arrival was met without a word of protest from French Canadians. In contrast with the reception reserved for the delegation from France, the arrival of the heir to the throne was greeted not only with the firing of cannons, but also with the ringing of the bells of the Basilica – a signal that the church was on side for this event. Even the *nationalistes* retained a polite silence regarding the prince's participation; they saw him as someone simply carrying out an assignment. After he had boarded the battleship that would take him back to Britain, they would sing a different tune, but no one could have known that on the day of his arrival.

There was no active protest against the prince; that being said, French Canadians participated little in the various events built around his presence. *Le Nationaliste* clearly overstated the point when it observed at the end of the celebration that French speakers 'did not figure to any great degree in the processions over the last few days; they have made little noise and have avoided raising their voices either to show their approval or to protest.'[90] Nevertheless, the reaction of French Canadians to two parades on 23 July, the prince's first full day in Quebec City, suggests that some aspects of the tercentenary were greeted with more enthusiasm than others. Of course, so many people were in town that any reluctance on the part of French speakers perhaps went unnoticed.

The first of these parades grew out of a massive military review scheduled for the Plains of Abraham on 24 July. However, as would be the case for the pageants, 'seating was limited, expensive, and the best seats were by invitation only.' The local French press lobbied hard for these militia units to take to the streets so that ordinary French Canadians could catch a glimpse of the militiamen, most of whom would have been English speakers. In a sense, this parade filled the void left by the cancellation of the military-style *défilé* of the SSJBQ. In one of the souvenir volumes produced after the fête, the holding of the parade was attributed to the 'request of the citizens of Quebec'; this made it the only tercentenary event with popular roots.[91]

The Canadian officers who had planned a rehearsal of their military review for the morning of 23 July did not need much convincing to take their 12,000 troops to the streets. In the process, they succeeded in staging an event that was not on the official program – no small feat for a celebration that had been orchestrated down to the smallest detail. There were no dignitaries on hand; most of these would have been readying themselves for the 'official' event that would come later in the afternoon. For his part, the Prince of Wales, with cannons booming in the background, was visiting the French and American battleships in the harbour. In spite of, or perhaps because of, the absence of dignitaries, an estimated 60,000 people came out for the parade. From the descriptions in the press, most of them were French-Canadian residents of Quebec City. As Desmond Morton put it, here was an opportunity for 'poorer people, unable to take their place in the grandstands [to] have a small share of the military excitement.'[92]

Other aspects of the tercentenary had seemed to marginalize ordinary French Canadians. In contrast, this event spoke to them on various levels. There were no imperial trappings to compromise the parade, so it was able to respond to the *nationaliste* desire to see Canadians, both English and French speaking, working together for the common good. Henri Bourassa himself might have enjoyed this event had he been in the country. As one newspaper observed, French Canadians could identify with this parade, which suggested a time 'when our fathers ... were passing through the streets of the young city founded by Champlain in order to rush to the defence of a country in danger.' Another remarked: 'Our soldiers were greeted with applause by the enormous crowd that was packed together as they passed by. Everything about this parade prompted the strongest feeling of proud admiration.'[93] The route itself had been chosen to bring the marchers to the people. On leaving the Plains of Abraham, the militiamen entered the old city, passing in front of the Basilica and along the rue St-Jean (which would be bypassed later in the day) before heading down to the St-Roch district. In light of the housing problems in the city, the parade then divided itself; some sections headed to their temporary quarters in a park to the west, others made their way to a ferry, which took them across the river to Lévis.

While the Lévis-based militiamen slipped quietly across the St. Lawrence, the harbour began drawing visitors for the second event of the day, one that was unambiguously official. The arrival of the reconstructed version of Champlain's ship the *Don de Dieu* marked the beginning of what the program referred to, perhaps ill-advisedly, as 'Champlain Day.' Some people saw a problem with assigning a single day to Champlain, since it suggested that the other twelve days were a celebra-

Military parade, 1908 (Archives nationales du Québec à Québec; Keystone View Co, 1908; P1000, S4, D62, P16206)

tion of empire. Other French Canadians were troubled by the greeting that had been arranged for the arrival of Champlain's ship. Clearly, the good spirit of the morning had evaporated by afternoon.

In a careful piece of choreography, the *Don de Dieu* approached the port exactly as had the HMS *Indomitable*, carrying the Prince of Wales, on the previous day. The prince had been taken from the battleship to the wharf by a small launch; on this day, Champlain (Charles Langelier in costume) and his party were transported in canoes by natives, in one of their many tercentenary appearances.[94] When Champlain disembarked, he was literally following in the footsteps of the prince. More than one French-language paper noted the rather glaring difference between the two events: the first had been marked by the booming of cannons and the pealing of bells; this one was shrouded in silence. In an article titled 'Déçus' (Deceived), one newspaper observed: 'Those who came out ... to enjoy the salute of the cannons upon the arrival of Champlain have been deceived ... Aside from the whistling noises coming from the steam ships which saluted him, not even the smallest cannon raised its voice.' Abbé Paré, who had spent the morning at the military parade, which he called 'an immense and brilliant procession,' watched the arrival of Champlain's ship with dismay: 'There was neither the thundering of the cannons, nor the pealing of the bells of the city, as had been advertised. This troubled more than one "canayen," who might have come to the conclusion that the event had been staged by the English, in a manner that would sap its dramatic appeal.'[95]

The sense that Champlain was being upstaged was reinforced by the organizers' decision to have the prince officially declare the start of the tercentenary in front of the Monument Champlain, just as the *Don de Dieu* was pulling into port. Here, the prince and the *fondateur* were being placed in direct conflict with each other; the estimated 150,000 spectators were being forced to choose between the two.[96] Those standing on Dufferin Terrace, who had arrived hours earlier for a good view, might have been able to steal glances at what was going on down below, but they would not have been able to appreciate the details of the re-creation of Champlain's arrival. One observer remarked in terms of the natives welcoming Champlain: 'Unfortunately, not many people saw the Indians in their canoes close enough to appreciate the scene.'[97]

Probably, most spectators focused on the events near the Monument Champlain, where many of the important figures in attendance addressed the crowd. Predictably, Mayor Garneau, Earl Grey, Vice-President Fairbanks, and Admiral Jauréguiberry all participated. Perhaps a bit more surprising was the presence of Adélard Turgeon, who had been asked by Laurier to represent the Canadian government. Though Turgeon had a reputation as an orator, his presence probably also had to do with the fact that he was president of the SSJBQ, and so in a position to mollify the tercentenary's critics, including those within the society who were still annoyed that they were not formally participating in the fête. Clearly, however, the star of the show was the Prince of Wales, who reflected some of the tensions in the whole celebration by speaking in both French and English but making different points in each language. In the first part of his address he played to the specific concerns of French Canadians. Only in the second, in English, did he refer to the larger diplomatic significance of the tercentenary.[98]

While these events were taking place in front of the Monument Champlain, Abbé Paré was among the smaller crowd observing developments down by the waterfront. He saw Champlain being greeted by the troops of Wolfe and Montcalm (the latter had also taken part in the ACJC rally), who took him into a replica of *l'Abitation*, the fort-like structure that the 'real' Champlain had constructed shortly after his arrival in Quebec. The actors, all of whom would participate in the pageants, waited inside for the signal that they, along with others from the cast, should begin the historical procession – the one that had pushed the SSJBQ parade from the program. The route would take marchers up the steep Côte de la Montagne; for this reason some participants – including all the women – preferred to join in only after Champlain and his hardy companions had reached the Monument Laval.[99] Those spectators who had forgone the formal ceremonies and positioned themselves along the Côte de la Montagne saw something less than the full procession.

When Champlain and his entourage reached the Monument Laval, the speech making was far from over. The entire cast, dressed in period costume on a hot summer's day, had to wait over an hour before covering the last 500 metres to the next monument. While the procession was waiting, some participants left and did not return; still others amused themselves, and annoyed the marshals by spontaneously singing 'O Canada' and other patriotic songs. Eventually the crowd and the marchers became intertwined, forming 'an inseparable and mixed up jumble of lords and ladies, heralds, troopers and pages, in their striking costumes of velvet, with the more sedately clad citizens of the present day.' Discipline so broke down that Frank Lascelles, the director of the pageants, was seen 'directing, counselling and instructing the different groups of participants.'[100]

Finally, late in the afternoon, the procession marched to the Monument Champlain, where the prince reviewed this heavily edited version of the pageant's cast. The spectacle he would view a few days later would present the history of Quebec from the arrival of Champlain to the loyal defence of Canada by de Salaberry during the War of 1812. For this occasion, however, two pageant scenes touching on the role of Catholicism in New France – one focusing on Marie de l'Incarnation and the other on Mgr de Laval – had been cut. Some scenes did include priests, but only as bit players. As if to further declericalize French-Canadian history, several new groups of characters were added, who would perform this one time only. One group of 'discoverers and founders of cities' presented such figures as Maisonneuve, La Salle, and Jolliet (though not Père Marquette); another consisted of a group of *coureurs de bois*; a

Historical procession, 1908 (Archives nationales du Québec à Québec; Keystone View Co, 1908; P1000, S4, D62, P16071)

third focused on Madeleine de Verchères as a lay alternative to Marie de l'Incarnation. While it is impossible to know who was responsible for the changes to the cast, this selective editing reinforced the sense – on this day at least – that Quebec's French Catholic legacy was being sacrificed to create a much more secular celebration.

From the start of the afternoon's festivities, the prince had been the centre of attention. This was reinforced by some accounts that viewed the procession as over when the last actor had passed the reviewing stand. As one commemorative volume put it: 'The procession has passed. The Prince now returns to the Citadel. The soldiers vacate the streets. Champlain has been honoured.'[101] Whether Champlain or the prince had been honoured was open to debate. What *was* clear was that the procession had been designed to continue long after the departure of the heir to the throne. It had been slated to pass by the prince, much as the St-Jean-Baptiste parade connected with the unveiling of the Monument Champlain had stopped to pay its respects to both the mayor and

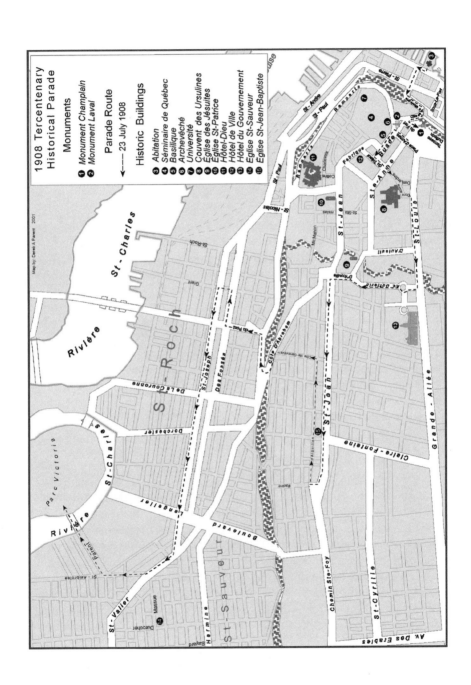

1908 Tercentenary
Historical Parade

Monuments

1 Monument Champlain
2 Monument Laval

Parade Route

——— 23 July 1908

Historic Buildings

3 Abitation
4 Séminaire de Québec
5 Basilique
6 Archevêché
7 Université
8 Couvent des Ursulines
9 Église des Jésuites
10 Église St-Patrice
11 Hôtel-Dieu
12 Hôtel de Ville
13 Hôtel du Gouvernement
14 Église St-Sauveur
15 Église St-Jean-Baptiste

Map by: Derek A Parent 2001

archbishop. The procession was then supposed to follow a winding route through the streets of the old town. It would bypass the shops on rue St-Jean so as not to impede the prince's departure, but it would pause in front of the Ursulines' convent in honour of Montcalm, who was buried inside. In the Fête-Dieu procession honouring Mgr de Laval, the nuns had come out from their convent to march; on this occasion they were given permission to watch the parade from behind their curtains.[102] The parade then passed the legislative assembly buildings (and the bust of Champlain) before heading downhill to the St-Roch and St-Sauveur districts. It finally dispersed in Parc Victoria, some four kilometres beyond the Monument Champlain.

This last part of the procession was a resounding failure. Abbé Paré observed that certain actors were forced to drop out due to heat exhaustion shortly after being reviewed by the Prince. Others took refuge from the sun in the Basilica. Still others left because the procession had gone overtime and they had other duties. For instance, regarding the soldiers of Wolfe's army, the 'commanding officers decided that it would not be fair to keep the men any longer and so it was decided to curtail a portion of the route that they had to traverse.' Paré was forced to conclude in regard to this section of the procession: 'This was far from being a success.' Indeed, two photographs, one showing the marchers in front of the Basilica and another depicting their procession down a stretch of rue St-Jean far from the commercial district, recorded a rather small gathering of onlookers. To all intents and purposes, the ceremony had ended with the prince; so much for Champlain Day.[103]

Performing on the Plains

The two parades staged on Champlain Day offered the public free glimpses of the much more elaborate performances that were to be mounted on the Plains of Abraham. The military parade was a preview of the elaborate review to be staged the following day; the historical procession was a shortened version of the pageants that would be performed eight times before the fete was over. In addition, on the only Sunday of the tercentenary (if the day of the ACJC rally is excluded), mass was to be celebrated on the plains. While there was a seemingly endless series of private receptions, dinners, and balls, these three very different performances constituted, aside from the processions, the major public events of the fête.

The term 'public' must be used advisedly, since the great majority of the roughly 100,000 people who attended these events had to pay for the privilege.[104] Every spectator at the pageants had to purchase a seat to enter the 10,000-seat amphitheatre, which had been constructed specifically for these events. For the mass, also held at the amphitheatre, individuals who wanted to be seated had to pay. Access to the grounds was free for those willing to stand, but it seems that few chose this option. As for the military review, it was mounted before a 'special stand where sat three thousand spectators,' while thousands of others watched from the ground.[105] Regardless of which stands were employed, the plains were repeatedly used as the stage; this seemed entirely appropriate in light of the central role it had been accorded in the celebration by both Laurier and Grey.

It was easy to find fault with the historical procession, which looked rather improvised, but hardly anyone failed to be impressed by the dramatic power of the performances on the plains, each of which was unique. With the military review, the Canadian authorities had an opportunity to stage a display of the country's military power for British officials as well as for thousands of Canadians, French and English speaking alike. Government and military leaders struggled to assemble a military presence that would be both impressive and affordable; the latter concern loomed large in light of the expenses already incurred for the tercentenary. There was also the practical problem of how to get the soldiers to Quebec City, since the rail system was already overloaded with travellers heading in the same direction. Ultimately, it was decided to send a force of 12,000, mostly members of militia units.[106]

On the morning of the military review, the men who had taken part in the parade the previous day retraced their steps from the various encampments toward the plains. They were joined there by sailors from the French and American vessels in port, thus forming a multinational force of more than 15,000. Once assembled in the constricted space in front of the reviewing stand, the troops in their various uniforms provided a visual feast. There were the British sailors ('bluejackets') alongside Highland regiments and even a detachment of the RCMP. But the show really started with the arrival on horseback of the Prince of Wales, who began his formal activities by placing a wreath on the monument to Wolfe. Later in the day he would balance this gesture by placing a second wreath at the Monument des Braves. The prince then inspected the troops before making his way to the grandstand, where he turned over $450,000 – cobbled together from individual contributions and the grants from the various levels of government – to finance the acquisition of the lands that would one day form the battlefields park. The ceremony ended with an intricately choreographed parade of 15,000 men and more than 2,000 horses that required an hour and a half to pass before the prince.

The military had had its day. Two days later it was time for another hierarchical organization to perform: the archdiocese of Quebec staked its own claim to the plains by conducting a pontifical mass. This was the one moment during the tercentenary that was entirely under the control of the church, and Mgr Bégin and his colleagues were determined to take full advantage. Early in the morning, long before mass was to begin, the Zouaves, the Garde Indépendante Champlain (till now shut out of the tercentenary), and similar groups from across the city made their way to the archbishop's palace across from the Monument Laval; from there they were to accompany the leaders of Quebec Catholicism, who were to be transported by carriage, to the pageant grounds. Conspicuously absent was the apostolic delegate, Mgr Sbarretti, who presumably stayed away so as not to encounter any Frenchmen. As it turns out, he had nothing to fear: the French delegation had decided not to participate because it had not received a special invitation from the archbishop. Though most of the other dignitaries in town were in attendance, the governor general and the prince spent the morning at an Anglican service. In 1898 Lord Aberdeen had attended the mass preceding the unveiling of the Monument Champlain; on this occasion the representatives of the Crown feared that they might offend some Protestants, ever sensitive to the federal government working too closely with the Catholic church.[107]

The spectators knew that the mass was about to begin when Mgr Bégin arrived with his entourage, which included the various *gardes*, who made their way on foot onto the pageant grounds, en route to an altar that had been constructed for this day. One observer described this *procession du clergé* as 'impressive, solemn, of an incomparable stateliness.' Mgr Bégin and the clergy entered the grounds to the music of a brass band, wearing clerical garb in shades of white, red, and violet that had been specially made for the occasion. The visual impact of the event was strengthened by the altar, which was decorated in shades of red and gold. The papal flag and the Drapeau de Carillon were prominently displayed.[108]

Having made his way to the altar, Bégin officiated over the mass, which had been planned down to the last detail. Musical interludes were provided by the band and by a 400-voice choir assembled for the occasion. There was even a reference to the legacy of Champlain – often left out of other tercentenary events – as the *Don de Dieu* made an appearance on the St. Lawrence just behind the altar. In the end, however, the aspect of the mass that attracted the most comment was the key role assigned to the Zouaves and the other French-Canadian independent military corps, which had been on the scene since early in the morning and which now formed an honour guard in front of the altar. When Mgr Bégin raised the host – the signal for those in attendance to drop to their knees – the Zouaves and their comrades performed the manoeuvre known as *genou terre*, whereby soldiers genuflected while presenting arms. All of the French-language papers commented on this part of the ceremony; one observed that the *genou terre* was 'performed by the group with a level of precision that reflects honour upon our volunteer "soldiers."' Here was French Canada's army performing on the same site occupied by the military two days earlier.[109]

Because the mass was so spectacular – or perhaps because it was so out of keeping with the spirit of much of the tercentenary – some commentators went out of their way to express their preference for it over the pageants. Some of these performances had already taken place on the same ground on the plains. *Le Soleil*, the official organ of the Liberal Party and not usually prone to excessive praise when it came to religious events, observed that 'yesterday's religious demonstration was much more impressive than the historical representations that have taken place upon these vast battlefields.' Even more emphatic was Mgr Camille Roy, who took a swipe at the pageants, dismissing them as make-believe, in contrast to the mass, which was real: 'Today, as the long pontifical procession passed by, one understood that all theatre, all fiction had come to a halt, and that one was in the presence of the most profound truth. This was not history being imperfectly revived, but rather a living religion which was represented by its priests, its faith, and its blessings. And this is why the crowd, overwhelmed by the power of the truth, was so respectful towards this spectacle; and it is also why it appeared to the crowd as more important and more venerable that all the other spectacles.'[110]

Many others would probably have preferred the pageants precisely *because* they were so unlike real life. People went to mass every week, and even saw military parades from time to time. Admittedly, the versions of these two events that were staged during the tercentenary were quite out of the ordinary. That being said, there was simply no precedent for the pageants, which brought more than 3,000 actors together for eight performances on the plains.

Because the pageants were unique, there was no bureaucratic structure in place for handling the hundreds of small details they involved.

This is why, when the local organizing committee responsible for the tercentenary program (until the NBC was formally constituted) endorsed the idea of holding pageants in January 1908, it had to start from scratch, beginning with the search for someone to take charge of the project. At first the committee considered hiring both French and English directors, perhaps hoping in this way to difuse French-Canadian ambivalence about the entire fête. Chouinard was supposed to follow up on leads for a director from France provided by Alfred Kleczkowski (from his perch in Uruguay); Louis Napoleon Parker, the father of the art form, would be contacted about directing the English part of the production. In the end, there is no evidence that Chouinard came up with any names, and Parker was unavailable. However, when the latter's shoes were filled by Frank Lascelles, who would succeed in charming French and English speakers alike, there was no need to look any further for a pageant master.

Lascelles was already well known for his production of a pageant in Oxford, and came available for the tercentenary only after another extravaganza in London was cancelled. It was probably fortunate both for the Champlain celebration and for Lascelles himself that he was able to come to Quebec, for he seems to have found his niche there: the telling of historical stories that touched on the experiences of diverse populations. He would never have encountered such a challenge in Oxford or London. In 1908 Lascelles succeeded in building a spectacle that brought together English-speaking Protestants and French-speaking Catholics (some of whom were clerics), as well as Canada's original inhabitants. Several years later, in 1910, he would pull off the same sort of trick when he directed the pageant of the Union of South Africa.

Lascelles was chosen for the South African job on the basis of his work in Quebec, which had impressed the Chief Justice of the Cape Colony, who had been a guest at the tercentenary. In South Africa, Lascelles drew together members of both the Dutch and English speaking communities to present a history which showed the two groups as collaborators rather than as enemies. Although the Black and 'coloured' populations played minor roles, Lascelles's efforts to integrate them into the story earned him recognition as an honourary chief of the Basuto, 'with the name of Rathkello, "father of wonderful thoughts,"' – an honour much like the one extended by native participants in the 1908 pageant, who made him an Iroquois chief with the title 'Tehonikonraka,' the man of infinite resources.[111]

Lascelles apparently had a knack for producing pageants that transcended ethnic, national, linguistic, and racial divisions, but he was not entirely responsible for the story that was told by the tercentenary pageants.[112] Rather, he inherited a scenario that had already gone through several drafts by the time he arrived. The first version was the work of the indefatigable Chouinard, who understood that pageants consisted of a series of discreet scenes, or *tableaux vivants*. He saw the event beginning with a scene depicting Columbus's discovery of the New World and ending just after the Conquest, either with Carleton's defence of Canada against the Americans in 1775 (Chouinard's preference) or with de Salaberry's defence against the same invaders in 1812.

Chouinard's script focused mainly on the history of French Canada, beginning with Jacques Cartier. After Cartier came Champlain, who was to arrive aboard a reconstructed *Don de Dieu* greeted by 'a salvo of artillery from the Citadel and from warships assembled at Quebec City.' This Champlain fared better than the one who had arrived on Champlain Day. Chouinard inserted two scenes dealing with New England, 'out of courtesy towards and to provide entertainment for our visitors.' However, most of the characters were the mainstays of textbooks of the time: Laval, Talon, Frontenac, Montcalm, Lévis, Dollard des Ormeaux and his fellow 'héros de Long-Sault,' as well as groups of French soldiers who had stayed on to settle New France. Though Chouinard balanced the presence of Montcalm and Lévis with actors representing Wolfe and Murray, there was something less than conciliatory about his inclusion of the Acadians, the memory of whose deportation would only have added fuel to the nationalist fire. Also, he had proposed a scene depicting French soldiers encamped at Beauport, just downstream from Quebec, who would be shown readying themselves for *la défense nationale* in 1759. One can only imagine that Chouinard was once again looking for ways to blunt nationalist animosity toward the tercentenary.[113]

By April Lascelles had been on the job for a month, and the scenario had been polished into its final form. Columbus was cut from the pageants early on, after it was decided that he would be sufficiently celebrated through the performances of 'Christophe Colomb' by Felicien David. This symphonic ode, staged with four hundred vocalists and a one-hundred-piece orchestra, was to be the main musical event of the fete, especially in the absence of any performance of the 'Cantate en l'honneur de Mgr de Laval,' which had been a mainstay of celebrations like this since the late nineteenth century. Though the cantata had been performed on Champlain's previous celebration in 1898, it seems that this time no one even considered incorporating it into the program.[114]

Left on the cutting room floor along with Columbus were the scenes dealing with New England; perhaps Lascelles himself cut these, in line with Parker's proviso that pageants should be performed for the local community rather than for tourists.[115] Not surprisingly, also cut were the Acadians and the French soldiers at Beauport, along with 'soldiers who had cleared the land'; the exclusion of all these meant that the pageants would not make any reference to the original settlers of New France. This gap led to complaints from 'the descendants of the earliest families,' who felt that their ancestors should have been included somewhere in the tercentenary program.[116]

What remained were the 'great men' of the French and early English regimes, beginning with Cartier and finishing with de Salaberry. Now joining them were various characters from the past who had been absent from Chouinard's draft. Consistent with the ecclesiastical blessing of the tercentenary was the addition of a scene portraying the arrival of the Ursuline and Augustine nuns (who had marched in the Fête-Dieu procession a month earlier), along with the Jesuits; all were led by Mère Marie de l'Incarnation, who was the only women given a lead role. Native people, who had been mere bit players in the original scenario, were given considerably more prominence in Lascelles's final version. They would appear in many scenes.

Chouinard had treated the Conquest very gingerly, avoiding any real reference to the battle of the Plains of Abraham by assigning Wolfe and Montcalm to separate scenes. Another version of the Conquest was developed by a committee chaired by Thomas Chapais and including Abbé Gosselin and Narcisse Dionne (the biographers of Laval and Champlain respectively). Chapais and his colleagues proposed to present the battle through a mock bombardment of Quebec; however, this idea was never pursued, as it would only have stirred up the wrong sentiments.[117] In the end, Lascelles hit on the idea of bringing the two generals together (along with Lévis and Murray) as comrades rather than enemies; to drive the point home, that rapprochement would take place on the plains, where the pageants were being staged.

With the story now in place, Lascelles began assembling his cast of thousands. There would be plenty of tourists to fill the stands and line the streets of tercentenary events if French Canadians turned out not to be interested, but to actually perform the pageants, local volunteers would have to be found. The only exception here: natives would be imported *and* paid for their services.[118] Native involvement in projects like this was nothing new. Indeed, Hurons from Ancienne-Lorette had appeared at the unveiling of the Monument Laval. These natives were positioned at the foot of the monument, paralleling the presence of the native figure on the monument itself. When it came to the pageants, however, Lascelles wanted to provide them with a much more dynamic role. Some of the native performers would be from Ancienne-Lorette; others would be brought from as far away as Sault Ste Marie. So that they might seem truly exotic and play their role in the script as threats to French-Canadian settlement, they would all be dressed as Plains Indians, 'brandishing tomahawks and shouting war whoops, determined to look and act the part expected of them.' In the end, they stole the show, even though they had first been seen as bit players.[119]

Natives could be 'purchased'; Lascelles had to find other means of recruiting the thousands of Quebec City residents the pageant required. The lead roles were filled fairly quickly by middle-class citizens, who were divided between French and English speakers in a ratio mirroring that in the local population. However, if roughly 85 per cent of the lead roles were filled by French Canadians, only 67 per cent of the supporting roles were. In other words, French speakers were seriously underrepresented in the cast as a whole, just as they had been among contributors to the battlefields fund.

The marginal role of francophones among the pageants' extras was at least in part a result of the recruiting process. In early June it looked as if the ranks of participants would never be filled. But then the city's clerical and economic elite went to work. Roughly thirty priests were pressed into service for the pageant scene focusing on Mgr de Laval. Far more performers were recruited through the city's business elite, in which English speakers were overrepresented. In the end, though many French speakers were brought into the pageant by these business leaders, the local linguistic minority was enlisted in numbers far outstripping its proportion in the population as a whole. The French-speaking presence might have been larger had Lascelles's recruiters enjoyed more success in the working-class districts. But these were precisely the parts of town where enthusiasm for the tercentenary had always been lukewarm at best.[120]

Having assembled his cast, Lascelles turned his attention to a daunting list of practical concerns. By and large, the cast members were assigned roles consistent with their place in society: priests played priests, nuns were played by graduates of the Ursuline school (in the absence of the nuns themselves), and 'sailors from the Yacht Club manned the *Don de Dieu*.'[121] As for the other matters that he had to attend to, Lascelles had

Champlain scene and crowds at the Tercentenary Pageant, 1908 (Archives nationales du Québec à Québec; Keystone View Co, 1908; P1000, S4, D62, P16078)

his job facilitated by his access to over $150,000 – almost half the total budget for the entire tercentenary.[122] Costumes designed by the artist Charles Huot ate up nearly half the available funds and would have eaten up even more had it not been for the volunteer labour of women (both lay and religious), who prepared the dresses for the pageants. The next biggest expense was for the grandstand, followed by wigs, hats, 'Indians,' props, tickets, and music performed by the local symphony (when it was not busy playing the ode to Columbus).[123]

Although it took some time for Lascelles to impose order on a pageant this vast, which was largely staffed by volunteers, it is almost impossible to find a negative comment about the result. Audiences were enthralled by the landscape of the plains, with the St. Lawrence in the background, and by the costumes, choreography, and music. Moreover, they were generally receptive to the stories being told. Natives were presented as both exotic and potentially dangerous, thus confirming popular conceptions. For their part, the native performers perhaps enjoyed the chance to be on the winning side for once: they were portrayed murdering Dollard and his men (which reinforced Dollard's place in the pantheon of local heroes). As for French Canada, the story told here was largely one of church and state working together harmoniously for the common good – a perspective not dramatically different from the one that had been offered at the Laval celebration. In fact, the scene that brought together Laval and the Marquis de Tracy replicated one of the bas-reliefs engraved on the base of the bishop's monument.

English speakers and French speakers alike could not help but be moved by the final scene of the pageant, in which the armies of 1759–60 and those which repelled the Americans in 1775 and 1812 marched onto centre stage, led by Wolfe and Montcalm, Murray and Lévis. The scene was choreographed so that the troops marched past the two generals who died on the plains; this gave them the same role that the Prince of Wales had filled in the military review. The story of rapprochement was one that most could accept, as long as the past was kept separate from the present. English Canadians could not help but feel good about a story that spoke about both victory and the humane treatment of the vanquished. As for French Canadians, such diverse characters as Laurier, Bourassa, and Mgr Bégin might have disagreed about the precise nature of the benefits arising from the Conquest, but all would have agreed that benefits there were. As long as no one talked too explicitly about the early-twentieth-century British Empire, the grumbling about the marginal role occupied by Champlain could be kept to a minimum, and everyone could go home feeling reasonably happy.

Performances and the People

All three of the performances staged on the plains packed an emotional punch, and the military review, the pontifical mass, and the pageants were almost universally praised. Typical of the commentary in the press was the response to the pageants in the journal of the Quebec archdiocese, *Semaine religieuse*, which otherwise had little positive to say about the tercentenary. It was forced to admit that the pageants constituted 'the *pièce de résistance* of the celebration. We are prepared to say without hesitation that we were absolutely incapable of expressing the great and powerful emotions that we felt.'[124]

The press lavished praise on these spectacles as dramatic performances; it also saw them as popular successes that had drawn large and diverse crowds of spectators who were actors in their own right. Regarding the mass, *Le Soleil* drew attention to the presence in the grandstand of sailors from the three navies, and of performers from the pageants dressed in their costumes, who contributed collectively to 'the particular cachet of the spectacle.' As for the pageants, in its description of the first full dress rehearsal, *L'Événement* conceived of the grandstand as a stage: 'The first spectacle and not the least noteworthy is that which was provided by the huge grandstand and its immediate surroundings with the masses that were crowded together: spectators, actors, soldiers, etc.

They formed an immense human bouquet within which were interspersed the colours of all the outfits being worn, the various languages
spoken, a wide variety of movements, and the display of every imaginable
emotion.'[125]

However, the press did not make any note of who had actually attended these performances – of how many ordinary French Canadians
were in the crowds. This question was especially pertinent, since admission was charged for some if not all of the seats at the various performances. This was a departure from the norm, in that commemorative
events were usually free. Various events stretching back to the reburial of
Laval had required that spectators pick up tickets in order to secure
entry, but no thought had ever been given to charging admission; organizers were happy to have immense crowds on hand and were not about
to scare people away by charging for tickets.

In contrast, the spectacles staged on the plains were treated as businesses that required income to defray expenses. In this they were rather
similar to the various forms of popular entertainment that were emerging at the turn of the century. With vaudeville halls, amusement parks,
world's fair midways, and baseball parks, no one thought it unusual to
charge admission for the right to view the product on display. This
market orientation was evident in the thinking of tercentenary organizers, who were incurring considerable costs to create a spectacle that
might attract tourists, and who were forced to charge admission to
prevent their finances from spinning out of control.[126]

The NBC spent much of its time dealing with the financial implications of the pageants, which ended up absorbing roughly half its total
budget. Among members of the NBC, Lascelles passed himself off as
someone who lived for art alone, and he repeatedly refused to accept
any payment for his services. Since he was willing to forgo any financial
gain, members of the commission found it hard to say no to him when
he kept revising upwards his cost estimates. His original budget was
$155,000, which included the construction of a 15,000-seat grandstand.
Only days later he reassured NBC commissioners that they were running
no financial risk, since ticket sales would bring in as much as $300,000.
Recognizing the importance of these funds to the fiscal well-being of the
tercentenary, J.M. Courtney wrote to Edmund Walker, one of the commissioners. As president of the Canadian Bank of Commerce, Walker
presumably was sensitive to the need for balancing the books. Courtney
insisted that Walker and his colleagues 'should take some steps or should
arrange for some highly responsible man to take charge, and sell the

tickets and place proper assistants at the several entrances. I am afraid that, with all due respect, if it is left to the local people who have never had any experience in such a business that we might not get all the advances that we should.'[127]

By early May, as fundraising efforts fizzled, the commissioners had become frantic. Notwithstanding Lascelles's assurances, they felt that something significant had to be done to avert financial disaster. Focusing on the pageants, they asked Lascelles to reduce his budget and his cast. At the same meeting, prices were set for the 7,500 seats that would be sold to the public in the grandstand. Its capacity had already been reduced from 30,000 to 15,000; it was now to be slashed even more, to 10,000. Even though selling all of the seats would have been consistent with the NBC's desire to avoid a deficit, the commissioners decided just the same to reserve one-quarter of the seats for non-paying guests. Still not comfortable with the economics of the pageants in late May the NBC created a subcommittee on tickets, which called for an increase in the original prices set for the sale of tickets and a reduction in the number of seats reserved for dignitaries. The most revealing initiative of this subcommittee was that it struck a deal with Thomas Cook to take charge of ticket sales through its agencies in New York, Boston, Toronto, Montreal, and other cities. It was to return to Quebec City those tickets it had not sold by 15 July. Thus, residents of Quebec City could buy pageant tickets only days before the first official performance.[128]

In the end, for all the commission's efforts, the pageants lost money. Lascelles had been told to keep his expenses down to $100,000; he ended up going 50 per cent over budget despite Courtney's best efforts to scrutinize every last expense. The deputy minister of finance was similarly frustrated by Lascelles's unrealistic forecast toward the end of the tercentenary that ticket sales would allow expenses to be covered with only a $75,000 contribution from the NBC's coffers. Courtney scoffed at this estimate: 'I am informed that the net revenue derived from the sale of tickets will be about $30,000 and no more.' Courtney's estimate of ticket revenue was slightly below the final figure of $36,000. Nevertheless, with expenses of $150,000, the commission had to come up with $114,000 to cover the pageants' deficit.[129] Ultimately, the costs of the tercentenary forced the commissioners – who had promised not to use publicly raised funds for the Quebec City celebrations – to employ the entire federal government grant of $300,000 to foot the bill. This reduced the funds available for acquiring lands to complete the battlefields park.

Given the costs of the affair, the commissioners' decision to charge admission to the pageants was perhaps understandable. Even so, this decision made it harder for ordinary Quebecers to take in the spectacle. This troubled Thomas Chapais, who at a meeting of local tercentenary organizers in April wondered whether it might be possible 'to set aside a certain number of seats which would be sold at a rather high price and to open the rest for free to the public.'[130] In the end, there was no free lunch: tickets sold for as little as 10 cents for a dress rehearsal and peaked for the performance attended by the Prince of Wales, for which the best seats cost 5 dollars. However, most tickets went for somewhere between 75 cents and 2 dollars.

These prices were within the range charged for admission to other public amusements of the time, which catered not to the working classes but rather to the growing ranks of white-collar employees. For example, the St Louis World's Fair of 1904 charged 50 cents just to enter the grounds – a policy that served 'to filter out a significant proportion of the urban population. If the fair directors had set out to reach a larger and wider cross section of the urban public, they would not have kept the admission prices so high.'[131]

Troubled that poorer elements of the local population were being excluded, L'Événement, a popular Catholic paper, which took a particular interest in the price issue, campaigned for free admission for the dress rehearsals. This paper seemed shocked 'that one would have to pay to attend any of the performances, even the dress rehearsals ... If the tercentenary celebrations, paid for by the people, are in any way being staged for the people, how can one argue about being more generous so as to allow the people of Quebec City to attend the two dress rehearsals for free.' This paper recognized that revenue would be lost in the process, but argued: 'Wouldn't it be better to sacrifice these gate receipts than to deprive the poor of the opportunity to gain entry?' Having failed on its first attempt, L'Événement tried again halfway through the fêtes: 'We are asking once more that there be a free performance of the Pageants for the families of the performers and for the public which does not have the means of paying the price of admission. In the midst of the grandeur of the fetes currently underway, we must not forget that money does not exist in great abundance everywhere. It would be a great shame if the entire population of Quebec City could not see the beautiful history lesson provided by these historical scenes.' Toward the close of the festival, Action sociale added its voice: '25 or 30 cents are small sums of money, but when they are multiplied five or six times, as would be the case for our heads of households with many mouths to feed, the result is the taking of large chunks out of small budgets. We understand that the majority of workers have not been able to take on such a responsibility, especially during this time of monetary crisis which they suffer just like everyone else.'[132]

This reference to *la crise monétaire* was a recognition that the tercentenary was being held in the midst of difficult economic times. In late 1907 there had been a run on a number of American banks; the impact of this was strong enough that the Federal Reserve System was created soon after. Financial institutions in Canada had also been affected by this panic; in response, they tightened their credit, which contributed to a slowdown in economic activity. In November 1907 the journal of the Canadian Manufacturers' Association reported: 'Six months ago there was no cloud on the horizon of Canada's commercial prosperity. Since that time conditions have developed which have aroused more or less anxiety, and businessmen in every part of the Dominion are preparing to face what threatens now to be an actual depression in trade. It would be unwise at the present time to predict that Canada is on the verge of "hard times," but it would be even more imprudent to shut our eyes to such significant factors as reduced crop returns and financial stringency, with their attending results already facing us.'

Among those who were prepared to shut their eyes were the tercentenary organizers, who chose to ignore the onset of a financial crisis in late 1907. As one official put it: 'This is said to be a time of financial depression. Would it not be a good proof of the stability and confidence of Canada in its own country and its people to show that by generosity, and if necessary, some self-sacrifice, it can get over that and show the world at large that we are equal to a great occasion, even in bad times?'[133]

By early in the new year, financial conditions had improved somewhat; however, economic activity did not fully recover until late in the summer. In fact, most economic historians mark the bottom of the trough in the business cycle as having come in July, just as the tercentenary was about to begin.[134] This economic downturn resulted in higher levels of unemployment as well as reduced wages for many of those who were able to keep their jobs. A federal government report noted that in 1908 'as the effects of the depression were more fully felt, decreases in wages were made in factories, and in the building and other trades.' In Quebec the erosion of workers' wages was especially noticeable in the textile industry, one of the mainstays of the economy. In May, the wages of textile workers were slashed by 10 per cent. In Quebec City the *Labour*

Gazette reported a 'poor' situation for unskilled labourers throughout the summer of 1908; local workers were in an even more precarious situation than their counterparts elsewhere in the province. Paradoxically, the tercentenary, though it did provide some employment in the city, also contributed to the unemployment problem. The blocking off of many of the city streets meant that gas and water lines could not be installed; the demand for unskilled labour decreased as a consequence.[135]

Even in the best of times, the necessities of life consumed nearly all that workers earned. In the precarious economic climate of 1908 there would have been little room in any family's budget for an extravagance such as tickets to the pageants.[136] Indeed, the stands were only partially filled for several performances, including the first dress rehearsal, for which ticket prices were at their lowest. This supports the view that even 25 cents was a significant expense for the poor. In the end, it seems plausible that the nearly 80,000 people who attended these performances were much like the performers recruited by Lascelles. The comfortable classes, both local residents and tourists, French and English speakers alike, came out in droves. No doubt some members of the working class also made the trek from the St-Roch and St-Sauveur districts, but it is doubtful that they came in great numbers. At very expensive performances, such as the one attended by the Prince of Wales, many if not most of the spectators would have been English speaking. There was something absurd about a situation in which the actors' dialogue was almost entirely in French, presumably to avoid offending the local linguistic majority, who would have constituted the minority of spectators.[137]

The pageants were the only events staged on the plains for which tickets were mandatory. For the other events, spectators had the choice of either sitting for a price or standing for free. The latter option was chosen by the vast majority of those who attended the military review. The logistics of staging a display of 15,000 men and another 2,000 horses made it impossible to use the pageant grounds, which were too small. Recognizing that a second grandstand would have to be built, the NBC at first opted for a small stand of only 1,000 seats, which would hold mainly dignitaries. As the day of the big event approached, however, J.H. Gignac, who also built the pageant grandstand, asked if he could add another 2,000 seats, at his own expense and on the understanding that he would charge no more than $3 per seat.[138] Needless to say, ordinary Quebecers did not even think of paying for seats for the military review. While many watched the review for free while standing on the plains, it is

Empty seats at the Messe Solennelle, 1908 (reproduced with permission of *La Presse*, 27 July 1908)

clear that a much larger number had come out for the military parade. This reinforces the impression that this last-minute addition to the tercentenary had been its only truly popular event.[139]

In the case of the pontifical mass, again, people could stand for free or pay for a seat, which on this occasion cost 25 cents. Nearly all who attended chose to pay. The many photographs and sketches of the mass indicate that few people chose to stand. One sketch, published in *La Presse*, shows that few people were standing and that many seats in the pageant amphitheatre were empty. Published estimates were that the pageants drew far more people than the mass. *L'Action sociale*, never one to underestimate the size of the crowd at the Laval celebrations, observed that just before the start of the mass the stands were only two-thirds full: 'Seeing that there were numerous empty seats, it was permitted to allow everyone [and presumably in particular those who had chosen to stand so as to avoid paying admission] to climb up the stairs and choose a seat.'[140]

Although it was not necessary to purchase a ticket to enter the pageant grounds, the requirement to pay for seats must have played some role in discouraging working class families, who were still reeling from the recession. At roughly the same time that mass was being celebrated on the plains, services were also taking place in churches across the city, including the Basilica, the archbishop's own church. During the Laval celebrations, when mass was celebrated at the bishop's monument, competition from the various parishes in the city was not allowed, just as competition among various Fête-Dieu processions was banned. In the case of the tercentenary, the archdiocese put on a show, but by setting a price for the tickets and allowing the other masses to go on as usual, the faithful had other options for the Sunday morning of the fête.

Furthermore, some of the grandstand seats at the mass were occupied by Protestants. The presence of the 'other' religion was commented on not only in the local press, but also by Abbé Paré, who attended relatively few tercentenary events. Our diarist attended the historical procession and the military parade but did not travel out to the plains for either the military review or the pageants. As one might have expected, however, he was on hand for the mass, which he described – perhaps predictably – as a great success: 'Never have the Plains of Abraham seen a spectacle that was as grand or as moving.' More interesting, however, was his further remark that the crowd was 'composed largely of Protestants.'[141] Paré had no reason for overstating the place of Protestants in the stands. Among the dignitaries, Catholics dominated; the two leading Protestants in town stayed away so as not to suggest that they were soft on Catholicism. Among run-of-the-mill tourists – mostly English-speaking Protestants – the mass was just another performance, not unlike the pageants and the military review, whose colour and exoticism were not to be missed.

'Ils sont restés silencieux' (They remained quiet)

Unlike the reburial of Mgr de Laval thirty years earlier, which was organized by the seminary without the involvement of other interested parties, the tercentenary was run by a modern bureaucracy that had to deal with the general public, various levels of government, and many other organizations. Though Mgr Hamel, the superior of the seminary, had been able to prepare a rough draft of the reburial ceremony, which was subsequently carried out almost to the letter, the tercentenary program went through various drafts and was so far-reaching that central control over the various elements was almost impossible. In the end, this relative absence of control made it possible for various messages to be communicated to the larger public. For instance, Frank Lascelles was given the freedom to run the pageants as he wished; in the process, natives were given the opportunity to emerge as performers, and insisted on making the most of it. In a similar manner, the give-and-take of commemorative politics made it possible for a mass to be staged in the midst of the pageant; this gave the French Catholic hierarchy – always sceptical about the tercentenary's celebration of British-French co-operation – the opportunity to stage a show of its own.

While the structure of the tercentenary allowed most bruised feelings to heal, there was a certain lingering sense of alienation among French Canadians that never entirely disappeared. This sentiment might have easily been missed in the midst of so many spectacles, which were carried off successfully in front of crowds swollen by the presence of so many visitors. No one who attended the fête would have been aware of any particular anger among local French Canadians, especially as so many prominent French Canadians were running the show, so many others were performing in the pageants, and so many thousands were attending the various events. Indeed, the dismissive comments of an ultramontane newspaper such as *La Vérité* – which simply wrote the celebration off as unabashed propaganda 'in support of the whole of Canada and of the Empire' – could easily be ignored.[142]

There was no palpable hostility among French Canadians, but there was a consistent undertone of suspicion and a certain reluctance to embrace the tercentenary too warmly. The years leading up to the celebration in late July 1908 had witnessed frequent squabbling between French and English speakers; this ultimately led to the separation of the Laval and Champlain celebrations. As the tercentenary program was being cobbled together, the SSJBQ, which had been marginalized in previous celebrations, found itself out in the cold once again. The sense in the French-Canadian community that this was not quite their celebration was reflected in the particular difficulties faced by fundraisers seeking donations for the park on the Plains of Abraham and by pageant organizers looking for performers. Ultimately, when the fête finally arrived, the decision by organizers of certain events to make the spectators pay resulted in many ordinary French Canadians staying home – a fact that could have been missed, since visitors were available to fill most if not all of the seats in the pageant amphitheatre.

In the end, perhaps the most cogent commentary on the tercentenary's reception by the larger French-Canadian community came from *Le Nationaliste*, the paper that advanced the *Bourassiste* view of affairs prior to the founding of *Le Devoir*. An article by the recently appointed editor Jules Fournier was taken seriously enough by several English-language publications for it to be rebuked in their columns. This piece, in the form of an open letter to the Prince of Wales several days before his departure from Quebec City, was not written with any anger. In fact, Fournier went out of his way to express the loyalty of French Canadians to an empire that had long been based on the principles of fair play. Fournier calmly explained to the Prince that though he had seen large crowds, which included many French Canadians, there were significant parts of that population, beyond the ranks of the politicians, who had not participated in large numbers. He included in this category 'the worker hunched over his tool, the industrialist in his factory, the merchant behind his counter, the farmer bending over the furrows in his field, [and] the settler opening up new lands for cultivation.' Those who had been left cold by the tercentenary had not come out to protest, nor had they self-consciously boycotted the fête; they had simply stayed away. As Fournier put it: 'Ils sont restés silencieux' (They remained quiet).[143]

Fournier undoubtedly exaggerated the extent of this silent disenchantment with the tercentenary, by trying to generalize it to most French Canadians. Nevertheless, the evidence indicates that he did put his finger on something significant. Though many French speakers both supported and participated in the fête, many others complained – albeit never too loudly – about the shape it was given during the years of planning. When July 1908 finally arrived, there were also those who simply chose to stay out of the way during the last two weeks of the month, attending only those events offered for free and counting the days for the visitors to go home so that life could return to normal. Fournier here was identifying a sentiment that would surface much more dramatically a few years later with the outbreak of the First World War. Again on that occasion, while some French Canadians were prepared to support the war effort, large numbers felt no emotional attachment. They did not come out into the streets to protest until conscription was imposed; even then, they largely expressed the sentiment that they wanted to be left alone. In the aftermath of the war, an angrier tone, embodied by Abbé Lionel Groulx, would take hold, but during the war, as had been the case in 1908, when the imperialists became assertive French Canadians did not get angry, but rather kept to themselves.

Epilogue: Champlain and Laval beyond the Summer of 1908

The Last Gasp of the Tercentenary

Just as there was debate as to when the tercentenary really began, so too was there some question as to when it ended. For the overwhelming majority of the roughly 200,000 people, counting both residents and tourists, who had been crammed into Quebec City in late July, this was a rather straightforward question: the final events on the program took place on the last day of the month. By then the Prince of Wales had already headed home, along with the navies, soldiers, dignitaries, and visitors from four countries. The return to 'normal' life was signalled by one of the local papers only days after the official end of the tercentenary. In a dramatic page-one headline, the Conservative newspaper *L'Événement* summoned 'all honest people [presumably excluding Liberals] to get ready for the general elections.'[1] Although Laurier would not call the federal election until mid-September, the time had come for the population to turn its thoughts away from spectacles toward more mundane matters.

For some residents of Quebec City, however, the election campaign took a back seat in late September to an event staged at Université Laval, which had hosted commemorative celebrations as far back as Laval's reburial. A large crowd came out to pay tribute to members of 225 French-Canadian families that had occupied the same land for at least two hundred years. This celebration had first been proposed in 1906, when the tercentenary was just getting off the ground. Though the event was placed on the program early in 1908, it was dropped when the National Battlefields Commission took charge of the planning. The tribute in September to *les anciennes familles* was designed to right that wrong.[2]

Several of the speakers went out of their way to tell a story that had been missing in July. Abbé David Gosselin, who organized the event, recognized Champlain's claim to fame, but insisted that equal credit was owed to the families that had committed themselves to the land: 'They are the real founders of New France, or at least of that part which is now called the Province of Quebec.' After this, the auxiliary bishop of Quebec, Mgr Paul-Eugène Roy, referred even more emphatically to the tercentenary. He seemed to feel the need to state what had been repressed in July. He saw the celebration of these families as 'the very dignified and practical epilogue to the tercentenary fetes. And this time, we can be sure that the spectre of imperialism will not show up to haunt and trouble our plans. It is a question here, in fact, of glorifying our race and our land, both of which are French-Canadian.'

Roy's speech may well have made the audience feel like it was June again – as if they had been transported back to the unveiling of the Monument Laval. The evening's final speaker would have reinforced this impression. H. de Lanrezac, a young French soldier and member of the Société de Géographie de Paris had distinguished himself as an eloquent advocate for the rebirth of a truly Catholic France. Echoing the words of Pierre Gerlier from earlier in the summer, he reminded Quebecers that they hailed from a *France catholique* that had not yet been extinguished. Abbé Paré did not much care for Lanrezac's speech, observing that it 'vibrates with patriotism from the other side of the Atlantic, and so it does not have much meaning to our people, left cold by the moral valour of our French cousins.'[3] Paré's reservations aside, this emphasis on Quebec's French Catholic roots was reinforced by the presence of the brass band of the Garde Indépendante Champlain, which played throughout the evening. There was also a choir, which performed 'France! France!' thus re-creating yet another moment from the Laval celebration.

But the music and the speeches merely added colour to the event, whose primary purpose was to distribute medals, which had been designed by Eugène-Étienne Taché, who had also designed the bust of Champlain erected in front of the legislative buildings during the tercentenary. The medals were made of gold-plated silver. Abbé Gosselin regretted that the gold was not pure: 'If such medals had ever been warranted, it is surely by those who continue the work of the first founders of New France.' He hoped that in 2008, 'when we will celebrate the four-hundredth anniversary of the founding of Quebec, medals of the purest gold will be awarded to the grandsons, more fortunate that their grandfathers [we fête today].'

On the face of the medal was a cross surrounded by a large crown of maple leaves, at the centre of which was a green banner with a Latin inscription. Latin had been pushed to the side during the raising of the monuments to both Champlain and Laval out of deference to tourists, but this tribute was aimed solely at the local population. The inscription paid tribute to the farmers who had triumphed: 'By the sword, by the cross, and by the plough.' This message contributed to the sense that the Laval celebration had been revisited; however, the reverse side of the medal made it clear that this event had been conceived as an extension of the tercentenary. Along with the name of the family, the medal had chiselled into it: 'Troisième centenaire de Québec, 1908.' Clearly, the organizers were trying to add an element to the tercentenary that they thought had been missed. Mgr Roy included this event as an 'épilogue' to the souvenir volume that he published to keep the tercentenary fresh in the public's mind.[4]

Echoes of the Tercentenary

This time the tercentenary really was over. However, there were further opportunities in the years to come for Quebecers to express their conflicting opinions regarding what should have been celebrated in 1908. The first of these occasions was in 1909, on the tercentenary of Champlain's 'discovery' of the lake that would later bear his name. The plans for this celebration had clearly been inspired by the one held in Quebec City. Within weeks of the official conclusion of the *tricentenaire*, representatives from New York and Vermont, the states bordering on Lake Champlain, committed themselves to staging an event of their own. As the Americans' plans began to take shape, Frank Lascelles was consulted about the mounting of a pageant. In late 1908, L.O. Armstrong, who had assembled the natives for the Quebec pageants, was hired to do the same for the theatrical events that would be performed during the Lake Champlain celebrations. These were scheduled to take place over several days in early July 1909 at various sites in the two states.[5]

Dignitaries from the same four countries that had been represented in 1908 travelled from town to town, accompanied by a cast of some 150 natives, most of whom were from Kahnawake, the Mohawk reserve near Montreal. A floating stage three hundred feet long was transported from one site on the lake to another for performances of a pageant titled 'Hiawatha, the Mohawk.' This was based on a story by the Montrealer William Douw Lighthall.[6] The floating stage was supposed to represent the island of Montreal where the story began with Hiawatha, a Mohawk warrior, trying to save his people from defeat at the hands of the Hurons. In spite of his supernatural powers, the Mohawks were sent fleeing to the Champlain Valley. Hiawatha helped them develop close ties with other Iroquois nations. They might have lived in peace after that had it not been for the arrival of the Hurons, who forced them to flee once again. This time, the Huron attackers were accompanied by the French led by Champlain, played by Charles Langelier in a reprise of his role in the Quebec pageants. On the Plains of Abraham, Lascelles had been careful to depict the French positively; in this new pageant, Champlain only appeared very briefly at the end of the drama, 'departing with [the Mohawk] spoils.'[7]

Langelier was not the only French Canadian to repeat a performance from 1908 on the Lake Champlain stage. There was also Mgr Paul-Eugène Roy, who at the assembly honouring the *anciennes familles* had expressed his frustration with the tercentenary. Roy did not have a place on the official program in 1909. Rather, the day before the celebration began he officiated over an open-air mass on Île La Motte. This island was noteworthy for having been the 'first land visited by Champlain in what is now the United States.' But the mass had little to do with Champlain; the significance of the island was that Fort Ste-Anne had been built there in 1666, the same year the Jesuits celebrated the first mass and erected the first chapel in what would become Vermont. By 1909 the island was the site of the Shrine of Ste-Anne, where mass was celebrated. In his comments, delivered in English, Mgr Roy had little to say about Champlain, focussing instead on the other founding father. Roy viewed himself as 'a successor to Laval' who, thanks to the intervention of providence, was now 'presiding over such an imposing religious ceremony.'[8]

Mgr Roy's perspective on the Quebec tercentenary was given further publicity by one final echo, this one coming from France. In 1908, Louis Herbette had been the most publicized member of the French delegation because of his anticlericalism. However, another French delegate had been as unsympathetic toward 'Uncle Herbette' as the local ecclesiastical establishment. Mayor Brandelis of Brouage had been included in the delegation because his town was Champlain's birthplace. On returning home he found himself facing a problem, which he hoped to resolve through the connections he made in Quebec.

The mayor's problem was that the church where Champlain had been baptised was deteriorating. Following the separation of church and state in France in 1905, municipalities had taken control of nearly all parish churches in the country. Catholics were permitted free use of these churches, but upkeep was left in the hands of *associations cultuelles*. In effect, the ecclesiastical entities known as parishes had been reconstituted as civil institutions under the new law. Under orders from the Vatican, which refused to participate in a process it saw as theft, the French clergy were not allowed to form these *associations*; as a result, there was no one with the authority to repair ageing churches like the one in Brouage. Mayor Brandelis turned to the municipal council for the needed funds, but was turned down; he now appealed to his French-Canadian friends. He explained to them that Brouage had been incorporated into a 'commune' along with the larger town of Hiers. The councillors from Brouage were in favour of funding the repairs to the church; those from Hiers were not. Early in 1910, despite the mayor's efforts, the communal council of Hiers-Brouage refused to earmark the 2,500 francs needed to repair the church's roof, which was about to collapse.[9]

Brandelis closed the church for safety reasons, but he was not willing to accept defeat. Instead, he drew on his tercentenary contacts to launch an appeal to the residents of Quebec City for funds, noting that 'this regime is becoming incredibly cruel towards us ... We ask you, in the name of the great Champlain whom you celebrated last year, to come to our aid and to look favourably upon our request.'[10] This call for the defence of *la France catholique* was printed in most of the Quebec City newspapers, some of which took advantage of the situation to express old grievances that had surfaced during the tercentenary. *La Vérité* explained that what was happening in Brouage was only the tip of the iceberg: 'We have already explained how the system works. The confiscated church having become the property of the municipality is denied needed repairs; it then falls into disrepair and ends up being destroyed by dynamite in order to protect the public from a dangerous building ... Already a number of churches have been dynamited ... Today we are informing our readers about the possible destruction of the old, historic church of Brouage.'[11]

As a result of Mayor Brandelis's request, the Société St-Jean-Baptiste de Québec established a special committee to raise the needed funds. This committee included tercentenary organizers such as H.J.J.B. Chouinard, as well as detractors such as J.E.A. Pin, who had been openly dismayed that the society had been marginalized in the summer of 1908. Within months the committee had collected 6,000 francs ($1,200), more than twice the amount Brandelis had solicited. This sum was amassed through modest contributions from two hundred individuals and associations. No gift exceeded $50, and the only individual to contribute that sum was Wilfrid Laurier. The prime minister apparently was not bothered by the rather obvious anti-French sentiment of the drive, and perhaps was hoping to cast himself in a good light with *nationaliste* voters, who would soon help defeat him. Political figures such as Laurier and Premier Gouin were joined by Mgr Bégin and other leaders of the church as well as ordinary individuals, some of whom identified themselves only as *un ouvrier* or *un Patriote* and contributed less than a dollar.[12]

Even after the residents of Quebec City had done their duty, they continued to be drawn into the politics of celebrating Champlain. Citizens of Brouage kept them informed of developments surrounding the reopening of the church, which was scheduled for late December 1912. In particular, the SSJBQ was kept up to date by Louis Augé, president of the Comité catholique Samuel de Champlain, which had overseen the work on the church. Augé reported that only forty-eight hours before the ceremony that would consecrate the repaired church, the same municipal council that had denied the funds in the first place issued 'an edict forbidding any religious demonstration in the streets.' As Augé put it, the council viewed Catholics 'as some wild Apaches.' He also told his friends in Quebec City that two separate committees were considering raising a monument to Champlain; one was headed by good Catholics such as himself, while the other was dominated by freemasons, whom he was sure would try to seek funds from Quebecers, in the process compromising his efforts. There is no evidence that Quebecers supported the monument project one way or the other; however, the tone of Augé's appeal must have sounded familiar to those who had lived through the commemorative politics of 1908.[13]

Laval and Champlain Fade from the Streets of Quebec

At roughly the same time the SSJBQ was raising funds to commemorate Champlain outside Quebec, another hero's star was rising in the province. Dollard des Ormeaux was not a founding father, but rather a guardian angel, someone who had given his life to defend the civilization that Champlain and Laval had begun. His fame was linked to a battle in 1660 at Long-Sault, just up the Ottawa River from Montreal. All that is unambiguously clear is that Dollard was killed, along with a small group that included both Canadiens and natives, in a skirmish in which he and his men were outnumbered by their Iroquois enemies. Dollard's motives for being at Long-Sault would later be questioned by historians, who saw him as interested mainly in securing control over the fur trade. But in the late nineteenth century he was seen by both English and French Canadians as someone who had given his life to safeguard the future of European settlement.

By the early twentieth century, a new French-Canadian version of the Dollard story had begun to gain a following. In this telling of the tale, Dollard and his colleagues had knowingly embarked on a suicide mission to dissuade the natives from attacking the nearby evangelical settlement of Ville-Marie, later known as Montreal. This new interpretation of Dollard as a selfless hero who had given his life so that a French-Canadian civilization might survive was perfectly suited to the mood in early-twentieth-century Quebec, where numerous nationalist leaders were loudly warning about the dangers posed by the modern world. Dollard's sacrifice in 1660 became a symbol to encourage young French Canadians to join groups such as the Association catholique de la jeunesse canadienne-française, the organization that had taken to the streets the day before the start of the tercentenary.

Dollard had been celebrated occasionally as a bit player in some of the commemorative events described in earlier chapters. He appeared sometimes on *chars allégoriques* in St-Jean-Baptiste parades in both Montreal and Quebec City, and he was featured in a scene dedicated to his exploits in the pageants of 1908. But it was only after the tercentenary – after it was widely accepted that he had made the supreme sacrifice for his people – that he emerged as a figure worthy of celebrations exclusively in his honour. Patrice Groulx identified the fête of 1910, on the occasion of the 250th anniversary of the Battle of Long-Sault, as a watershed in terms of Dollard's place in the collective memory of French Canadians. In the same year that the SSJBQ was raising the funds to repair Champlain's church in Brouage, Dollard was being celebrated in Montreal by 20,000 people who saw him as a symbol of their fight against the forces of assimilation. Dollard became 'a stark reminder about the fate of French Canada in the face of the challenges from its enemies.'[14]

Beginning with the 1910 fête, Dollard was celebrated on an annual basis. Abbé Lionel Groulx – soon to become a prominent university professor – was his most enthusiastic promoter. Groulx's efforts were assisted by the First World War, which made the threats to French Canada seem more concrete. Beginning in 1918, annual pilgrimages were staged to Long-Sault. In 1920 a monument to Dollard was unveiled in Montreal's Parc Lafontaine, with tens of thousands attending. As

Patrice Groulx has put it, Dollard received a form of popular beatification in 1910 and canonization in 1920; this put him in the same league as Joan of Arc, another Catholic hero who had given her life to save her people. Joan of Arc was proclaimed a saint the same year Dollard was immortalized with a monument.[15]

This public perception of Dollard as a champion of traditional French Catholic values held sway until after the Second World War, when modernity was more firmly embraced by the leaders of French-speaking Quebec, now interested in sharing in the fruits of a booming economy. Dollard, the symbol of francophone defensiveness, was swept away by the Quiet Revolution, during which the French Canadian, 'conquered, humiliated, and demoralized,' disappeared, and was replaced in the popular mind by the Québécois, 'successful, entrepreneurial, and ambitious.'[16] As Quebecers came to see themselves as a modern people, their interest in the history of New France evaporated. This development was reflected in the preoccupation of professional historians with the nineteenth and twentieth centuries. Around the same time, heroes from the French regime – both saviours such as Dollard and founders such as Champlain and Laval – were pushed aside. To the extent that there have been heroes in post–Quiet Revolution Quebec, they have tended to be modern figures such as Maurice Richard and René Lévesque.

After the tercentenary, Laval and Champlain largely disappeared from the streets of twentieth-century Quebec. For Laval there was a rather lacklustre celebration in May 1923 on the 300th anniversary of his birth. Perhaps it was a sign that Laval had retreated from the public consciousness that the editorial in Le Soleil marking the occasion observed, incorrectly, that the 1908 celebrations had marked 'the tercentenary [not the bicentenary] of the death of Mgr de Laval.' In any event, the same editorial noted that the 1923 celebrations were to be much more 'modest' than those of 1908, and that they would be 'more intimate' – the event would be open only to current and past students of the seminary that Laval had founded.[17] The program included a concert, a high mass, and a celebration at the foot of the Monument Laval, but there was no effort to draw in the public by marching from one site to another, as on previous occasions.

The clerical leaders ultimately took Laval to the streets, but the streets in question were in Laval's hometown of Montigny-sur-Avre. Quebecers had supported the reconstruction of Champlain's church only after a plea for help from the mayor of Brouage; this time the idea of celebrating a Quebec hero in France was the idea of French Canadians, who felt they owed something to France, which was suffering badly in the wake of the First World War. The project first surfaced in March 1922, when a committee headed by Mgr Paul-Eugène Roy was formed to oversee the raising of a monument at Montigny-sur-Avre and another, smaller one in Paris at the Église St-Germain-des-Prés, where Laval had been consecrated as bishop.

Roy's committee raised the required funds by appealing to the various dioceses, parishes, and Catholic *collèges classiques* in the province, as well as the Quebec City municipal government. But the largest contribution by far came from the provincial government; this earned the province the right to have 'la Province de Québec' inscribed in red letters on the panel that was installed in the church of Laval's hometown. Roy's committee had first hoped to erect a monument in some public place for all to see, but the only good site in town had been taken by the memorial to the dead of the Great War. So one had to enter the church to see the multicoloured panel, which was dominated by a scene depicting Laval being sent off to Quebec by France, with the holy family watching over the affair. As for the panel in Paris, it depicted Laval kneeling to receive his consecration.[18]

In 1923, clerical leaders resisted the temptation to celebrate Laval publicly in Quebec, perhaps feeling self-conscious about compromising the bishop's case for sainthood – a concern that had never stopped them before. However, on this occasion Cardinal Bégin (he had been promoted in 1908) encouraged prayers for Laval's eventual canonization, though adding to his priests that 'it would be a good idea to explain to the people that there can be no question about a public cult to the Venerable Servant of God. What we request from public prayer, is for the glorification [the eventual canonisation] of Mgr de Laval, and nothing more.'[19] In contrast with this restrained celebration of Laval at home, a pilgrimage was organized to take Quebecers – with $935 (nearly $10,000 in 2001 funds) and two months of free time at their disposal – to the two celebrations of Laval as well as to various sites across Europe, including Rome.[20] Laval might have received another grand public celebration in Quebec had he achieved sainthood. However, in the early twenty-first century, French-speaking Quebecers are profoundly indifferent to religious matters, and one must wonder whether much of a spectacle would be staged if he were canonized tomorrow.

Champlain largely disappeared from the streets of Quebec City until a celebration was mounted on the 350th anniversary of his founding of the town. The 1958 celebration went on for two weeks, but few of the events were especially imposing, except perhaps for the one staged on Canada Day, which featured a procession during which two hundred *personnages historiques* and eighty *chars allégoriques* passed through the old town before heading out to the Plains of Abraham. *Le Soleil* questioned this event's significance. Newspapers had once gone out of their way to promote celebrations like this; now, the editorialist made it clear that other, more important events had taken place on Canada Day of 1958: 'The majority of Québécois [the term still referred to residents of Quebec City in 1958], preoccupied with the celebration of the 350th anniversary of their city, managed to ignore the most important event that took place on 1 July. While tens of thousands of people took to the streets or watched from their balconies to see the great parade pass by, Radio-Canada was introducing its transcontinental television network.'[21]

The editorial writer hoped that the new television network would allow the creation of 'a truly Canadian sense of identity.' In 1908 some had believed – albeit rather naively – that public celebrations of the past could achieve that goal. By 1958 commemorative events were being seen as little more than trivial distractions, hardly worth serious comment. This impression was reinforced in the pages of *Le Soleil* by the photos of the various floats from the Canada Day parade; all were sponsored by large firms whose names were prominently displayed. The same paper also published pictures of the individuals who played the various historical personalities. Though all of the participants looked as if they were having fun wearing odd costumes, none of them looked as if they were involved in something as special and emotionally gripping as Lascelles's pageants.[22]

After 1958 Champlain's memory was trotted out from time to time on Canada Day by a group called the Société nationale Samuel de Champlain. But whatever Champlain might have represented had been lost – he was simply an ornament for the celebration of Canada.[23] His disappearance has become almost complete, judging from the advance publicity for the quadricentenary of the founding of Quebec. Though Champlain's name always figured prominently in the various official titles attached to the tercentenary, he has been elbowed aside since then: the 2008 event has been named the '400e anniversaire de Québec.' The mission statement of the organization created to stage this celebration points to the need to 'create an event ... that is festive, national and international; which brings people together and encourages further developments.' One has to look long and hard at the official website of the organizing committee to know that Champlain has anything to do with the celebration.[24]

The Divorce of the Past from the Present

The gradual retreat of Laval and Champlain from the streets of Quebec was to a considerable degree a reflection of various changes in Quebec society – first the shift to the defensiveness embodied by Dollard, and subsequently the embrace of the modern that left little room for ancient heroes. At the same time there were larger changes in the public's connection with the past that transcended provincial or national boundaries. The founding fathers had been lavishly celebrated at the turn of the century not only because their legacies were pertinent to French Canadians, but also because local leaders were able to draw on a repertoire of commemorative techniques in use on both sides of the Atlantic in order to reinforce the place of traditional elites in a rapidly urbanizing world. This debt to larger currents in commemorative practice was especially evident in the form chosen for the statues to the founding fathers and in the mounting of the pageants of 1908.

The monuments adhered to what Maurice Agulhon described as the standard formula for statues in the second half of the nineteenth century. Most of them were designed to pay tribute to great men whose lives told stories that leaders felt needed to be communicated. The hero invariably stood on a pedestal, dressed in period costume. The pedestal itself usually had an inscription presenting the pertinent virtues and accomplishments. There were usually allegorical figures – commonly women – to link the subject being held up for emulation with values that might have contemporary meaning. There was nothing subtle about the *sculpture réaliste*, which was designed to send a message to the larger population – a message grounded in the past but with relevance to the present. In that context, considerable energy was invested in sweating over the details of the monuments to the founding fathers.[25]

But conventions changed. A new approach to commemorative monuments was suggested by Rodin's statue of Balzac, which was first displayed in 1898, the year the Monument Champlain was unveiled. Balzac was presented in a slightly abstract manner, without any inscription explaining why he was important and without any allegorical figures to link him to larger lessons the public might absorb. Because all of this so flagrantly violated the accepted conventions, Rodin was heavily criticized. After the First World War, however, this 'modern' form became widespread, since it reflected the postwar sense that the ties between the past and the present had been severed; lessons from the past could no longer provide direction for ordinary people, who were now increasingly under the sway of such popular amusements as motion pictures, radio, and professional sports. In the late nineteenth and early twentieth centuries, art had been used to reach the public. The gulf between the masses and the artist grew following the war.

Many of the same processes also led to the demise of historical pageantry by the 1920s. As with public statues before the First World War, pageants were designed to depict the past in order to provide lessons about the present. This had certainly been the point of the exercise in Quebec in 1908. After the war, as David Glassberg has explained, there was a growing sense that 'the past [was] receding from the present and the future, rather than leading to it.' To the extent that there continued to be historical re-enactments, they 'were more likely to highlight the differences, rather than the continuities, between what souvenir programs labelled "past," "present" and "future."' An even more dramatic indication of the divorce of the past from the present was the emergence of the restored village, which offered a past frozen in time, without any links to the present. In Glassberg's words: 'The visitor to the carefully reconstructed sites valued history primarily for the opportunity it offered to escape temporarily to a world perceived as different from their own.'[26] This was a far cry from the pageants of Frank Lascelles, which had been designed to make spectators feel some kinship with the soldiers of Wolfe and Montcalm, who had been presented burying ancient grievances, in the process becoming brothers in arms. There was an implicit message of progress in such a story, but the certainty that the past held the answers for the future had been undermined by the war.

Statues would still be raised after the First World War, just as various types of historical re-enactments would continue to be offered to the population. But in the absence of an overriding belief that these commemorative techniques could profoundly transform society, it would prove impossible to mount lengthy and lavish public celebrations such as those that had been staged for Champlain and Laval. After all, why would leaders invest the vast quantities of time, energy, and money required to stage these spectacles if they could not imagine some return on their investment? In the end, the sumptuous celebrations of these two heroes could only have taken place during a very narrow window of opportunity in the late nineteenth and early twentieth centuries, when the messages that could be derived from their legacies seemed pertinent to French Canadians, and when there was sufficient belief in the power of these messages to mobilize leaders, lay and clerical alike.

Notes

Abbreviations

AAQ   Archives de l'archidiocèse de Québec
ANQQ   Archives nationales du Québec (Quebec)
AVQ   Archives de la Ville de Québec
MCSQ   Musée de la civilisation, fonds Séminaire de Québec
NAC   National Archives of Canada

Introduction

1 (Toronto, 1997).
2 Jocelyn Létourneau, 'La production historienne courante portant sur le Québec et ses rapports avec la construction des figures identitaires d'une communauté communicationnelle,' *Recherches sociographiques* 36 (1995): 9–45.
3 Pierre Nora, 'Between Memory and History: Les Lieux de Mémoire,' *Representations* 26 (1989): 15.
4 Eric Hobsbawm, 'Mass-Producing Traditions: Europe, 1870–1914,' in Hobsbawm and Terence Ranger, eds, *The Invention of Tradition* (Cambridge, 1983), 265.
5 Paul Commerton, *How Societies Remember* (Cambridge, 1989), 64.
6 Two studies touching on turn-of-the-century commemoration have deservedly been awarded the highest prize of the Institut d'histoire de l'Amérique française: Patrice Groulx's *Pièges de mémoire: Dollard des Ormeaux, les Amériendiens et nous* (Hull, 1998) deals with the changing image of a seventeenth-century hero; H.V. Nelles, whose masterful *The Art of Nation-Building* (Toronto, 1998) has also won the Canadian Historical Association's

Macdonald Prize, discusses the Quebec tercentenary of 1908. More recently, Colin Coates has addressed the varied representations of a Quebec heroine, Madeleine de Verchères, in a book co-authored with Cecilia Morgan, *Héroines and History: Representations of Madeleine de Verchères and Laura Secord* (Toronto, 2002). However, none of these studies deal with commemorative celebrations spanning the late nineteenth and early twentieth centuries. Most of the public events commemorating Dollard came after the First World War, while Nelles's study focuses on a single event and does not take a longer view of commemorative activity. As for Madeleine de Verchères, Coates shows that she received her most public celebration with the unveiling of a statue in her honour in 1913. The work closest to this one in its attention to late-nineteenth- and early-twentieth-century commemorative activity in Quebec is Alan Gordon's *Making Public Pasts: The Contested Terrain of Montreal's Public Memories, 1891–1930* (Montreal, 2001). While Gordon focuses on the conflicts between different interested parties vying to present the past, he pays little attention to the changing nature of commemorative celebrations across the western world.

7 Throughout the book I use the term 'French Canadian' to refer to the French-speaking population of Quebec. This term might have included French speakers living outside Quebec, but I have consistently used the term in a geographically limited sense.

8 For examples of the renewed interest in cultural matters, see Yvan Lamonde, *Histoire sociale des idées au Québec* (Montreal, 2000); and Ollivier Hubert, *Sur la terre comme au ciel la gestion des rites par l'Église catholique du Québec: fin XVIIe–mi-XIXe siècle* (Ste-Foy, 2000). Just as the revisionists' focus on economic matters was related to the concerns of the Quiet Revolution, historians' increased interest in cultural matters emerged beginning in the 1990s alongside the larger questioning in Quebec society of the assumptions that had been dominant since the 1960s. For a fuller discussion of these matters, see *Making History*, ch. 5.

9 ANQQ, Fonds Société St-Jean-Baptiste de Québec, P412/2, form letter from Albert Jobin (president of SSJBQ), 10 March 1904.

10 Peter Pope, *The Many Landfalls of John Cabot* (Toronto, 1997).

11 Chouinard, *Fête nationale des Canadiens-français célébrée à Québec, 1881–1889* (Quebec, 1890), vi.

12 *La Presse*, 2 July 1895. This and all subsequent material that was originally published in French has been translated into English by the author to make the book more accessible. The sculptor of the Monument Maisonneuve, Louis-Philippe Hébert, will emerge later as a failed participant in the competition for the Monument Champlain and as the artist responsible for the Monument Laval.

13 This point has been made in David Waldstreicher, *In the Midst of Perpetual Fetes: The Making of American Nationalism, 1776–1820* (Chapel Hill, 1997); and Simon P. Newman, *Parades and the Politics of the Street: Festive Ritual in the Early American Republic* (Philadelphia, 1997).

1. The Discovery and Display of Mgr de Laval, 1877–1878

1 In the following pages I refer to either the Cathedral or the Basilica, depending upon the context.

2 MCSQ, MS 679, Légaré journal, 20 September 1877.

3 MCSQ, Université, 119, CD, Taschereau to Rev. B. Paquet, Rome, 22 September 1877.

4 For a fuller account of Laval's life, see André Vachon's biography in *Dictionary of Canadian Biography* (hereafter *DCB*) 2: 358–72.

5 Ibid., 366.

6 Garneau, *Histoire du Canada depuis sa découverte jusqu'à nos jours.*, 4th ed, (Montreal, 1882), 1: 188. I have discussed the various editions of Garneau in *Making History*; the issue is also discussed at length in Serge Gagnon, *Le Québec et ses historiens* (Quebec, 1978).

7 H.-R. Casgrain, 'Histoire du Canada' (review of the fourth edition of Garneau), *Opinion publique*, 15 November 1883, 541–2.

8 MCSQ, Université 140, AC: Hamel to Casgrain, 4 December 1883.

9 MCSQ, Fonds Casgrain, lettres, vol. 16, no. 154, Casgrain to Abbé Verrault, 9 October 1892. In spite of these criticisms, when Casgrain testified during the second phase of Laval's trial for sainthood, he took a positive view of the bishop. See, Gagnon, *Quebec and Its Historians*, 103–4.

10 Vachon, 371.

11 A. Leblond De Brumath, *Bishop Laval* (Toronto, 1910), 256–7.

12 Cited in Jean-Marie Lebel, 'Les tombeaux du premier évêque de Québec,' *Cap-Aux-Diamants*, Hors Série (Spring 1993), 42.

13 Cited in Auguste Gosselin, *Vie de Mgr de Laval* (Quebec, 1890), 2: 544.

14 Gosselin, 2: 638. I can attest to the existence of cloth soaked in Laval's blood, since I came across one such relic in the seminary archives (MCSQ, SME, 12.3/59/1L).

15 Gosselin, 2: 645–7.

16 *Le Canadien*, 5 June 1854.

17 'Mémoires' of Olivier Robitaille, reproduced in H.J.J.B. Chouinard, *Fête nationale des Canadiens-français célébrée à Québec en 1880* (Quebec, 1881), 61.

18 Shortly after the discovery of the bones, the SSJBQ lobbied hard, in spite of the absence of any evidence, for the archbishop to acknowledge that

'the bones ... were those of Catholic soldiers' (Robitaille, 'Mémoires' in Chouinard, *Fête Nationale 1880*, 56).

19 Ibid., 69.

20 Cited in Eveline Bossé, *La Capricieuse à Québec en 1855* (Montreal, 1984), 45.

21 *Le Canadien*, 16, 20 July 1855.

22 J.-C. Taché, *Notice historiographique sur la fête célébrée à Québec, le 16 juin 1859, jour du deux centième anniversaire de l'arrivée de Mgr de Montmorency-Laval en Canada* (Quebec, 1859), 6–7.

23 The name was spelled in this manner in the official volume produced for the 1859 celebration of Laval. The DCB entry suggests either La Rue or Larue. During the morning of 15 June, LaRue was examined 'solely before members of the medical profession,' and in the afternoon before 'a larger assembly of people' (*Journal de l'instruction publique*, 3: no. 7 [July 1859], 112).

24 *Le Canadien*, 13 June 1859.

25 Taché, *Notice historiographique*, 14–15. LaRue's findings are interesting in light of Quebec's distinction at the start of the twenty-first century as home to one of the highest rates of suicide in the Western world.

26 Ibid., 53.

27 The debate was on the subject of the education provided in Quebec's collèges classiques. The discussion focused on the relative merits of a classical as opposed to a more 'practical' education. In the end, the winning side showed that a practical education had its place, but that leaders needed to have their knowledge tempered by values grounded in Catholicism. Effectively, this was the same message that had been communicated in LaRue's thesis.

28 *Le Canadien*, 17 June 1859.

29 *Journal de l'instruction publique*, 3, no. 7 (July 1859), 112.

30 *Quebec Morning Chronicle*, 14 June 1859; also published in *Le Canadien*, 13 June 1859.

31 *Le Canadien*, 17 June 1859.

32 Crémazie's contribution to the 1859 celebration of Laval included a lengthy poem ('Deux centième anniversaire de l'arrivée de Mgr de Montmorency-Laval en Canada'), which was widely circulated at the time of the fête, along with a shorter tribute to the Seminary ('Envoi à Messieurs du Séminaire de Québec').

33 Letter from Crémazie to Casgrain, reprinted in Casgrain, *Octave Crémazie* (Montreal, 1912), 34.

34 There were several slightly different published versions of the Cantate. The complete text reproduced below is taken from Odette Condemine, *Octave Crémazie, Oeuvres*, vol. 1–Poésie (Ottawa, 1972), 355.

Connaissez-vous sous le soleil,
Un fleuve à nul autre pareil
Dont les rivages enchantés
Encadrent les flots argentés,
Sous un ciel brillant et serein?
Fils de Laval et de Champlain, Le Canadien de ses aieux,
Garde le souvenir pieux,

> Protégé par la croix
> Brillant sur nos montagnes
> Dans nos vertes campagnes
> Il conserve nos droits
> Et fier de son destin
> Français et catholique
> Il montre à l'Amérique
> Deux noms: Laval, Champlain.

Ouvrant tes portes immortels
Gloire, couronne ces héros,
Et que tes pages éternelles
Gardent à jamais leurs travaux.
Soleil, qui vis sur nos parages
Mourir ces deux héros français,
Tu vois aujourd'hui nos rivages
Couverts des fruits de leurs bienfaits.

Et de la croix et de l'épée
Ces deux champions glorieux
Font briller dans notre épopée
L'éclair de leurs noms radieux.
Sur les bords de la jeune France,
O Laval! ton nom respecté
S'élève comme un phare immense
Rayonnant d'immortalité

Vive, vive, Laval! que notre voix sonore
Sache redire encore
La gloire et les bienfaits
Des deux héros Français.
Amis, chantons:
  Vive, vive, Laval!
  Vive, Champlain! vive, Laval!

35 Ernest Gagnon, *Feuilles volantes et pages d'histoire* (Quebec, 1910), 78.

36 Taché, 64.

37 Ibid., 68; *L'Abeille*, 22 June 1859.

38 The Taché volume was published 'with the authorization of the rector of Université Laval.'

39 The elevation of the Cathedral to the status of a Basilica placed the archbishop's church in a very select category. Though the number of Basilicas increased in the late nineteenth and early twentieth centuries, this was still a considerable honour. As a result, certain privileges were extended to the archbishop and his staff, especially on special occasions such as processions, when they would be allowed to wear elaborate garb and be surrounded by other trappings of their new status.

40 The words to this ode can be found in Felicien David, 'Christopher Columbus, or, The Discovery of the New World: A Symphonic Ode in Four Parts, ' trans. James A. Lanigan (Buffalo, 1892). 'Christopher Columbus' would return during the tercentenary of 1908, when Laval's legacy was marginalized by organizers trying to downplay his French Catholic message. All of the other celebrations of Laval and Champlain between 1878 and 1908 opted for the cantata. In this context, the decision by the local ecclesiastical establishment to ignore Crémazie's tribute to Laval can only be seen as a snub of the first bishop.

41 *Le deuxième centenaire de l'érection du diocèse de Québec* (Quebec, 1874), v.

42 MCSQ, Séminaire, 59, no. 13, Langevin to Taschereau, 17 April 1878.

43 The earliest reference that I could find to the planning of the fête was in a letter from the superior of the seminary, Thomas Hamel, who went on to be the advocate of Laval's case for canonization. MCSQ, Université, 123, AZ: Hamel, to Mgr B. Paquet, 21 February 1878.

44 MCSQ, Manuscrit 33, Journal Personnel de Mgr T.-E. Hamel, 5 August 1878. The emphasis is Hamel's. In the text I have referred to Hamel as 'Abbé,' the title that he bore from 1854 to 1886, thereafter being referred to as 'Monseigneur.' His journal was catalogued using the latter title. The issue of the role of the clergy in politics is discussed at length in Roberto Perin, *Rome in Canada: The Vatican and Canadian Affairs in the Late Victorian Age* (Toronto, 1990); for the university question, see, André Lavallée, *Québec contre Montréal: la querelle universitaire, 1876–1891* (Montreal, 1974).

45 Archives de la paroisse de Notre-Dame de Québec, Cahiers de prônes, 7 April 1878. Auclair's comments were in line with his sympathy for the Quebec City working class. As René Hardy has observed, 'Auclair was particularly sensitive to the destitution caused by the chronic unemployment in Quebec City at that time' (DCB, 11: 38).

46 Bruce Levine et al., *Who Built America: Working People and the Nation's Economy, Politics, Culture and Society* (New York, 1989), 1: 515–6.

47 These various strikes are discussed in Jean Hamelin, et al, *Répertoire des grèves dans la province de Québec au XIXe siécle* (Montreal, 1971).

48 *L'Événement,* 22 May 1878.

49 *Translation des restes de Mgr de Laval à la chapelle du séminaire de Québec: Relation complète de tout ce qui s'est passé depuis l'exhumation des ossements de Mgr de Laval le 19 sept 1877 jusqu'à leur déposition au séminaire le 23 mai 1878.* (Quebec, 1878), 7; *L'Événement,* 22–3 May 1878.

50 Serge Gagnon, *Mourir hier et aujourd'hui* (Ste-Foy, 1987), 72.

51 The rules as they existed at the time of the introduction of Laval's candidacy are described in Thomas Macken, *The Canonisation of Saints* (Dublin, 1910).

52 MCSQ, SME, 12.3/59, file File 12, Hamel to P.-B. Delpeck, 11 April 1878.

53 Ibid., Université, 123, AZ: Hamel, to Mgr B. Paquet, 21 February 1878; Université 123, CJ, Paquet to Hamel, 10 March 1878.

54 Gosselin, 2: 662, 664.

55 *Translation des restes,* 36, 44.

56 Ibid., 36; MCSQ, Manuscrit 33, Journal Personnel de Mgr T.-E. Hamel, 8 May 1878.

57 *Translation des restes,* 36.

58 Gosselin, 2: 664.

59 The name also appears as Sawatanin, which means 'man of memory' ('homme du souvenir').

60 MCSQ, SME, 12.3/59, file File 62, letter from P. Vincent (Sawatannen), vicaire à l'Ancienne-Lorette, 20 May 1878.

61 Michel Lessard, *The Livernois Photographers* (Quebec, 1987), 96, 93.

62 *L'Événement,* 17 May 1878. Years later, one priest remarked that his mother 'kept until her death in her prayer book the photograph of the Venerable Mgr de Laval' (MCSQ, 'Sacra Rituum Congregatione, Quebecen, Beatifications et cannonizationis ven servi Francisci de Montmorency-Laval Primi Quebecensis Episcopi. Summarium Super Dubio, 1904,' testimony of the Rev. Georges-Pierre Côté, p. 1128).

63 The use of this glass coffin was in line with the increasingly extravagant trappings of funerals in urban Quebec during the nineteenth century (Gagnon, *Mourir,* 35).

64 There is a considerable literature dealing with the symbolism of public processions. See for instance Robert Darnton, 'A Bourgeois Puts His World in Order: The City as a Text,' in Darnton, *The Great Cat Massacre* (New York, 1985), 107–43; Mona Ozouf, *Festivals and the French Revolution,* trans. Alan Sheridan (Cambridge, Mass, 1988); Susan Davis, *Parades and Power. Street Theatre in Nineteenth-Century Philadelphia* (Philadelphia, 1986); Roberto Da Matta, 'Carnival in Multiple Planes,' in John J. MacAloon, ed., *Rite, Drama, Festival, Spectacle* (Philadelphia, 1984), 208–40.

65 In spite of the ubiquitous nature of Fête-Dieu processions in Quebec, historians have given them scant attention. This reflects the general disinclination among historians in post–Quiet Revolution Quebec to deal with religious issues, no matter how central they may have been to the life of the community.

66 The Fête-Dieu always fell on the Thursday following the eighth Sunday after Easter. In practice, however, in Quebec the Fête-Dieu festivities, including the procession, were always held on the subsequent Sunday (or nine weeks after Easter).

67 Miri Rubin, *Corpus Christi: The Eucharist in Late Medieval Culture* (Cambridge, 1991), 214.

68 Ibid., 78–9.

69 Mervyn James, 'Ritual Drama and Social Body in Late Medieval English Towns,' *Past and Present* 98 (February 1983), 6–9.

70 Rubin, 263; 266–7.

71 Claude Macherel, 'Corpus Christi: Cosmos et société,' in Antoinette Molonié, ed., *Le corps de dieu en fêtes* (Paris, 1996), 56. Macherel observed that this positioning of the host at the centre of the marchers stood apart from the organization of a royal procession, in which the monarch would have been at the front.

72 Rubin, 267; Macherel, 55.

73 Christine Sheito, 'Une fête contestée: la procession de la Fête-Dieu à Montréal au XIXe siècle,' MA thesis (anthropology), Université de Montréal, 1983, 127.

74 Rubin, 355–6.

75 Cited in Philippe Sylvain et Nive Voisine, *Recueil et consolidation: Histoire du catholicism québécois* (Montreal, 1991), vol. 2, tome 2, p. 356.

76 *Translation des restes*, 47.

77 MCSQ, SME, 12.3/59, file File 12, Hamel to P.-B. Delpeck, 11 April 1878.

78 *Congrégation des jeunes gens de la Haute-Ville de Québec érigée sous le titre de l'Immaculée-Conception* (Quebec, 1902), 3, 15.

79 *Annales de l'Hôtel-Dieu de Québec*, 3: pp. 20–24.

80 The ties between the French-Catholic hierarchy of Quebec City and the local Irish community were reinforced at the time by the fact that Archbishop Taschereau had attended to the Irish immigrants at the quarantine station on Grosse-Île in 1847, the year of the largest movement of those escaping the potato famine. Taschereau contracted typhus for his efforts, which were immortalized on the monument constructed in his honour, unveiled in Quebec City in 1923.

81 *Translation des restes*, 60–1.

82 Ibid., 63. The image of the French colonial governor passing the torch to the lieutenant-governor of Quebec was also advanced during celebrations in Laval's honour in 1891. Regarding this celebration, see chapter 3.

83 *L'Abeille*, 31 May 1878.

84 MCSQ, SME, 12.3/59: File 62, Bar of the Province of Quebec, Section of the District of Quebec to Hamel, 22 May 1878; File 61, Jean-Thomas Taschereau to Hamel, 18 May 1878; Taschereau sent a further complaint to Hamel two days later: File 62, Taschereau to Hamel, 20 May 1878; NAC, MG 5 C 1: Ministère des affaires étrangères, France, Correspondance consulaire avec le consulat de Québec, Lefaivre to Hamel, 28 May 1878.

85 *Courrier du Canada*, 4 May 1878.

86 Ibid., 15 May 1878. The conspiracy theories regarding Joly were also reported, so as to refute them, in *L'Événement*, 15 May 1878.

87 *Le Canadien*, 25 May 1878.

88 *L'Événement*, 27–8 May 1878.

89 *Journal de Québec*, 28 May, 25 May 1878.

90 *L'Événement*, 20 May 1878. The same rules, which had originally been read to the congregation at the Basilica on the Sunday preceding the fête, were also reported in other local papers. The emphasis comes from these published versions.

91 *Translation des restes*, 64–6.

92 Ibid., 79.

93 *Quebec Morning Chronicle*, 24 May 1878.

94 *Translation des restes*, 81. This inscription was in French. There is no evidence that anyone had considered using a Latin one, but the issue of using Latin on monuments in the public eye would emerge in subsequent celebrations of the founding fathers.

95 Ibid, 86.

96 Ibid., 88.

97 Ibid., 94, 100.

98 Ibid., 108–10. These letters were originally published in Latin. They were translated into English by Crista McInnis, to whom I am extremely grateful.

99 Various aspects of Laval's candidature for sainthood – in particular the public celebration of the Vatican's declaration that he was 'venerable' – are discussed in chapter 3.

100 MCSQ, 'Sacra Rituum Congregatione, Quebecen, Beatifications et cannonizationis ven servi Francisci de Montmorency-Laval Primi Quebecensis Episcopi. Summarium Super Dubio, 1904' (hereafter Summarium 1904), 1193, 1209–10. The testimony of these and subsequent witnesses referred

to in this chapter was not available to the general public. The 'Summarium' was produced in the early twentieth century exclusively for the internal use of the seminary, which was promoting Laval's candidacy for sainthood.

101 Ibid., 1202, 1196–7, 1206–7.

102 Mgr Henri Têtu, *Les évêques de Québec* (Quebec, 1889), 74; Summarium 1904, 1206–7.

103 Summarium 1904, 1117–8.

104 Laval did not accede to the second step along the road to sainthood until his beatification in 1980. As I write these lines, he has still not reached the third and final step.

2. A Monument for Champlain, 1879–1898

1 *Journal de Québec,* 12 November 1866.

2 Marcel Trudel has observed: 'The supposition is that the bodies (Champlain was not alone) interred beneath [the chapel] were moved and placed beneath the new parish church (today the Basilica).' If such had been the case, Laval and Champlain might have been fairly close to one another before the bishop's remains were discovered (DCB, 1: 197).

3 J.M. Harper, 'Champlain's Tomb,' *Transactions of the Literary and Historical Society of Quebec* 19 (1889), 119.

4 Laverdière and Casgrain, *Découverte du tombeau de Champlain* (Quebec, 1866); Drapeau, *Observations sur la brochure de MM. les abbés Laverdière et Casgrain relativement à la découverte du tombeau de Champlain* (Quebec, 1866); Drapeau, *Le journal de Québec et le tombeau de Champlain* (Quebec, 1867); Drapeau, *La Question du tombeau de Champlain* (Ottawa, 1880).

5 Cited in François Drouin et Jean-Marie Lebel, 'Le Roman-Feuilleton du Tombeau de Champlain,' *Cap-Aux-Diamants,* vol. 4, no. 3 (1988), 45. This article offers an excellent summary of the search for Champlain's remains.

6 Maurice Agulhon, 'La "statuomanie" en l'histoire,' *Ethnologie française,* nos. 2–3 (1978), 145–72.

7 Harper, p. 143.

8 Champlain's promoters touted him as the founder of the first permanent settlement in Canada for his exploits at Quebec City. They were on firm ground in the sense that the only significant French settlements that predated Quebec were short-lived affairs. In 1604, Champlain and Pierre Du Gua de Monts established a settlement at Île Ste-Croix (on the current border between Maine and New Brunswick). However, this colony lasted only a single winter before Champlain and de Monts transplanted it to Port-Royal (in present-day Nova Scotia). The second effort ended when

the settlement was destroyed in 1613. Although these efforts were ephemeral, in 1898 and again in 1908 there was a sense that Champlain somehow was linked exclusively to Quebec City, as if he had never been involved in establishing any other settlement on what would become Canadian soil.

9 N.E. Dionne, *Samuel Champlain: fondateur de Québec et père de la Nouvelle-France. Histoire de sa vie et de ses voyages*, 2 vols. (Quebec, 1891–1906), 2: 361.

10 Trudel, 197; C.-H. Laverdière, ed., *Œuvres de Champlain* (Quebec, 1870).

11 Auguste Gosselin, 'Le vrai monument de Champlain: ses Œuvres éditées par Laverdière,' *Mémoires de la Société Royale du Canada*, Section 1 (1908), 3–23.

12 Trudel, 197.

13 Dionne, 1: 7.

14 Dionne, 1: 6.

15 Trudel, 188.

16 Garneau, *Histoire du Canada depuis sa découverte jusqu'à nos jours*, 1st ed. (Quebec, 1845), 1: 253. This observation was not altered in subsequent versions of Garneau's text.

17 Dionne, 1: xiii, ix; 2: 297.

18 Dionne, 1: 355, 342. The same depiction of Hélène can be found in H.-R. Casgrain, *Les origines du Canada: Champlain: Sa vie et son caractère* (Quebec, 1898), 41. Serge Gagnon made a similar observation in his *Québec et ses historiens*, 171.

19 This point is also made by Marie-Aimé Cliche in her discussion of Dionne's biography: 'Samuel de Champlain, fondateur de Québec et père de la Nouvelle-France,' in Maurice Lemire, comp., *Dictionnaire des œuvres littéraires du Québec*, 2nd ed., rev. (Montreal, 1980), 1: 775.

20 J.M. Harper, *Champlain: A Drama in Three Acts* (Toronto, 1908), 28; Charles Colby, *The Founder of New France: A Chronicle of Champlain* (Toronto, 1915), 80.

21 Harper, 51.

22 Colby, 1, 133–4.

23 Ibid., 151.

24 Minutes of Literary and Historical Society of Quebec, 9 April 1879, in *Transactions of the Literary and Historical Society of Quebec, 1879–80* (Quebec, 1880), 9.

25 *Quebec Morning Chronicle*, 13 December 1890. The society's involvement with the project resurfaced briefly in 1889 when J.M. Harper claimed that 'a proposition has already been made by the wealthiest corporation in the country to build such a monument for us at least in part ('Champlain's Tombeau,' 143). Although Harper did not name the corporation, it was

most likely the Canadian Pacific Railway, which was already interested in developing the Dufferin Terrace through its plans to construct the Château Frontenac. It must be noted, however, that research in the CPR archives did not confirm this hypothesis.

26 H.J.J.B. Chouinard, comp., *Annales de la Société St-Jean-Baptiste de Québec, 1889–1901* (Quebec, 1903), 21 (hereafter, *Annales, 1889–1901*).

27 Caouette, 'Une Statue à Samuel de Champlain,' *Le Glaneur* 1, no. 1 (1890).

28 *Inauguration du Monument Champlain* (Quebec, 1902), 5. The monument Short-Wallick was ultimately unveiled in 1891 on another site outside the walls of the old city.

29 *L'Électeur*, 11 December 1890. Mercier proposed this site because one of the terms for the purchase of the land for the city hall from the Jesuits was the construction of three statues, one of which would honour Champlain.

30 *Annales, 1889–1901*, 21–5.

31 Kirk Savage, *Standing Soldiers, Kneeling Slaves: Race, War and Monument in Nineteenth-Century America* (Princeton, 1997), 6.

32 Ibid., 31–4.

33 AVQ, QP1–4/73–8, Société St-Jean-Baptiste to Mayor, 18 October 1890.

34 I could not help but regret the abandonment by the SSJBQ of responsibility for the project. The Société's records have survived, but I could not find those for the Comité du Monument Champlain. One report suggested that they had been sealed in the pedestal of the monument!

35 *Inauguration*, 10. The remarks that follow regarding the balances in the committee's bank account come from figures in *Inauguration*, 22–3.

36 *L'Électeur*, 20 October 1894.

37 Ibid.

38 *Mandements, lettres pastorales et circulaires des Evêques de Québec*, 8: 179, Circulaire no. 233, 9 November 1894.

39 Meeting of Comité du Monument Champlain, 29 January 1895; reproduced in *Le Soleil*, 22 September 1898.

40 The federal and Quebec City governments contributed $3,000 each, while the Quebec provincial government contributed $2,000 and that of Ontario $1,000.

41 NAC, RG 6, Series A-1, vol. 87, file 3302, Petition from a meeting of citizens in Quebec City, 19 May 1894.

42 *L'Électeur* was in especially bad repute among the clergy in 1896 because it had published extracts from L.-O. David's *Le clergé canadien, sa vie, son œuvre*, which had been banned from public view by the bishops. To escape the wrath of the clergy, the name of the journal was changed and a more mod-

erate approach toward church–state affairs was adopted (André Beaulieu and Jean Hamelin, *La presse québécoise: des origines à nos jours*, 3: 13).

43 MCSQ, Journal, 17 September 1895, 4: 541.

44 *Inauguration*, 11. The Château Frontenac opened in 1893. In 1904, Adolphe-Basile Routhier, touting the future prospects for Quebec City, observed that tourists would be attracted by the Monument Champlain: 'Should they be stopping at the Frontenac, from the very windows of their hotel they will see the statue of Champlain with his back turned to the old continent, proudly standing in the open space, upon a high pedestal' (Routhier, *Quebec: A Quaint Medieval French City in America at the Dawn of the Twentieth Century* (Montreal, 1904), 285).

45 Dominick Malack, 'Le développement du tourisme: l'exemple du Château Frontenac,' in Serge Courville and Robert Garon, eds., *Atlas historique du Québec: Québec, ville et capitale* (Ste-Foy, 2001), 318.

46 Savage, 7.

47 AVQ, QP1–4/73–8, letters from Baillairgé, 27 February 1895.

48 Christina Cameron, 'Charles Baillairgé,' DCB, 13: 30–1.

49 *Inauguration*, 193.

50 Agulhon, 'Statuomanie,' 61. The jury evaluated twenty submissions, some of which only amounted to sketches. There were fourteen maquettes; photographs of twelve of them can be seen in a dossier at the MCSQ (Ph1986–0850 to 0860; Ph1987–0842). The previous comments were based on these twelve.

51 The reporter's comments were published in *La Presse*, 26 February 1896. From those comments, it is possible to recognize these three 'Catholic' submissions as MCSQ photographs 1986-0853; 1986-0855; and 1986-0851.

52 MCSQ photograph, 1986-0857. Joanne Chagnon, 'Le Monument à monseigneur de Laval,' in Daniel Drouin, ed., *Louis-Philippe Hébert* (Quebec, 2001), 185.

53 *Canadian Magazine* 11 (September 1898), 431; MCSQ photograph, 1986-0860.

54 Agulhon noted that the use of *une allégorie féminine* was common in turn-of-the-century statues ('Statuomanie,' 61). As for the use of head dresses that symbolized the city that was being celebrated, see Marina Warner, *Monuments and Maidens: The Allegory of the Female Form* (New York, 1985), 259–60. The iconography of 'Fame' is explained in Lina De Girolami Cheney, 'Fame,' in Helene Roberts, ed., *Encyclopedia of Comparative Iconography* (Chicago and London, 1998), 1: 307–13.

55 *Inauguration*, 193.

56 MCSQ, Journal, 24–25 February 1896, 4: 610.

57 MCSQ, Univ. 58, no. 14, Mgr J.-C. K. Laflamme to Abbé H.A. Verreau, 26 February 1896; MCSQ, Journal, 26 February 1896, 4: 610. Hébert's failure to win the competition was also grumbled about after the Monument Champlain was unveiled by an anonymous writer in *Le Monde Illustré*, 24 September 1898.

58 Maurice Larkin, *Church and State after the Dreyfus Affair: The Separation Issue in France* (London, 1974), 37.

59 Hanotaux's handling of African affairs is discussed in Alf Andrew Heggoy, *The African Policies of Gabriel Hanotaux* (Athens, Georgia, 1972).

60 *Inauguration*, 27–50.

61 Legislation to create such a ministry was introduced early in 1898. It was passed by the Legislative Assembly but rejected in the upper house, the appointed Legislative Council. A Ministry of Education would not be established until the 1960s.

62 *Inauguration*, 62–4.

63 Ibid., 59. Boudin's first name was not provided, and his occupation could only be determined by various comments made by other speakers at the banquet.

64 Ibid., 60.

65 Heggoy, *African Policies of Gabriel Hanotaux*, 124.

66 *L'Événement*, 6 December 1898.

67 MCSQ, Journal, 4: 682, 13 November 1896. The French translation of the Latin text can be found in Casgrain, *Notes relatives aux inscriptions du monument de Champlain.* (Quebec, 1898), 21–2.

68 Cited in Casgrain, *Notes*, 19.

69 Cited in Casgrain, *Notes*, 7,21. The emphasis is Lindsay's. Casgrain's inconsistent support for Laval's canonization was discussed in chapter 1.

70 Chapais, cited in Casgrain, *Notes*, 22; Raoul Renault, 'Le monument Champlain: histoire de son inscription,' *Courrier du Livre*, 3 (1898), 378.

71 MCSQ, 'Souvenir Album given by Arthur Doughty to participants in the Champlain Ceremony, 21 September 1898.' This included the 'Latin inscription intended for the Monument Champlain, but which has been replaced by an English inscription' (np).

72 Casgrain, *Notes*, 23.

73 The two versions of the French inscription can be seen, one above the other, in *Semaine religieuse*, no. 24 (1899), 386. The English version, as it appears on the monument, translated (fittingly) by the rector of the Anglican Church in Quebec City, reads:

Samuel
de
Champlain
Born at Brouage in Saintonge
About 1567. Served in the French army as Marechal des Logis
under Henri IV. Explored the
West Indies from 1599 to 1601 and also
Acadia from 1604 to 1607
Founded Québec in 1608
Discovered the region of the Great
Lakes. Led several expeditions
against the Iroquois from 1609 to
1615. Was successively Lieutenant
Governor and Governor of New
France. Died at Québec December 25, 1635

74 Dionne, in *Le Soleil*, 21 January 1899.
75 Ibid.
76 Casgrain, *Notes*, 30.
77 *Le Soleil*, 21 January 1899.
78 Gagnon, *Réponse à la brochure de Monsieur l'abbé H.-R. Casgrain: intitulée 'Notes relatives aux inscriptions du monument de Champlain'* (Quebec, 1899), 5–6.
79 *Semaine religieuse*, 25 June 1898, 10: 694. In the same article, the journal also voiced its own complaint about Casgrain's version of the inscription in honour of Champlain.
80 MCSQ, Fonds Casgrain, Correspondance, Liasse 25, no. 2, 30 January 1899.
81 While many, perhaps most, French Canadians considered St-Jean-Baptiste as their patron saint, he only officially secured that title in 1908. St John the Baptist's role in French-Canadian culture is discussed in more detail later in this chapter.
82 ANQQ, Fonds SSJBQ, P412/8, Comité de régie, 31 May 1898.
83 Ibid., 3 June 1898.
84 *L'Événement*, 13 September 1898.
85 *Le Soleil*, 19–20 September; 17 September 1898.
86 *Annales, 1889–1901*, 50, 68, 85
87 *Le Soleil*, 3 September 1898; H.J.J.B. Chouinard, comp., *Fête Nationale des Canadiens-Français célébrée à Québec en 1880* (Quebec, 1881), 195.
88 *L'Événement*, 22 September 1898; *Le Soleil*, 23 September; 22 September 1898.

89 In fact, the declaration by the Vatican of St-Jean-Baptiste as French Canada's patron saint was a coup for Mgr Bégin in the context of the commemorative politics of 1908.

90 Pamphile LeMay, *Fêtes et corvées* (Lévis, 1898), 24; Benjamin Sulte, 'Les origines de la fête St-Jean-Baptiste,' in *Fête Nationale, 1880*, 4.

91 Sulte, 3.

92 John R. Porter, 'Processions et défilés,' in *Le grand héritage: l'Eglise catholique et des arts au Québec* (Quebec: Musée du Québec, 1984), 261.

93 Lemay, 25–6.

94 As we saw in chapter 1, in the aftermath of the rebellions the church was similarly interested in using the Fête-Dieu as a tool for consolidating its control over the people.

95 While the discussion that follows pertains to St-Jean-Baptiste processions in Quebec City, there is a much larger literature on such celebrations in Montreal. See for instance Michèle Guay, 'La fête de la St-Jean-Baptiste à Montréal, 1834–1909,' MA thesis, Université d'Ottawa, 1973; or Alan Gordon, 'Inventing Tradition: Montreal's Saint-Jean-Baptiste Day Re-Examined,' unpublished paper presented to Canadian Historical Association, 1996. Gordon also discusses this issue in his *Making Public Pasts* (Montreal, 2001), ch. 8.

96 *Fête Nationale, 1880*, 570.

97 Guay, 145–6. Guay more generally described the early Montreal festivities as having constituted 'a religious celebration' in which 'the participants marched as a procession to the church. The model for this solemn procession was most likely borrowed from the Fête-Dieu procession, which is celebrated in a similar fashion.'

98 Porter, 262.

99 Chouinard, comp., *Fête nationale des Canadiens-français célébrée à Québec, 1881–1889* (Quebec, 1890), 265.

100 Roberto Da Matta, 'Carnival in Multiple Planes,' in John J. MacAloon, ed., *Rite, Drama, Festival, Spectacle* (Philadelphia, 1984), 218–9.

101 The 'procession de la Fête-Dieu' was alternatively referred to as the 'procession du très St-Sacrement,' but it never would have been connected with any of the terms occasionally associated with 'la St-Jean.' In 1908, when both events would be staged in conjunction with the unveiling of the Monument Laval, one observer would contrast the 'pieuse procession des fidèles à la suite de l'Hostie' with 'l'enthousiaste défilé d'un cortège national' (*Le Vénérable François de Montmorency-Laval Premier Évêque de Québec; Souvenir des fêtes du deuxième centenaire célébrées les 21, 22 et 23 juin 1908* [Quebec, 1908], 124). For its part, the Quebec archdiocese distinguished

in 1908 between 'la procession du St-Sacrement' and 'le cortège de la St-Jean-Baptiste' (AAQ, 4A, 4-4. 'Procession du Très Saint Sacrement' (nd).

102 There were moments in the history of the Quebec City St-Jean-Baptiste parade when there were inklings of the presence of the host. In the mammoth 1880 procession, the 'char allégorique,' or float, of the SSJBQ was located in the middle of the procession, occupying the position of the host in the Fête-Dieu. Otherwise, on that occasion, the marchers were organized in the normal, ascending manner of St-Jean-Baptiste processions.

103 Benoît Lacroix, 'La fête religieuse au Québec,' in Diane Pinard, ed., *Que la fête commence* (Montreal, 1982), 55.

104 Because of the shift of the St-Jean-Baptiste celebrations to September, no festivities were held on 24 June. Normally, newspapers would not have published on the 24th, but in 1898 this was a regular day in Quebec City. *Le Soleil* observed that the city was oddly quiet, as it would be necessary to wait until September to celebrate 'the virtues and accomplishments of our fathers, to commemorate their sacrifices.'

105 John R. Porter notes that in the large St-Jean-Baptiste parade of 1880 in Quebec City, there were 22 'chars,' only four of which bore religious figures ('Processions et défilés,' 262–6).

106 Porter, 137. Regarding the same concern in Montreal, see Guay, 210, 216, 222.

107 *Le Soleil,* 20 September 1898.

108 Mgr Bégin, cited in *Programme-souvenir, 1894–1954: 60ième anniversaire de la Garde indépendante Champlain. de la paroisse St-Roch, Québec, 25, 26, 27 sept. 1954* (Quebec, 1954), np.

109 *Le Monde Illustré,* 2 October 1897. This was a description of the Garde Champlain's uniforms on Laurier's triumphant return from both London, where he had been knighted, and Paris, where he had been made an officer of the Légion d'honneur. The uniforms were apparently so popular that when they were first introduced in 1895, there was an immediate increase in the membership of the organization.

110 The Montreal St-Jean-Baptiste procession was apparently organized in a similarly hierarchical manner. See Gordon, 'Inventing Tradition,' 15.

111 *Le Soleil,* 20 September 1898; MCSQ, MS 746. Diary of Abbé Alfred Paré, 21 September 1898 (hereafter Paré diary). Born in 1864, Paré taught history at the seminary from 1898 to 1915. During this time he carefully recorded his observations. I owe a special thanks to Julie Bouchard of the Archives du Séminaire who brought his diary to my attention.

112 *Le Soleil,* 20 September 1898.

113 Ibid., 19–20 September 1898.

114 Ibid., 22 September 1898.
115 Ernest Gagnon, 'Notice sur le drapeau de carillion,' in *Fête nationale, 1881–1889*, 56–63.
116 *Inauguration*, 77–9.
117 MCSQ, *Journal*, 5: 164, 9 September 1898.
118 *La Vérité*, 1, 8 October 1898.
119 *Inauguration*, 81–2.
120 Ibid., 88; 93; 97.
121 *Le Soleil*, 22 September 1898; *L'Événement*, 22 September 1898.
122 *Le Soleil*, 19 September 1898.
123 *Annales 1889–1901*, 83.
124 *Inauguration*, 107. In 1878, on the reburial of Laval, an event run exclusively by French Catholics, the lieutenant-governor of Quebec was viewed as successor to the last French governor; this had the effect of turning Quebec into the 'state' that succeeded France. In contrast, the unveiling of the Monument Champlain was a celebration of a larger country in which both English and French speakers had a role to play. In that context, Aberdeen was presented as successor to Champlain.
125 Paré diary, 21 September 1898.
126 *Inauguration*, 109.
127 Archives de la Ministère des affaires étrangers (Paris), Nouvelle série Canada, vol. 3, Alfred Kleczkowski to Minister, 29 September 1898.
128 *L'Événement*, 24 September 1898; Paré diary, 21 September 1898.
129 Pierre Savard, *Le consulat général de France à Québec et à Montréal de 1859 à 1914* (Quebec, 1970), 98.
130 *Souvenir du punch d'honneur offert par la Colonie Française à M. Kleczkowski* (Montreal, 1894), 13–14.
131 Paré diary, 21 September 1898.
132 Inauguration, 114–5.
133 *La semaine religieuse de Montréal*, 8 October 1898, 233–5; 5 November 1898, 312–15.
134 Inauguration, 128; NAC, Laurier Papers, John Davidson to Laurier, 23 September 1898.
135 Paré diary, 21 September 1898; *La Vérité*, 1 October 1898.
136 Ibid.
137 Paré Diary, 20 September 1898.
138 *L'Événement*, 1 September 1898. According to this report, the ship slated for the Quebec festivities had just arrived in Nova Scotia. The French apparently had cold feet in the weeks that followed.

139 Archives de la Ministère des affaires étrangers (Paris), Nouvelle série Canada, vol. 3, Alfred Kleczkowski to Minister, 29 September 1898.

140 United States Consular Despatches, Quebec City (microfilm); SN Parent to General William Henry, 3 September 1898.

141 Ibid., General Henry to Secretary of State, 3 September 1898.

142 These issues are discussed at considerable length in R.C. Brown, *Canada's National Policy, 1883–1900: A Study in Canadian–American Relations* (Princeton, 1964).

143 This context is explained in greater detail in Charles S. Campbell, Jr, *Anglo-American Understanding* (Baltimore, 1957).

144 *L'Événement*, 3 September 1898; *Le Soleil*, 1 September 1898. The same justification was printed in *Le Soleil*, 3 September.

145 H. George Classen, *Thrust and Counterthrust: The Genesis of the Canada-United States Boundary* (Chicago, 1965), 326–7; John T. Saywell, ed., *Canadian Journal of Lady Aberdeen* (Toronto, 1960), 474.

146 *Inauguration*, 153; *Le Soleil*, 20 September 1898.

147 *Le Soleil*, 5 May 1898; Paré diary, 7 May 1898.

148 *New York Times*, 22 September 1898.

149 Ibid.; University of Toronto, Fisher Rare Book Library, Diary of John Charlton, 21 September 1898.

150 Paré diary, 21 September 1898.

151 *La Vérité*, 15 October 1898.

3. Immortalizing Laval, 1878–1908

1 The Jesuit martyrs, who were given public recognition of their own with the unveiling in 1889 of a monument that was partly in their honour, started on the road to sainthood in 1904. They were canonized in 1930.

2 Kenneth Woodward, *Making Saints: How the Catholic Church Determines Who Becomes a Saint, Who Doesn't and Why*. 2nd ed. (New York, 1996), 74–5.

3 MCSQ, SME 27 May 1878; *Mandements, lettres pastorales et circulaires des Evêques de Québec*, 7: 165, Mandement No 77, 6 November 1890. The expense of pro-moting a candidate for sainthood is discussed in Serge Gagnon, *Le Québec et ses historiens de 1840 à 1920* (Quebec, 1978), 98. An estimate of the cost of turn-of-the-century canonization can be found in Thomas Macken, *The Canonisation of Saints* (Dublin, 1910), pp. 287–91. Macken estimated that the entire process from beginning to end might cost £10,000. This was the equivalent of £500,000 in 2000, or over $1 million in Canadian funds.

4 Woodward, 76.

5 MCSQ, Journal Personnel de Mgr T.-E. Hamel, 23 November 1881. Some of this unpublished testimony was discussed in chapter 1 in relation to the impact of the reburial celebrations on the public perception of Laval.

6 Sacra Rituum Congregatione, Quebecen, *Béatificionis et canonizationis servi dei Francisci de Montmorency-Laval. Primi Quebecensis Episcopi. Positio Super Introductione Causae* (Rome, 1890), 14–15.

7 Laval's candidacy was also supported publicly by the publication in 1890 of Abbé Gosselin's biography of the bishop, which the author hoped would hasten 'the day when our mother the Holy Church ... will permit us to honour him with a public cult!' (Gosselin, 1: xxxviii) Since the public needed to believe that the candidate had a reputation for saintly behaviour, works of hagiography, such as Gosselin's, which showed the triumph of Laval over adversity, constituted a central part of the process. For an interesting discussion of the role of hagiography, see Allan Greer, 'Savage/Saint: The Lives of Kateri Tekakwitha,' in Dépatie et al., *Vingt ans après 'Habitants et marchands'* (Montreal and Kingston, 1998), pp. 138–59.

8 Pierre Delooz, *Sociologie et canonisations* (Liège, 1969), 70.

9 MCSQ, Journal, 17 November 1890, 3: 550; 24 November 1890, 3: 553. Laval's remains were still beneath the seminary, where they had been deposited in 1878,

10 The Monument Cartier-Brébeuf is discussed in the preface.

11 *Le Courrier du Canada*, 13 May 1891. The event was also given extensive coverage in *La Vérité*, 16 May 1891. The latter journal, which represented what was left of ultramontanism within Quebec Catholicism, was convinced that a conspiracy by state officials against the church had resulted in the failure of authorities to bring charges against those responsible for the disappearance of the Jesuits' remains. The journal viewed this failure as indicative of the 'petty hatred against the Jesuits and the even pettier desire to prevent these bones from becoming the object of an honourable ceremony such as the one which has just taken place.'

12 *Le Canadien*, 14 May 1891.

13 *Courrier du Canada*, 20 May 1891.

14 *Quebecen Beatificiones et Canonizatonis ven servi dei Francisci de Montmorency Laval. Primi Episcopi Quebecensis. Positio Super Non-Cultu* (Rome, 1892), 6. Many thanks to Eric Reiter, who translated this passage from the Latin.

15 *L'Événement*, 14 May 1891.

16 AAQ, 31–21–A, Fonds Louis-Nazaire Bégin, vol. 21–4.

17 MCSQ, MS671, Benjamin Paquet, superior of seminary, to Abbé A. Gingras, curé of Ste-Claire, 1 December 1890.

18 *Courrier du Canada*, 14 May 1891.

19 J.-A. Poisson, *Chants canadiens à l'occasion du 24 juin 1880* (Quebec, 1880).

20 *Courrier du Canada*, 14 May 1891.

21 Delooz, 62; *Quebecen Beatificiones et Canonizatonis ven servi dei Francisci de Montmorency Laval. Primi Episcopi Quebecensis. Positio Super Non-Cultu*

22 MCSQ, Summarium 1904, 1127; Paré Journal, 24 May 1908.

23 MCSQ, SME, 1 February 1904.

24 *La Semaine Religieuse de Québec*, 12 July 1902, 763.

25 The term is borrowed from Graham S. Lowe, *Women in the Administrative Revolution: The Feminization of Clerical Work* (Toronto, 1987).

26 Letter from Jobin, 10 March 1904, reprinted in *La Semaine Religieuse de Québec*, 16 April 1904, 550–1.

27 AAQ, Comité du Monument Laval, Comité général, 14 March 1904.

28 *La Semaine Religieuse de Québec*, 16 April 1904, 588; 616–7.

29 Letter from Jobin, 10 March 1904, reprinted in *La Semaine Religieuse de Québec*, 16 April 1904; AAQ, Letter from S.-N. Parent, 1 March 1904; MCSQ, Université 56, no. 74, Laflamme to Carlo Nicoli (sculpteur), 1904, nd.

30 Mgr Laflamme's reaction was discussed in chapter 2. Hébert's career is dealt with in great detail in a volume published to accompany an exhibition of the sculptor's work. See Daniel Drouin, ed., *Louis-Philippe Hébert* (Quebec, 2001); one chapter of this volume deals with the Monument Laval.

31 Musée du Québec, Fonds Louis-Philippe-Hébert, Hébert to Mgr Marois, 11 April 1904. The emphasis is Hébert's.

32 The opposition to Hébert's 'monopoly' is discussed in MCSQ, Journal, 7: 110, 6 April 1904; also in MCSQ, Paré Journal, 25 April 1904.

33 AAQ, 2–2 (b) 8: 'Légende envoyée par l'artiste Hébert, en même temps que sa première maquette.'

34 Ibid. For the link between Hébert's design for the Monument Champlain and this maquette, see Joanne Chagnon, 'Le Monument à monseigneur de Laval,' in Drouin, ed., *Louis-Philippe Hébert*, 185.

35 AAQ, Comité de construction, 8 July 1904; MCSQ, Université 56/80, 'Observations sur la maquette présentée pour le futur monument de Mgr de Laval,' panel report from Chanoine Bouillon, G. Emile Tanguay and E.-E. Taché, July 1904.

36 Ibid. This part of the story is not reported in Joanne Chagnon's telling of the tale (Drouin, ed., *Louis-Philippe Hébert*, 183), which tends to ignore details that might present Hébert in a less than flattering light. This is perhaps to be expected in a volume accompanying an exhibition of the artist's work.

37 AAQ, 2–2 (c) 15, 'Observations sur la maquette'; MCSQ, Université 56/80, 'Observations sur la maquette.'

38 MCSQ, Univ. 58, no. 89, Chevré to Mgr Laflamme, 5 August 1904.

39 MCSQ, Journal, 7: 174, 30 October 1904.

40 Ibid., 6 November 1904; Paré Journal, 8 November 1904.

41 MCSQ, Université 56, no. 77, Report from Maurice Lefebvre, October 1904.

42 MCSQ, Journal, 7: 176–7, 6 November 1904.

43 MCSQ, Université 56/81, Chauveau to Laflamme, 3 January 1905. The emphasis is Chauveau's.

44 AAQ, Comité de construction, 19 January 1905; 26 February 1905.

45 Jean-Baptiste Lagacé, 'Le Monument de Mgr de Laval à Québec,' *Revue Canadienne* 1 (1908): 20–1.

46 AAQ, Comité de construction, 8 July 1904.

47 Fr Valentin-M Breton, 'L'œuvre du sculpteur Hébert,' in *Le Vénérable François de Montmorency-Laval Premier Évêque de Québec; Souvenir des fêtes du deuxième centenaire célébrées les 21, 22 et 23 juin 1908* (Quebec, 1908), 84.

48 Musée du Québec, Fonds Louis-Philippe-Hébert, H-15–43, 'Notes sur le projet du Monument Laval'; Breton, 'L'œuvre du sculpteur Hébert,' 87–8.

49 Ibid., 83. This figure apparently had an exposed breast until Hébert was told by the committee in 1907 to cover it up. See Chagnon, in Drouin, ed., *Louis-Philippe Hébert*, 190.

50 AAQ, 2–2 (c) 28, Fagel to Mgr Marois, 7 August 1905.

51 Breton, 'L'œuvre du sculpteur Hébert,' 82; Lagacé, 'Le Monument de Mgr de Laval à Québec,' 18. The views of Garneau and Casgrain were discussed in chapter 1.

52 Paré Journal, 15 October 1905; 13 April 1908; 3 May 1908. There was an extremely negative commentary in *Le Soleil*, 14 April 1908. *La Vigie* mocked Hébert's effort by means of a conversation that might have passed between the monuments to Champlain and Laval (13 May 1908).

53 Paré Journal, 30 May 1908. In the same spirit, Paré repeated this sentiment several weeks later: 'Now that it is finally complete, this monument has a wonderful appearance ... Unfortunately it is located upon a detestable site' (12 June 1908).

54 AVQ, Comité des chemins, minutes of meeting, 14 January 1902; *Quebec Chronicle*, 18, 20 December 1901.

55 AVQ, Comité des chemins, minutes of meeting, 4 December 1902; *Le Soleil*, 11, 31 October 1902.

56 AVQ, Comité des chemins, minutes of meeting, 20 January 1903, letter from Mgr Têtu to Parent, 7 November 1902; letter from Mgr Mathieu (superior of seminary) to Mayor Parent, 20 January 1903.

57 *Le Vénérable François de Montmorency-Laval*, 100. The exclamation was in the original!

58 Paré Journal, 25 April 1904. In a letter to the prime minister, Mgr Têtu noted that the work on the *archevêché* would cost $40,000 (NAC, Laurier Papers, Têtu to Laurier, 20 February 1905, p. 94923).

59 In 1904 the Jardin Montmorency was still officially known as the Parc Frontenac, although there was already a movement underway (in association with the monument project) to change its name so as to honour Mgr de Montmorency-Laval (*Semaine religieuse de Québec*, 3 June 1905, 660).

60 The monument was forty feet high, and one source noted that it was sixty feet from the lowest point of the base to the top of Laval's mitre. The difference (twenty feet) had to be dealt with during construction.

61 MCSQ, Journal, 8–9 April 1906.

62 Letter from L.P. Sirois, 30 April 1906, reprinted in *Le Vénérable François de Montmorency-Laval*, v.

63 I can testify to this problem, having tried to take a picture of the front of the monument in the very short space between Laval and the *archevêché*. In fact, most photographs taken from the street in front of the monument look straight up since it is impossible to stand back from the structure. The only really good photographs of the monument have been taken from the archbishop's palace.

64 AAQ, 2–2 (c) 23: Fagel to Marois, 5 August 1905.

65 Paré Journal, 14 April, 13 April 1908. Someone, perhaps Paré himself, put the blame on Têtu through some clever artwork that was stuffed into the history professor's journal and dated 20 April 1908. Starting with a newspaper drawing of the Monument Laval, there was a bubble coming out of the bishop's mouth, so as to make him say, *'C'est un têtu qui avait dans sa tête de me faire mettre ici!'* Playing on the word *têtu* (someone extremely stubborn), the barb translated as, 'Someone extremely stubborn must have put me here!'

66 AAQ, Fonds du Comité du Monument Laval, dossier 1, Notes of Mgr Têtu, nd; *Le Vénérable François de Montmorency-Laval*, xx.

67 AAQ, Fonds du Comité du Monument Laval, dossier 3-2, letter to religious communities, 4 June 1904. The letter was signed by the archbishop, but had been prepared by Têtu.

68 These lists (hereafter referred to as Têtu lists) can be found in AAQ, Fonds du Comité du Monument Laval, dossier 3-2.

69 *Mandements, lettres pastorales et circulaires des Evêques de Québec*, 9: Circulaire no. 33, 2 June 1904; no. 36, 9 February 1905, p. 361.

70 Paré Journal, 10 December 1904.

71 AAQ, Fonds du Comité du Monument Laval, dossier 1, Comité de souscription, 25 March and 6 May 1906.

72 Letter from L.P. Sirois, 30 April 1906, reprinted in *Le Vénérable François de Montmorency-Laval,* v–vi; *Mandements, lettres pastorales et circulaires des Evêques de Québec* 10, Circulaire no. 42, 120, 5 June 1906.

73 AAQ, Têtu, list 51m, 10 August 1906.

74 Têtu's final financial statement indicated that only $7760 was raised from Quebec City residents during the entire fundraising drive. Accordingly, these ordinary people provided the bulk of funds raised from local residents.

75 Têtu interspersed his own observations along with the published lists.

76 AAQ, Têtu, list 63, 6 March 1908.

77 Ibid., list 64, 1 April 1908.

78 The Quebec government was the second-largest contributor, having pledged $2000. The Quebec municipal government cleared the land of the *pâté de maisons* and then gave it to the Comité du Monument Laval, thus precluding any cash contribution. According to Têtu, the municipal government spent $50,000 in this regard. (NAC, Laurier Papers, Têtu to Laurier, 20 February 1905, p. 94923.)

79 NAC, Laurier Papers, Têtu to Laurier, 17 July 1905, 99755–6; Laurier to Têtu, 18 July 1905.

80 AAQ, Fonds du Comité du Monument Laval, dossier 3-2, letter to religious communities, 4 June 1904. The letter was signed by the archbishop, but had been prepared by Têtu.

81 H.J.J.B. Chouinard, comp., *Fêtes du Troisième Centenaire de la Fondation de Québec par Champlain: Projets-Délibérations-Documents* (Quebec, 1908).

82 AVQ, QP1–4/55–2, 'Rapport du Comité Spécial du Programme' (the committee met on 9 and 12 October 1906). This program was then sent on to Laurier; see NAC, Laurier Papers, J.G. Garneau to Laurier, 20 November 1906, p115751–61; a slightly altered English version can be found in 'Programme for the Celebration of the Tercentenary,' nd, p. 118396.

83 AAQ, Comité de construction, 11 October; MCSQ, Université 170 no. 1, nd.

84 AAQ, Comité de construction, 21 February 1907.

85 AAQ, Dossier 4, 28 April 1907. For a complete discussion of the debate within the Comité du Monument Laval, see Nelles, *Art of Nation-Building,* 109–10.

86 AAQ, 4A, 4-4, 'Procession du Très Saint Sacrement,' nd, 1. This document, which presented the design for the 1908 procession, was written at roughly the same time (Fall 1907) that the decision was made to stage the three-day extravaganza in June 1908, free of any ties to the Champlain celebrations.

87 AAQ, Comité de Construction, 17 November 1907.

88 NAC, RG7 G21, Central Registry Files: File 335, pt 2a (microfilm T-1178), Mathieu to Grey, 13 January 1908.

89 The issue of St-Jean-Baptiste's formal declaration as French Canadians' patron saint is discussed later in the chapter.

90 *Quebec Chronicle*, 20 June 1908; the same ad appeared in *Action sociale*, 19 June 1908.

91 AAQ, dossier 2-2 (a) 3. The final text was approved at a meeting held on 25 March 1907. The French text on the monument reads:

FONDATEUR
de l'église de la Nouvelle-France et du séminaire de Québec.
HOMME D'ÉTAT
dans l'organisation du conseil souverain, dans de fructueuses missions auprès de la cour de France, dans la pacification des esprits et des peuples.
APÔTRE
de la foi, de l'éducation et de la tempérance.
VÉNÉRABLE
par ses vertus de charité, de force, et de mortification.

92 Guy Laperrière, '"Persécution et exil": La venue au Québec des congrégations françaises, 1900–1914,' RHAF, 36 (1982), 389–411. Laperrière is in the midst of publishing a series of three volumes on the question, the first two of which have appeared as *Les congrégations religieuses: De la France au Québec, 1880–1914*, 2 vols. (Ste-Foy, 1996–9).

93 Groulx, *Mes Mémoires*, 4 vols. (Montreal 1970–4), 1: 127, 167.

94 *Mandements, lettres pastorales et circulaires des Evêques de Québec* 10, Circulaire no. 44, 29 January 1907.

95 *Le Vénérable François de Montmorency-Laval*, 124.

96 An earlier version of the material in this and the following sections first appeared in 'Marching and Memory in Early-Twentieth-Century Quebec: La Fête-Dieu, la Saint-Jean-Baptiste, and le Monument Laval,' *Journal of the Canadian Historical Association* 10 (1999), 209–35.

97 AAQ, 'Procession du Très Saint Sacrement,' 1.

98 Testimony before special committee of Quebec legislative assembly, 1906–7, reproduced in *Réflexions d'Alphonse Desjardins* (Lévis, 1986), 52.

99 On this issue, see my *In Whose Interest: Quebec's Caisses Populaires, 1900–45* (Montreal, 1990).

100 AAQ, Dossier 4–4, letter from *archevêché* (but not signed) to each parish, 14 March 1908. In the case of the parish of Nôtre-Dame de Québec, whose parish church was the cathedral, $500 was paid to help cover 'the costs of the Great *Procession du St-Sacrement* (the Fête-Dieu procession) across the entire City, which will coincide with and will form part of the unveiling

celebrations for the Monument Laval' (Archives de la paroisse de Nôtre-Dame de Québec, Assemblée de fabrique, 5 avril 1908).

101 AAQ, 'Procession du Très Saint Sacrement,' 10.

102 In his book on the Champlain celebrations that were held later in the summer of 1908, H.V. Nelles provided a brief account of the Fête-Dieu procession noting that it 'was a special kind of parade' in which the marchers came 'to the people in their neighbourhoods and parishes.' In fact, the 1908 procession was distinguished by the way in which it was routed away from the parishes (*Art of Nation-Building*, 112).

103 AAQ, 'Procession du Très Saint Sacrement,' 3.

104 Ibid., 3; 17.

105 Archives des Sœurs de la Charité de Québec (Beauport, Québec), Annales, 21 June 1908. I am grateful to Sister Gemma Castonguay for giving me access to these annals.

106 AAQ, 'Procession du Très Saint Sacrement,' 17; ibid., dossier 4-4; 'Contributions à l'érection d'un arc sur le parcours de la procession de la Fête-Dieu, le 21 juin 1908.' This form could be used for any parish.

107 AAQ, 'Procession du Très Saint Sacrement,' 3; 11. There was also provision for the positioning of girls along the route, who would strew flowers as the host passed by.

108 AAQ, Têtu, list 66, 15 June 1908.

109 Ibid., 14–15.

110 *L'Événement*, 22 June 1908.

111 Annales des Sœurs de la Charité de Québec, 21 June 1908.

112 P. Courbon, 'La grande procession de la Fête-Dieu,' in *Le Vénérable François de Montmorency-Laval*, 110.

113 *L'Événement*, 22 June 1908; *Action Sociale*, 22 June 1908.

114 Paré Journal, 21 June 1908.

115 Archives des Ursulines de Québec, *Annales des Sœurs Ursulines*, 4: 65. I appreciate the help provided in these archives by Sœur Nancy Marchand. I also owe Viv Nelles a word of thanks for having led me to the Ursuline and Augustine archives. He referred to their participation in the events of the summer of 1908 in his *Art of Nation-Building*.

116 Archives des Sœurs Augustines de la Miséricorde de Jésus, Hôtel-Dieu de Québec, Annales, 21 June 1908, V, 193–4. My thanks to Sœur Marie-Paule Cauchon.

117 P. Courbon, 'La grande procession de la Fête-Dieu,' in *Le Vénérable François de Montmorency-Laval*, 111.

118 In this regard, Christine Seito has observed: 'By the 1870s the Fête-Dieu procession began to take on a nationalist tinge as the terms "Catholic" and

"French Canadian" were used synonymously' ('Une fête contestée: la procession de la Fête-Dieu à Montréal au XIXe siècle,' MA thesis, Université de Montréal, 1983, 164) For his efforts, Bourget earned opposition from English-speaking Protestants who resented French-speaking Catholics claiming Montreal's streets as their own. The provocative nature of claiming public space as holy was also evident in England at the turn of the century. In 1908, the same year as the unveiling of the Monument Laval, there was much controversy over the staging of a massive Corpus Christi procession through the streets of London as part of the Eucharistic Congress that was being held in England. On this issue see Carol Devlin, 'The Eucharistic Procession of 1908: The Dilemma of the Liberal Government,' *Church History* 63 (1994), 407–25.

119 *L'Événement,* 22 June 1908; Archives des Sœurs Augustines, Annales, 21 June 1908, V, 193.

120 *Le Vénérable François de Montmorency-Laval,* 115.

121 Ibid., 125, 132–3.

122 *L'Événement,* 24 June 1908.

123 AAQ, Dossier 4, Report of Special Committee for inauguration, 20 February 1908. The original plans for the event were literally crossed out in this document.

124 AAQ, Minutes of Comité de Construction, 6 May 1908. That this was a very sensitive dossier within the walls of the *archevêché* was made clear in the minutes of the Comité de Construction, which was watching over the unveiling ceremonies. The committee approved the arrangement with the governor general, but its secretary then placed a large 'X' over the minutes, which were labelled 'Confidentiel.' No one wanted to be responsible for taking such an initiative, which could be opposed from certain quarters, until approval came from Mgr Bégin, who was next sent the proposal, and who ultimately gave his assent.

125 NAC, Grey Papers, Grey to Crewe, 18 May 1908, pp. 4003–5.

126 *Le Vénérable François de Montmorency-Laval,* 144–5.

127 NAC, Grey Papers, Grey to Crewe, 24 June 1908, p. 4044.

128 Nelles, *Art of Nation-Building,* 114; Paré Journal, 22 June 1908.

129 NAC, Grey papers, Grey to Crewe, 18 May 1908.

130 *Le Vénérable François de Montmorency-Laval,* 156, 159.

131 Gerlier went on to a career in the priesthood, rising through the ranks to become both a cardinal and the Archbishop of Lyon in 1937. He was sympathetic to many of the principles advanced by Marshal Pétain in the creation of the Vichy régime, within which Gerlier's archdiocese was located. Nevertheless, the cardinal did express public outrage at the

treatment of Jews, so much so that Serge Klarsfeld, who became a tireless pursuer of Nazi war criminals, remarked: 'We must emphasize that it is to Cardinal Gerlier, a pillar of the Vichy regime that is owed, more than to any other, the abrupt slow-down of the massive police co-operation given by Vichy to the Gestapo' (Cited in W.D. Halls, *Politics, Society and Christianity in Vichy France* (Oxford, 1994), 142.

132 *La Semeur* 1, no. 1 (September–October 1904), 37–9.

133 The *loi Lavergne* guaranteeing the use of French in certain circumstances at the provincial level was passed in 1910. See, Michael Behiels, 'L'ACJC and the Quest for Moral Regeneration, 1903–14,' *Journal of Canadian Studies* 13 (1978), 27–41.

134 *Le Vénérable François de Montmorency-Laval*, 170–2. Alfred Paré viewed Gerlier as a strong representative of *la France catholique* (Paré Journal, 22 June 1908).

135 With words by J.F. Vaudin and music by Ambroise Thomas, the chorus concluded: 'France! France! Dieu protège la France!' (May God protect France!)

136 ANQQ, Fonds SSJBQ, 412/1, Letter from H.J.J.B. Chouinard to Mgr Bégin, 20 November 1907; *Mandements, lettres pastorales et circulaires des Evêques de Québec*, 10, Circulaire no. 52, 10 May 1908.

137 Chouinard, *Annales de la SSJB de Québec, 1889–1901*, 112–3.

138 On the issue of the 'invented' nature of the Montreal St-Jean-Baptiste festivities, see Gordon, 'Inventing Tradition.'

139 The growing antagonism in early 1908 toward the Champlain tercentenary was evident in ANQQ, SSJBQ, 412/1, Dossier 14, Comité de régie, 10 April 1908.

140 Ibid., 6 and 14 February 1908.

141 AAQ, 'Procession du Très Saint Sacrement,' 3.

142 ANQQ, SSJBQ, 412/3, Dossier 31, Comité de la Procession, 20 March 1908.

143 *Le Soleil*, 20 June 1908.

144 ANQQ, SSJBQ, 412/1, Dossier 14, Comité de régie, 10 April 1908. In the case of the Montreal St-Jean-Baptiste parade, there were apparently demands for the inclusion of women, but I have seen no evidence of their participation prior to 1908 (Guay, 291).

145 Ibid., 412/3, Dossier 31, Comité de la Procession, 20 March 1908.

146 Ibid., 412/1, Dossier 14, Comité de régie, 14 February; 6 March; 20 March 1908.

147 Paré observed that the ropes had separated the spectators from the speakers at the unveiling ceremony. Accordingly, 'the orators ... were speaking towards an empty space surrounded by spectators a bit further away' (Paré Journal, 22 June 1908).

148 Ibid., 23 June 1908.

149 ANQQ, SSJBQ, 412/5, Dossier 57, Report of Secretary General, 1907–8.

150 *Action sociale*, 24 June 1908.

151 ANQ-Saguenay, Fonds ACJC, dossier 64.23.31, letter from Archbishop of St-Boniface, 20 April 1908; letter from J.G. Garneau, 16 May 1908.

152 Paré Journal, 23 June 1908. The battles within the ACJC between these various factions were so intense that they paralysed its affairs. A new board of directors, committed to putting the organization back on track, took control shortly after the tercentenary, bringing with it more 'normal' organizational practices, including the keeping of minutes of meetings. Had this decision come only a few months earlier we would have a clearer view of the ACJC's activities in the summer of 1908. The terms *intégraliste* and *conciliatoristes* come from Laurier Renaud, *La fondation de l'ACJC: L'histoire d'une jeunesse nationaliste* (Jonquière, 1973), 69.

4. Champlain's Tercentenary?

1 While little has been written about the fêtes discussed in the previous chapters, the tercentenary has been the subject of Viv Nelles's deservedly acclaimed *The Art of Nation-Building*. Nelles focused on the perspective of a diverse collection of participants in and spectators of the tercentenary; the treatment here, in line with the rest of this book, focuses on French Canadians.

2 *L'Événement*, 31 July 1908.

3 *Montreal Star*, 1 May 1908; *Quebec Chronicle*, 16 July 1908.

4 Adolphe-Basile Routhier, *Quebec: A Quaint Medieval French City in America at the Dawn of the Twentieth Century* (Montreal, 1904); NAC, Grey Papers, Grey to Lord Strathcona, 11 December 1907. The attraction of Quebec City to tourists was discussed in more detail in chapter 2, with regard to the construction of the Monument Champlain

5 Reproduced in Yvan Lamonde et Claude Corbo, *Le rouge et le bleu* (Montreal, 1999), 303.

6 Mason Wade, *The French Canadians*, 2 vols. (Toronto, 1968), 1: 558.

7 Bourassa to Goldwin Smith, 26 June 1908, quoted in Jacques Mathieu and Eugen Kedl, *Plains of Abraham: The Search for the Ideal* (Sillery, 1993), 247; NAC, Grey Papers, Grey to Crewe, 18 May 1908, pp. 4003–5. For an early statement of alarm over the imperialist implications of the tercentenary, see *La Vérité*, 1 February 1908.

8 In 1909, with the tercentenary out of the way, Chouinard was unceremoniously relieved of his duties with the NBC for reasons that were never explained to him. When he went public about his dismissal, the president

of the commission, Sir George Garneau, observed: 'Mr Chouinard has a marvellous gift as regards works of imagination and is a talented writer. As an administrator he is useless' (*Quebec Chronicle*, 31 March 1910)

9 Chouinard, *Fêtes du Troisième Centenaire de la Fondation de Québec par Champlain: Projets-Délibérations-Documents* (Quebec, 1908), 11 [hereafter *Projets-Délibérations-Documents*].

10 Ibid., 96; Paré Journal, 27 October 1906. The negative reaction to this draft of the program was discussed at some length in chapter 3.

11 NAC, Crew Papers, Grey to Crewe, A1645, 17 August 1908; NAC, Grey Papers, Grey to Laurier, 29 February 1908.

12 Mary Hallett, 'The Quebec Tercentennial: Lord Grey's Imperial Birthday Party,' *Canadian Historical Review*, 54 (1973), 341.

13 NAC, Grey Papers, Grey to Lyttelton, 15 May 1905, as cited in Hallett, 'The 4th Earl Grey as Governor General of Canada, 1904–11' (PhD diss., University of London, 1974), 147.

14 NAC, Grey to J.-G. Garneau, 7 November 1907. When the Goddess of Peace idea did not pan out, Grey proposed another monument, this one to immortalize Madeleine de Verchères. The statue in her honour was unveiled in 1913, in the town downstream from Montreal that bore her name (Coates and Morgan, *Heroines and History*, 76–8).

15 NAC, NBC records, vol. 1, Courtney to Edmund Walker, 26 May 1908. Nelles provides an explanation of the Graham scam in *Art of Nation-Building*, 99–100.

16 NAC, Grey Papers, Grey to Laurier, 25 October 1907.

17 Paré Journal, 29 May 1908.

18 NAC, NBC records, vol. 1, Manager of Banque Nationale office at Chicoutimi to Courtney, 5 April 1908; a nearly identical letter was sent by the manager of the Banque Provinciale office at St-Eustache. Courtney sent the same response to the two managers, 9 and 11 April 1908.

19 Ibid., Louis Lavergne, Corporation du Comté d'Arthabaska, to Courtney, 9 May 1908.

20 Although the NBC did not formally create the Quebec Battlefields Association until April, the chapters in Montreal and Quebec City were already active in February and March.

21 *Montreal Daily Witness*, 14 March 1908. Similar lists were printed in *Montreal Daily Witness*, 22 February 1908; *Montreal Gazette*, 29 February 1908; *Montreal Star*, 28 March 08; *Montreal Daily Witness*, 11 April 1908. Needless to say, determining mother tongue by family name is far from foolproof. Nevertheless, the under representation of French speakers was so significant that even some mistaken categorization of French speakers with English-

sounding names (such as a Flynn who was a French speaker) would not fundamentally change the situation.

22 *Illustrated Witness*, 14 March 1908.

23 NAC, RG90, vol. 1, Colonel C.J. Turnbull (honorary treasurer of Quebec Battlefield Association in Quebec City) to Courtney, 16 June and 15 September 1908. In the end, Turnbull sent $2,570 to Courtney, out of the total of $7,200. In other words, the bulk of the funds collected were absorbed by administrative expenses such as the printing of thousands of appeals for the fundraising drive. Had this been known, it would have done little to encourage contributors.

24 NAC, Grey Papers, Grey to Laurier, 2 March 1908.

25 Canada, Parliament, House of Commons, *Debates*, 5 March 1908, p. 4410. Nelles refers to Lavergne as an 'ultra-nationalist,' although it is difficult to understand why he merited that title, or why Grey, to balance the ledger, should not be deemed an ultra-imperialist. See H.V. Nelles, 'Historical Pageantry and the "Fusion of the Races" at the Tercentenary of Quebec, 1908,' *Histoire sociale/Social History*, 29 (1996), 395.

26 Canada, Parliament, House of Commons, *Debates*, 5 March 1908, p. 4515.

27 Wade, *French Canadians*, 1: 553.

28 Meeting of Comité d'Action, 4 March 1908, reproduced in *Projets-Délibérations-Documents*, 211.

29 Chouinard, 'Mémoire, Les grandes scènes de notre histoire,' document tabled before the organizing committee in February 1908 and reproduced in *Projets-Délibérations-Documents*, 187.

30 For the American experience, see David Glassberg, *American Historical Pageantry: The Uses of Tradition in the Early Twentieth Century* (Chapel Hill, NC, 1990). For another experience within the empire, see Peter Merrington, 'Masques, Monuments and Masons: The 1910 Pageant of the Union of South Africa,' *Theatre Journal* 49 (1997), 1–14.

31 *Standard*, 11 January 1908.

32 The impact of the recession on the capacity of ordinary Quebecers to partake of the tercentenary is discussed in greater detail later in this chapter.

33 Robert Withington, *English Pageantry: An Historical Outline*, 2 vols. (New York, 1918–26), 2: 194–6.

34 *Projets-Délibérations-Documents*, 187.

35 Ibid., pp. 185–96.

36 Ibid., pp. 202, 211.

37 The tercentenary organizing committee rather laconically committed itself in late March to provide $3,500 to the national societies, of which $2,000

would go to the SSJBQ (Projets-Délibérations, 233). However, this sum does not show up in the expenditures of the NBC, nor is it ever acknowledged in the minutes of the SSJBQ.

38 ANQQ, SSJBQ, 412/1, minutes of Régie, 10 April 1908. The construction of the Monument des Braves was discussed in chapter 1.

39 A public meeting was set up by the tercentenary organizers for 6 July in order to create a committee of the national societies (*Action sociale*, 7 July 1908). SSJBQ records indicate that the Comité de la procession des sociétés nationales met three days later. There is no evidence of other meetings.

40 *L'Événement*, 18 July 1908; ANQ, SSJBQ, 412/2, Minutes of Comité de la procession des sociétés nationales, 9 July 1908; 412/5, Annual report, 1907–8. For his part, Nelles observed: 'Only weeks before the celebration and after the programs had been printed, the nationalist and patriotic societies who had turned out in such numbers for the Laval procession regretted that they could not muster enough strength for the advertised parade at a meeting with tercentenary organizers' (*Art of Nation-Building*, 140) Perhaps a bit unfairly, Nelles put the burden here on the SSJBQ, not taking into account the lack of enthusiasm among its partners in the Irish, English, and Scottish organizations.

41 *Congrès de la Jeunesse à Québec en 1908* (Montreal, 1909), 382.

42 Ibid., 382–5. Reflecting on his participation in the convention, Gerlier observed upon his return to France: 'Above everything else, I wanted to show French Canadians that they should avoid confusing official France and the true France.' He was gratified by the enthusiastic response that he received, which brought tears to his eyes (*Action sociale*, 4 August 1908).

43 *Congrès de la Jeunesse à Québec en 1908*, 390, 406.

44 Ibid., 407; *Projets-Délibérations-Documents*, 244. The issue of financing was no small matter for ACJC leaders. The Quebec regional committee ran up a debt of $392 in staging its rally, leading to considerable debate within the provincewide organization as to whether it had an obligation to help out. This debate over a rather small sum stands in contrast to the vast expenditures available for other tercentenary events (ANQ-Saguenay [Chicoutimi], Fonds ACJC, 61.221.02, 'Rapport annuel, 1908–9').

45 *Congrès de la Jeunesse à Québec en 1908*, 414; Camille Roy, *Les Fêtes du Troisième Centenaire de Québec, 1608–1908* (Quebec, 1911), 42; Arthur Doughty and William Wood, *King's Book of Quebec*, 2 vols. (Ottawa, 1911), 2: 227. For its part, *Le Soleil*, the organ of the Liberal Party in Quebec City, proclaimed on 21 July: 'Officially, the fetes of the tercentenary of the founding of Quebec by Champlain start today.'

46 A rally was held in St-Roch in January at which concerns about the 'English' character of the tercentenary fuelled opposition to Garneau's re-election as

mayor (*Le Soleil,* 17 January 1908). Only a week later, there were reports that a replica of a monument in honour of Jacques Cartier, unveiled in St-Malo, France in 1905, might be erected in the St-Roch district during the tercentenary. Perhaps this was an effort to buy some support from this section of town (*Le Soleil,* 23 January 1908)

47 *Action sociale,* 3 July 1908.

48 Ibid., 2 July 1908.

49 Ibid., 15 July 1908.

50 Nelles, *Art of Nation-Building,* 159.

51 *Congrès de la Jeunesse à Québec en 1908,* 418, 433.

52 Ibid., 413.

53 Paré Journal, 19 July 1908.

54 The photograph reproduced by Nelles (*Art of Nation-Building* 20) shows the emptied stands. In contrast, see the photo in *Congrès de la Jeunesse à Québec en 1908,* opp. 432.

55 Nelles, *Art of Nation-Building,* 119.

56 In the midst of the fête, Quebec City's newspapers announced that a French bishop had ordered that anyone in possession of church property that had been confiscated by the state would be excommunicated (*L'Événement,* 25 July 1908).

57 Paré Journal, 19 July 1908.

58 Ibid., 17 November 1906; *La Vérité,* 17 November 1906. Kleczkowski's personnel file indicates that he had wanted a promotion to a higher classification within the French diplomatic corps since 1904, and that he received that promotion as part of his transfer to Montevideo. His letter to the French foreign minister acknowledging his new posting indicated no bitterness whatsoever (Archives de la ministère des affaires étrangères [Paris], Personnel files, 2e série; file of Alfred Kleczkowski).

59 *Le Soleil,* 16 November 1906; *La Vérité,* 24 November 1906. The latter journal's position was echoed in *L'Événement,* 16–17 November 1906.

60 *Congrès de la Jeunesse à Québec en 1908,* 134.

61 Paré Journal, 16 January 1907.

62 NAC, Laurier papers, p. 130756, Grey to Edward VII, 21 October 1907.

63 Archivio Segreto Vaticano (Rome), Dossier, 52.10/1, Sinnott to Mgr Mathieu, 18 September 1905. I owe a great debt to Matteo Sanfilippo, who arranged for photocopying the pertinent dossiers.

64 MCSQ, Université 168, no. 261, Alfred Sinnott to Mgr Mathieu, 18 February 1907.

65 The history of the bad feeling provoked among Quebec's ecclesiastical leaders by the creation of the office of the apostolic delegate is discussed in Roberto Perin, *Rome in Canada* (Toronto, 1990); Sbarretti's career in

Canada is discussed in Giovanni Pizzorusso, 'Un diplomate du Vatican en
Amérique: Donato Sbarretti à Washington et Ottawa (1893–1910), *Annali
Accademici Canadesi* 9 (1993), 5–33. The plenary council of Canadian bishops
was ultimately held, with Sbarretti presiding, in 1909.

66 Archivio Segreto Vaticano, Dossier, 52.10/1, Mathieu to Sinnott, 17 February 1907; Paré Journal, 19 May 1906.

67 Ibid., Mathieu to Sinnott, 17 February 1907.

68 Ibid., Dossier, 52.10/2, letter from Sinnott, 28 November 1907. All such
letters were marked 'confidential.'

69 Nelles, *Art of Nation-Building*, 108, 116.

70 Archivio Segreto Vaticano, Dossier, 52.10/3, Mathieu to Sbarretti, 18 July
1908. This luncheon clearly captured the imagination of Abbé Paré, who
accorded nine full pages in his diary to a description of the event – much
more than he accorded to any other day of the tercentenary (Paré Journal,
27 July 1908).

71 This issue was discussed at length in chapter 3.

72 Archives de la ministère des affaires étrangères (Paris), Nouvelle serie
Canada, vol. 6, minister to consul in Montreal, 22 May 1908. The French
delegation also included the mayor of Champlain's hometown of Brouage,
who kept a low profile during the tercentenary, but who was not pleased by
the behaviour of his anticlerical colleague. We will see the mayor again in
the epilogue, in the context of his own efforts to advance Champlain's
Catholic legacy by campaigning for French-Canadian financial assistance
for the reconstruction of the church where *le fondateur* had been baptized.

73 Louis Herbette, 'La langue et la littérature françaises au Canada, la famille
française et la nation Canadienne,' in Charles ab der Halden, *Etudes de
littérature canadienne-française* (Paris, 1904). In this text, Herbette further
alienated certain elements in Quebec by criticizing Consul Kleczkowski for
his close ties to the clergy, which had resulted in his being 'out of touch
with the old country' (lxxx).

74 Ruby Heap, 'La ligue d'enseignement (1902–4): héritage du passé et
nouveaux défis,' *Revue d'histoire de l'Amérique française* 36 (1982), 339–73.

75 Archives de la ministère des affaires étrangères (Paris), Nouvelle série, vol.
6, Herbette to Montreal consul, 12 June 1908.

76 *La Vérité*, 27 June, 1 August 1908; Archives de la ministère des affaires
étrangères (Paris), Nouvelle serie Canada, vol. 6, telegram to minister sent
from *Léon Gambetta*, 29 July 1908.

77 Cited in Paré Journal, 27 July 1908.

78 Archives de la ministère des affaires étrangères (Paris), Nouvelle série, vol.
6, consul to minister, 10 August 1908, including letter from consul to Mgr

Bégin (22 July 1908); and Mgr Bégin's reply, 24 July 1908. The mass was celebrated on 26 July.

79 *L'Événement* found it shocking that the lieutenant-governor 'of an essentially Catholic province' might have boycotted the mass out of support for Herbette (29 July 1908). If Herbette is to be believed, he actually stayed at the lieutenant-governor's residence while at the tercentenary (NAC, MG 28 I 38, file 1-2, Herbette to president of Société Royale, 21 July 1908). This claim is corroborated by the fact that Herbette's letter was written on 'Hôtel du Gouvernement' letterhead.

80 *L'Événement*, 18 July 1908.

81 It is not clear why this tribute to the royal line began with William iv. Perhaps it is understandable that the story did not begin with George iii, the monarch at the time of conquest, but there was still his own successor, George iv.

82 *Le Soleil*, 10 July 1908. The reference to Laval wearing both the mitre and the ecclesiastical hat is puzzling, since they were different forms of headgear. Perhaps the reporter was referring to the mitre as the triangularly shaped item worn at the front, and the cap as the part of the mitre that covered the rest of the head.

83 Brouage was Champlain's birthplace; Richelieu, the power behind the French throne, was involved with Canadian affairs in the later years of Champlain's governorship.

84 Frank Carrel and Louis Feiczewicz. *The Quebec Tercentenary Commemorative History* (Quebec, 1908), 72, 169. Quite aside from the decorations before the legislative buildings, Taché was also credited by Chouinard with the creation of 'a superb design ... which depicted the [French] Canadian nation in the form of a women who was striking because of her youth and beauty, but who was also imbued with power and energy, and who was proclaiming her faith in God and her confidence that she had bright prospects for the future.' Chouinard had hoped to stage as part of the pageants *une brillante allégorie* inspired by this design. However, it seems that no trace of it has survived (*Projets-Délibérations-Documents*, 196)

85 Roy, *Fêtes du troisième centenaire*, 37; Mario Béland, 'L'apport du sculpteur Louis Jobin aux grandes festivités de la fin du XIXe siècle, à Québec,' in John R. Porter, ed., *Questions d'art québécois* (Quebec, 1987), 258–9; 276–7.

86 Letter to editor by H.E. Lavigueur, *L'Événement*, 21 July 1908.

87 Abbé Paré tells the story of Fairbanks being rescued by someone who took him back to the Château Frontenac. The vice-president is quoted as saying, 'O, nice people of Quebec.' Colonel Denison found himself stranded in St-Sauveur, overcome by heat during the military parade on 23 July. He was

befriended by locals, who provided him with water, lemonade, and *bière de tempérance* (non-alcoholic beer). According to Paré, Denison, who had been a *mange canayen-français* (a francophobe), was won over by this kind treatment (Paré Journal, 23 July 1908).

88 A lengthy description of these decorations is in *L'Événement*, 21 July 1908.

89 *Montreal Star*, 22 July 1908; *Action sociale*, 24 July 1908.

90 *Le Nationaliste*, 26 July 1908. In its report on the tercentenary, the *Canadian Annual Review* held this article up for ridicule, not giving its expression of dismay any credibility (1908, p. 244).

91 Nelles, *Art of Nation-Building*, 204; Carrel and Feiczewicz, 71. There are no data regarding the linguistic makeup of the militiamen in town. However, Desmond Morton has shown that most were from Ontario, with only a small percentage from Quebec (*The Canadian General: Sir William Otter* [Toronto, 1974], 287). Furthermore, *The Militia List* indicates that nearly all of the Quebec militia units that took part were at least led by English speakers. The source provides no information about the other men in these units.

92 Morton, *The Canadian General*, 287.

93 *Action sociale*, 24 July 1908; *L'Événement*, 24 July 1908.

94 Champlain's landing at Quebec in 1908 was similar to the one staged at St John, New Brunswick, in 1904, as part of the tercentenary of Champlain's 'discovery' of the St John River. On that occasion, natives were not employed, but rather locals dressed up for the occasion. Nevertheless, they set out in canoes to meet Champlain's reconstructed ship, much as would be the case in Quebec City four years later. There is no evidence, however, to suggest that the Quebec tercentenary organizers, in this or any other context, drew inspiration from the various tercentenary celebrations held in the Atlantic provinces in 1904.

95 *Action sociale*, 24 July 1908; Paré Journal, 23 July 1908. For its part, *La Croix* was troubled that 'the cannon sounded only for the Prince and the visitors' (30 July 1908).

96 *Action sociale*, 24 July 1908. If this figure is even roughly accurate, it would have been the single most attended event of the tercentenary.

97 Doughty and Wood, *King's Book*, 2: 247.

98 Carrel and Feiczewicz, 59–61. Also speaking, although not even listed in the Carrel and Feiczewicz volume, was the mayor of Brouage, Champlain's hometown in France, who was unhappy about the involvement of godless France in the tercentenary. If Mayor Brandelis had expressed his feelings, which only became known after the event, he would have broken with the secular character of the moment.

99 NAC, RG 90 vol. 2, minutes of NBC, 12 June 1908. A letter was received from the English secretary of the Ladies' Pageant Committee to inform the NBC

that 'the Ladies who are to take part in the pageant absolutely refuse to walk or ride in the procession.'

100 *Quebec Chronicle*, 24 July 1908.

101 Carrel and Feiczewicz, 70.

102 Nelles, *Art of Nation-Building*, 119.

103 Paré Journal, 23 July 1908; *Quebec Chronicle*, 24 July 1908; Carrel and Feiczewicz, 168; AVQ, 'Défilé des Pageants,' negative 19660. The St-Roch and St-Sauveur districts received only one other event during the tercentenary – a visit by the Prince of Wales to Parc Victoria, *le parc du peuple travailleur* (the park of the working people), on his last full day in town. He made his way to the park by travelling through 'the working-class sections of the city,' but the visit seems to have generated little interest among the population, and not much more in the French press, which gave it little coverage (Roy, *Fêtes du troisième centenaire*, 314).

104 The figure of 100,000 is based on the assumption that roughly 70,000 attended the pageants, 20,000 the military review, and 7,000 the mass. The amphitheatre for the pageants seated 10,000 and was not always full for the eight performances; and there were reports that the same stands were less than full for the mass. Although most descriptions from 1908 claim that there were 15,000 seats in the grandstand, the NBC absorbed the expense of trimming the seating back to 10,000 in order to limit expenses that were spiralling out of control (RG 90, NBC minutes, 7–8 May 1908). As for the military review, newspaper reports cited 20,000 as the number of spectators on hand.

105 Carrel and Feiczewicz, 77.

106 The military view of the matter is outlined in NAC, RG9 II A 2, vol. 27: Minutes of the Militia Council, vol. IV, 1908.

107 This touchiness was evident in the complaint received by the battlefields commission from the Montreal and Ottawa synod of the Presbyterian Church, which did not want to see parliamentary funds for the tercentenary going to 'defray the cost of any religious service by any particular church in Canada.' Of course, none of those funds were being used in this case, but the complaint indicated a certain hypersensitivity just the same (RG 90, vol. 2, minutes of NBC, 29–30 May 1908).

108 Roy, *Fêtes du troisième centenaire*, 284–6.

109 *Le Soleil*, 27 July 1908; also see *L'Événement*, 27 July 1908.

110 Roy, *Fêtes du troisième centenaire*, 287; *Le Soleil*, 27 July 1908.

111 In 'Masques, Monuments and Masons,' Merrington viewed Lascelles's honours as a sign of the subordinate status of Black or native performers. In contrast, Nelles found that the natives and Lascelles had somehow been transformed by the whole experience of working together. As he put it, at

the moment that Lascelles was initiated he 'was visibly moved ... shook hands and embraced his new brothers' (*Art of Nation-Building*, 166).

112 After his work in South Africa, Lascelles faced another multinational challenge in producing a pageant in Calcutta in 1911.

113 Chouinard, 'Mémoire,' in *Projets-Délibérations-Documents*, 189.

114 Columbus was purged from the pageants by a subcommittee of the tercentenary bureaucracy that had been convened to consider Chouinard's report in early February 1908. The subcommittee also purged other elements of Chouinard's plan, but provided no justification (AVQ, 'Rapport du sous comité d'histoire et d'archéologie sur le mémoire présenté par Monsieur Chouinard au sujet de la procession et du "pageant" historiques,' 3 February 1908).

115 Nelles, *Art of Nation-Building*, 144.

116 *L'Événement*, 18 July 1908. In the epilogue we will see that these descendants were at the centre of what some would have viewed as the final act of the tercentenary – a celebration held in September 1908, long after the dignitaries had gone home.

117 AVQ, 'Rapport du sous comité d'histoire et d'archéologie,' 3 February 1908.

118 The colonization agent for the CPR was given $5,500 to recruit, transport, and pay '100 Algonquin savages equipped with their outfits for war.' (AVQ, Tercentenary Executive Committee, 30 March 1908).

119 Nelles, *Art of Nation-Building*, 176.

120 The figures for the linguistic division of the performers are derived from Nelles, 'Historical Pageantry and the "Fusion of the Races" at the Tercentenary of Quebec, 1908.' Even though the French-speaking population was underrepresented, Nelles claims that the cast constituted 'almost a mirror reflection of the general population of the city' (*Art of Nation Building*, 155).

121 Nelles, *Art of Nation-Building*, 156.

122 Lascelles had originally asked for $155,000, before settling on slightly more than $100,000. In the end, however, he overspent this amount by 50 per cent.

123 This list is based on a budget prepared by Lascelles in April 1908 (MCSQ, lettres A, no. 9D).

124 *Semaine religieuse*, 20 (8 August 1908), 806.

125 *Le Soleil*, 27 July 1908; *L'Événement*, 17 July 1908.

126 For an interesting discussion of the market orientation of public amusements, see David Nasaw, *Going Out: The Rise and Fall of Public Amusements* (New York, 1993).

127 NAC, RG 90, vol. 2, Courtney to Walker, 6 April 1908. Walker responded to

this letter noting that there was some resentment over Courtney's assumption of control over tercentenary finances: 'The French members of the Commission did not like the idea of the money being kept at Ottawa' (ibid., Walker to Courtney, 8 April 1908).

128 Ibid., meetings of 4 April, 7–8 May , 29–30 May, 12–13 June 1908. There were dress rehearsals on 14 and 16 July, but the first 'real' performance was on 21 July. The grandstand was commonly referred to in publications of the time as seating 15,000, even though the NBC's internal documents make it clear that funds were spent for the redesign of the stands to reduce its capacity to 10,000. Indeed, the total value of receipts from the pageants makes no sense unless it is understood that there were only 10,000 seats per performance, or 80,000 over the course of the tercentenary – a significant percentage of which were given away to dignitaries. If 25 per cent of the seats were not sold, the remaining 60,000 would have cost 60 cents on average for the NBC to take in a total of $36,000. This figure is plausible in light of the price structure for the seats.

129 Ibid., meeting of 29–30 July 1908; the final costs of the pageants were presented in a finance department document dated 23 February 1909 (as above, vol. 2).

130 *Projets-Délibérations-Documents*, 236.

131 Nasaw, *Going Out*, 71.

132 *L'Événement*, 10 and 25 July 1908; *Action sociale*, 28 July 1908.

133 *Industrial Canada*, November 1907; NAC, MG 28 I 38, file 1–17, n.d, no author.

134 Keith AJ Hay, 'Early Twentieth Century Business Cycles in Canada,' *Canadian Journal of Economic and Political Science*, 32 (1966), 354–64. The roots of Canada's economic downturn are sketched out in Georg Rich, 'Canadian Banks, Gold and the Crisis of 1907,' *Explorations in Economic History*, 26 (1989), 135–60.

135 Canada, *Report of Board of Inquiry into Cost of Living*, 2 vols. (Ottawa, 1915), 1: 501; the *Labour Gazette* provided monthly assessments of employment prospects in various Canadian cities; the assessments for Quebec City throughout the summer of 1908 were uniformly gloomy – *Labour Gazette*, June 1908, p. 1402.

136 This point has been made by various authors, including Terry Copp, *The Anatomy of Poverty* (Toronto, 1974), 32. Focusing on the Quebec textile industry in the early twentieth century, Jacques Rouillard has found that the cost of living outstripped increases in workers' wages – a point confirmed by the previously cited inquiry into the cost of living (Rouillard, *Les travailleurs du coton* [Montreal, 1974], 76).

137 One also has to wonder who could actually hear what the actors were saying.

138 NAC, RG 90, vol. 2, NBC, meeting of 12–13 June 1908.

139 If 20,000 people attended the military review, 17,000 of them would have been there for free. In contrast, there were an estimated 60,000 people at the military parade.

140 La Presse, 27 July 1908; Action sociale, 27 July 1908. The latter journal estimated the crowd at 10,000 even though the stands (with 10,000 seats) were not full. As I noted earlier, the local papers operated on the assumption that there were 15,000 seats even though only 10,000 had been installed. Accordingly, Action sociale may have been inadvertently signalling that the stands were roughly two-thirds full (10,000/15,000) – an impression confirmed by the sketch published in La Presse.

141 Paré Journal, 26 July 1908. The presence of Protestants was also commented on in L'Événement, 27 July 1908, but one has to wonder how these observers concluded that many in the crowd were Protestants. One possible explanation relates to the much commented on dropping of the spectators to their knees when the host was held before them. Perhaps Protestants did not react instinctively to such aspects of Catholic ritual.

142 La Vérité, 8 August 1908.

143 Le Nationaliste, 26 July 1908. Fournier's piece earned responses from the Canadian Annual Review (1908, p. 244), as well as both the Toronto World and the Globe (27 July 1908).

Epilogue: Champlain and Laval beyond the Summer of 1908

1 L'Événement, 4 August 1908.

2 AVQ, Procès-verbaux, Comité exécutif du tricentenaire, 25 September 1906; 24 February 1908.

3 Paré Journal, 23 September 1908.

4 This account was compiled from the 24 September 1908 issues of Le Soleil, Action sociale, and L'Événement, along with Roy, Fêtes du troisième centenaire, 339–53.

5 New York Lake Champlain Tercentenary Commission, Report on the Champlain Tercentenary (Albany, 1911), 15; Lake Champlain Tercentenary Commission of Vermont, The Tercentenary Celebrations of the Discovery of Lake Champlain and Vermont (Montpelier, 1910), 15.

6 The pageant was based on Lighthall's The Master of Life: A Romance of the Five Nations and of Prehistoric Montreal (Toronto, 1908).

7 New York Lake Champlain Tercentenary Commission, 462.

8 Ibid., 301–3. Roy's proficiency in English came from his experience as a parish priest in Hartford, Connecticut.

9 The legal intricacies of the Brouage case are explained in Larkin, *Church and State after the Dreyfus Affair*, 152–4; 170.

10 This appeal and other correspondence pertinent to the Brouage affair were published in *Brouage – Québec* (Quebec, 1911). The people of Brouage were, of course, mistaken in believing that the tercentenary had taken place in 1909.

11 *La Vérité*, 30 April 1910. The appeal was also printed in *Le Soleil*, 26 April 1910; *Action sociale*, 12 May 1910; *Semaine religieuse de Québec* 22 (1910), 667–8. The French consul in Montreal carefully monitored the reporting of this appeal to his superiors in Paris. See NAC Fonds Ministère français des affaires étrangers, letter from consul, 3 May 1910, microfilm reel 2181, p. 174.

12 *Brouage – Québec*, 73–6.

13 ANQQ, Fonds SSJBQ, 412/2, dossier 18, letter from Louis Augé, 27 December 1912. A column had been built in Champlain's honour in Brouage in 1878; no further monument to Champlain was subsequently constructed.

14 Patrice Groulx, *Pièges de mémoire: Dollard des Ormeaux, les Amériendiens et nous* (Hull, 1998), 200.

15 Ibid., 243n. Joan of Arc had been beatified in 1909. On the face of it, Madeleine de Verchères had all the ingredients to be feted as a guardian angel, in the mold of Dollard. However, as Colin Coates has observed, her gender stood in the way of her securing the cult status achieved by Dollard in pre–Quiet Revolution Quebec (Coates and Morgan, *Heroines and History*, ch. 4).

16 Létourneau, 'La production historienne courante portant sur le Québec et ses rapports avec la construction des figures identitaires d'une communauté communicationnelle,' *Recherches sociographiques* 36 (1995), 12.

17 *Le Soleil*, 16 May 1923.

18 *Troisième Centenaire de Mgr François de Montmorency-Laval. Compte rendu des fêtes de Montigny-sur-Avre et St-Germain-des-Près* (Mamers, France, 1924).

19 *Semaine Religieuse de Québec*, 24 May 1923, p. 594.

20 This tour was organized by the Thomas Cook travel agency. The itinerary is described in the company's brochure, *Au berceau de la foi et au pays des aïeux* (Montreal, 1923).

21 *Le Soleil*, 3 July 1958. The program of the 1958 fete was published in *Québec 1608–1958: l'album du 350e anniversaire* (Quebec, 1958).

22 The relevant photos were published in *Le Soleil*, 25 and 30 June 1958.

23 These activities were described in the *Annuaire Samuel de Champlain / Samuel de Champlain Yearbook,* published for a time in the 1950s and 1960s by the Société nationale Samuel de Champlain.

24 http://www.quebec400.qc.ca. These comments pertain to the version of the website in July 2002.

25 Maurice Agulhon, 'La "statuomanie" et l'histoire,' *Ethnologie française* (1978), 145–72.

26 David Glassberg, 'History and the Public: Legacies of the Progressive Era,' *Journal of American History* 73 (1984), 972–5.

Bibliography

Primary Sources

Manuscript Collections

Archives de la Ministère des affaires étrangères (Paris)
    Nouvelle série, Canada
    Personnel file of Alfred Kleczkowski
Archives de la paroisse de Notre-Dame de Québec (Quebec)
    Cahiers de prônes
    Assemblées de la fabrique
Archives de l'archidiocèse de Québec
    Fonds du Comité du Monument Laval
    Fonds Louis-Nazaire Bégin
Archives de la Ville de Québec
    Dossiers dealing with Monument Champlain and tercentenary
    Minutes of Comité des chemins
Archives des Sœurs Augustines de la Miséricorde de Jésus, Hôtel-Dieu de Québec, *Annales*
Archives des Sœurs de la Charité de Québec (Beauport, Québec), *Annales*
Archives des Ursulines de Québec, *Annales*
Archives nationales du Québec (Chicoutimi), Fonds Association catholique de la jeunesse canadienne-française
Archives nationales du Québec (Quebec)
    Fonds Société St-Jean-Baptiste de Québec
    Fonds Jean-George Garneau
    Fonds Tricentenaire de Québec

Archivio Segreto Vaticano (Rome), Dossiers relating to the Monument Laval
    and the tercentenary
Musée de la civilisation, fonds Séminaire de Québec
    Diary of Abbé Alfred Paré (MS 746–755)
    Diary of Cyrille Légaré (MS 679)
    Diary of Mgr T.-E. Hamel (MS 33)
    Fonds Henri-Raymond Casgrain
    Journal of the Superior, Séminaire de Québec
    'Sacra Rituum Congregatione, Quebecen, Beatifications et cannonizationis
        ven servi Francisci de Montmorency-Laval Primi Quebecensis Episcopi.
        Summarium Super Dubio, 1904'
    'Souvenir Album given by Arthur Doughty to participants in the Champlain
        Ceremony, 21 September 1898'
    Translation des restes de Mgr de Laval (SME 12.3/59)
Musée du Québec, Fonds Louis-Philippe-Hébert
National Archives of Canada
    Wilfrid Laurier Papers
    Ministère des affaires étrangères, France, Correspondance consulaire avec le
        consulat de Québec
    Earl Grey Papers
    National Battlefields Commission Papers
    Quebec Battlefields Association Papers
University of Toronto, Fisher Rare Book Library, Diary of John Charlton.
United States, Department of State, Despatches from United States Consuls in
    Quebec City, 1878–1906 (National Archives Microfilm Publication M1267).

Other Printed Materials

Association catholique de la jeunesse canadienne-française. *Congrès de la Jeunesse
    à Québec en 1908*. Montreal, 1909.
Brouage – Québec. Quebec 1911.
Carrel, Frank, and Louis Feiczewicz. *The Quebec Tercentenary Commemorative
    History*. Quebec, 1908.
Casgrain, Henri-Raymond. *Notes relatives aux inscriptions du monument de
    Champlain*. Quebec, 1898.
Chouinard, H.J.J.B. *Annales de la Société St-Jean-Baptiste de Québec, 1889–1901*.
    Quebec, 1903.
– *Fête nationale des Canadiens-français célébrée à Québec, 1881–1889*. Quebec,
    1890.
– *Fête nationale des Canadiens-français célébrée à Québec en 1880*. Quebec, 1881.

– *Fêtes du Troisième Centenaire de la Fondation de Québec par Champlain: Projets-Délibérations-Documents.* Quebec, 1908.

David, Felicien. *Christopher Columbus, or, The Discovery of the New World: A Symphonic Ode in Four Parts*, trans. James A. Lanigan. Buffalo, 1892.

Le deuxième centenaire de l'érection du diocèse de Québec. Quebec, 1874.

Diocèse de Québec. *Mandements, lettres pastorales et circulaires des Evêques de Québec.* Quebec, 1878–1908.

Doughty, Arthur, and William Wood. *King's Book of Quebec*, 2 vols. Ottawa, 1911.

Drapeau, Stanislas. *Le Journal de Québec et le tombeau de Champlain.* Quebec, 1867.

– *Observations sur la brochure de MM. les abbés Laverdière et Casgrain relativement à la découverte du tombeau de Champlain.* Quebec, 1866.

– *La Question du tombeau de Champlain.* Ottawa, 1880.

Gagnon, Ernest. *Réponse à la brochure de Monsieur l'abbé H.-R. Casgrain: intitulée 'Notes relatives aux inscriptions du monument de Champlain.'* Quebec, 1899.

Inauguration du Monument Champlain. Quebec, 1902.

Lake Champlain Tercentenary Commission of Vermont. *The Tercentenary Celebrations of the Discovery of Lake Champlain and Vermont.* Montpelier, 1910.

Laverdière, C.-H., and Henri-Raymond Casgrain, *Découverte du tombeau de Champlain.* Quebec, 1866.

New York Lake Champlain Tercentenary Commission. *Report on the Champlain Tercentenary.* Albany, 1911.

Quebecen Beatificiones et Canonizatonis ven servi dei Francisci de Montmorency Laval. Primi Episcopi Quebecensis. Positio Super Non-Cultu. Rome, 1892.

Roy, Camille. *Les Fêtes du Troisième Centenaire de Québec, 1608–1908.* Quebec, 1911.

Sacra Rituum Congregatione, Quebecen. *Béatificionis et canonizationis servi dei Francisci de Montmorency-Laval. Primi Quebecensis Episcopi. Positio Super Introductione Causae.* Rome, 1890.

Taché, J.-C. *Notice historiographique sur la fête célébrée à Québec, le 16 juin 1859, jour du deux centième anniversaire de l'arrivée de Mgr de Montmorency-Laval en Canada.* Quebec, 1859.

Thomas Cook et Fils. *Au berceau de la foi et au pays des aïeux.* Montreal, 1923.

Translation des restes de Mgr de Laval à la chapelle du séminaire de Québec: Relation complète de tout ce qui s'est passé depuis l'exhumation des ossements de Mgr de Laval le 19 sept 1877 jusqu'à leur déposition au séminaire le 23 mai 1878. Quebec, 1878.

Troisième Centenaire de Mgr François de Montmorency-Laval. Compte rendu des fêtes de Montigny-sur-Avre et St-Germain-des-Près. Mamers, France, 1924.

Vaudin, J.F., and Ambroise Thomas. *France! France!* Paris, 1860.

Le Vénérable François de Montmorency-Laval Premier Évêque de Québec; Souvenir des fêtes du deuxième centenaire célébrées les 21,22 et 23 juin 1908. Quebec, 1908.

Secondary Sources

Agulhon, Maurice. 'La "statuomanie" en l'histoire,' *Ethnologie française* nos. 2–3 (1978), 145–72.

Behiels, Michael. 'L'ACJC and the Quest for Moral Regeneration, 1903–14,' *Journal of Canadian Studies* 13 (1978), 27–41.

Béland, Mario. 'L'apport du sculpteur Louis Jobin aux grandes festivités de la fin du XIXe siècle à Québec,' in John R Porter, ed., *Questions d'art québécois*, 235–77. Quebec, 1987.

Bossé, Eveline. *La Capricieuse à Québec en 1855*. Montreal, 1984.

Casgrain, Henri-Raymond. *Octave Crémazie*. Montreal, 1912.

Coates, Colin, and Cecilia Morgan. *Heroines and History: Representations of Madeleine de Verchères and Laura Secord*. Toronto, 2002.

Colby, Charles. *The Founder of New France: A Chronicle of Champlain*. Toronto, 1915.

Commerton, Paul. *How Societies Remember*. Cambridge, 1989.

Condemine, Odette, comp. *Octave Crémazie, Oeuvres*. Vol. 1. *Poésie*. Ottawa, 1972.

Courville, Serge and Robert Garon, eds. *Atlas historique du Québec: Québec, ville et capitale*. Ste-Foy, 2001.

Darnton, Robert. *The Great Cat Massacre*. New York, 1985.

Davis, Susan. *Parades and Power: Street Theatre in Nineteenth-Century Philadelphia*. Philadelphia, 1986.

De Brumath, A. Leblond. *Bishop Laval*. Toronto, 1910.

Delooz, Pierre. *Sociologie et canonisations*. Liège, 1969.

Dionne, Narcisse-Eutrope. *Samuel Champlain: fondateur de Québec et père de la Nouvelle-France. Histoire de sa vie et de ses voyages*. 2 vols. Quebec, 1891–1906.

Drouin, Daniel, ed. *Louis-Philippe Hébert*. Quebec, 2001.

Drouin, François et Jean-Marie Lebel, 'Le Roman-Feuilleton du Tombeau de Champlain,' *Cap-Aux-Diamants* 4, no. 3 (1988), 45–8.

Gagnon, Serge. *Mourir hier et aujourd'hui*. Ste-Foy, 1987.

– *Le Québec et ses historiens*. Quebec, 1978.

Garneau, François-Xavier. *Histoire du Canada depuis sa découverte jusqu'à nos jours*, 1st ed., Quebec, 1845; 4th ed., Montreal, 1882.

Glassberg, David. *American Historical Pageantry: The Uses of Tradition in the Early Twentieth Century*. Chapel Hill, NC, 1990.

– 'History and the Public: Legacies of the Progressive Era,' *Journal of American History* 73 (1984), 957–80.

Gordon, Alan. 'Inventing Tradition: Montreal's Saint-Jean-Baptiste Day Re-Examined.' Unpublished paper presented to Canadian Historical Association, 1996.

- *Making Public Pasts: The Contested Terrain of Montreal's Public Memories.* Montreal, 2001.

Gosselin, Auguste. *Vie de Mgr de Laval.* 2 vols. Quebec, 1890.

Groulx, Patrice. *Pièges de mémoire: Dollard des Ormeaux, les Amériendiens et nous.* Hull, 1998.

Guay, Michèle. 'La fête de la St-Jean-Baptiste à Montréal, 1834–1909,' MA thesis, Université d'Ottawa, 1973.

Hallett, Mary. 'The Quebec Tercentennial: Lord Grey's Imperial Birthday Party,' *Canadian Historical Review* 54 (1973), 341–52.

Harper, J.M. *Champlain: A Drama in Three Acts.* Toronto, 1908.

- 'Champlain's Tomb,' *Transactions of the Literary and Historical Society of Quebec* 19 (1889), 113–44.

Hobsbawm, Eric, and Terence Ranger, eds. *The Invention of Tradition.* Cambridge, 1983.

James, Mervyn. 'Ritual Drama and Social Body in Late Medieval English Towns,' *Past and Present* 98 (February 1983), 3–29.

Lagacé, Jean-Baptiste. 'Le Monument de Mgr de Laval à Québec,' *Revue Canadienne* 1 (1908), 20–1.

Laperrière, Guy. *Les congrégations religieuses: De la France au Québec, 1880–1914.* 2 vols. Ste-Foy, 1996–9.

- '"Persécution et exil": La venue au Québec des congrégations françaises, 1900–1914,' *Revue d'histoire de l'Amérique française* 36 (1982), 389–411.

Larkin, Maurice. *Church and State after the Dreyfus Affair: The Separation Issue in France.* London, 1974.

Lebel, Jean-Marie. 'Les tombeaux du premier évêque de Québec,' *Cap-Aux-Diamants,* Hors Série (Spring 1993), 40–6.

LeMay, Pamphile. *Fêtes et corvées.* Lévis 1898.

Létourneau, Jocelyn. 'La production historienne courante portant sur le Québec et ses rapports avec la construction des figuresidentitaires d'une communauté communicationnelle,' *Recherches sociographiques* 36 (1995), 9–45.

Macken, Thomas. *The Canonisation of Saints.* Dublin, 1910.

Mathieu, Jacques and Eugen Kedl. *Plains of Abraham: The Search for the Ideal.* Sillery, 1993.

Merrington, Peter. 'Masques, Monuments and Masons: The 1910 Pageant of the Union of South Africa,' *Theatre Journal* 49 (1997), 1–14.

Molonié, Antoinette, ed. *Le corps de dieu en fêtes.* Paris, 1996.

Nasaw, David. *Going Out: The Rise and Fall of Public Amusements.* New York, 1993.

Nelles, H.V. *The Art of Nation-Building.* Toronto, 1998.

- 'Historical Pageantry and the "Fusion of the Races" at the Tercentenary of Quebec, 1908,' *Histoire sociale* 29 (1996), 391–415.

Newman, Simon P. *Parades and the Politics of the Street: Festive Ritual in the Early American Republic*. Philadelphia, 1997.

Nora, Pierre. 'Between Memory and History: Les Lieux de Mémoire,' *Representations* 26, (1989), 7–25.

Ozouf, Mona. *Festivals and the French Revolution*. trans. Alan Sheridan. Cambridge, MA, 1988.

Perin, Roberto. *Rome in Canada: The Vatican and Canadian Affairs in the Late Victorian Age*. Toronto, 1990.

Pinard, Diane, ed. *Que la fête commence*. Montreal, 1982.

Pizzorusso, Giovanni. 'Un diplomate du Vatican en Amérique: Donato Sbarretti à Washington et Ottawa (1893–1910),' *Annali Accademici Canadesi* 9 (1993), 5–33.

Pope, Peter. *The Many Landfalls of John Cabot*. Toronto, 1997.

Porter, John R. *Le grand héritage: l'Eglise catholique et des arts au Québec*. Quebec, 1984.

Renaud, Laurier. *La fondation de l'ACJC: L'histoire d'une jeunesse nationaliste*. Jonquière, 1973.

Renault, Raoul. 'Le monument Champlain: histoire de son inscription,' *Courrier du Livre* 3 (1899), 323–79.

Roberts, Helene, ed. *Encyclopedia of Comparative Iconography*. Chicago and London, 1998.

Routhier, Adolphe-Basile. *Quebec: A Quaint Medieval French City in America at the Dawn of the Twentieth Century*. Montreal, 1904.

Rubin, Miri. *Corpus Christi: The Eucharist in Late Medieval Culture*. Cambridge, 1991.

Rudin, Ronald. *Making History in Twentieth-Century Quebec*. Toronto, 1997.

Savage, Kirk. *Standing Soldiers, Kneeling Slaves: Race, War and Monument in Nineteenth-Century America*. Princeton, 1997.

Savard, Pierre. *Le consulat général de France à Québec et à Montréal de 1859 à 1914*. Quebec, 1970.

Sheito, Christine. 'Une fête contestée: la procession de la Fête-Dieu à Montréal au XIXe siècle,' MA thesis (anthropology), Université de Montréal, 1983.

Souvenir du punch d'honneur offert par la Colonie Française à M. Kleczkowski. Montreal, 1894.

Trudel, Marcel. 'Samuel de Champlain,' *Dictionary of Canadian Biography*. 1: 186–99.

Vachon, André. 'François de Laval,' in *Dictionary of Canadian Biography*. 2: 358–72.

Waldstreicher, David. *In the Midst of Perpetual Fetes: The Making of American Nationalism, 1776–1820*. Chapel Hill, 1997.

Warner, Marina. *Monuments and Maidens: The Allegory of the Female Form.* New York, 1985.

Withington, Robert. *English Pageantry: An Historical Outline.* 2 vols. New York, 1918–26.

Woodward, Kenneth. *Making Saints: How the Catholic Church Determines Who Becomes a Saint, Who Doesn't and Why.* 2nd ed. New York, 1996.

Index